Roger S. Collins

Melting Point

A Novel

Roger – thanks for helping me with the second edition of "Melting Point"

– Roger C.

This is a work of historical fiction. Apart from the well-known actual people, events, and locales that figure in the narrative, all names, characters, places, and incidents are the products of the author's imagination or are used fictitiously. Any resemblance to current events or locales, or to living persons, is entirely coincidental.

Copyright © 2009 by Roger S. Collins

All rights reserved.

ISBN 978-1-4357-1321-5

Dedication

This book would not have been possible without the support and encouragement of my incredible wife Cindy and my super-genius daughter Melissa.

Thanks, too, to all the friends and acquaintances who reviewed my book, each from their own perspective. You all provided valuable input that made this book as good as it is. I only wish I were a better writer to do your help justice. Reviewers include: Tony, Amanda, Janice, Deanna, Roger House, Paula and her book club, Susan and her book club, Dave, and especially Margaret Hakkinson and William Greenleaf. If I left anyone out, I apologize and will include you in a future revision. Honest.

Prologue

Southern Poland, June 1944

The doll clutched tightly in her hands, the little girl looked away from the man she had asked the question of, the man standing next to the brick building on a shaded side path. The man who had looked at her in shock and disbelief. He wasn't going to answer the question.

The old woman who was holding her hand said to her, "Don't worry. We'll be fine. Everything will be fine."

The woman and the little girl continued along the dusty path towards a steep downwards stairway where all the people in line before them were descending into the darkness of the building. The girl looked up and saw a huge chimney towering over the building, black smoke billowing out from it, darkening the sky above them. It reminded her of when she boarded the train just two days ago, the way the train's engine had similar black smoke billowing out of it.

It was back then, when she had looked up, watching the steam engine belching out smoke, that she lost hold of her mother's hand. A large crowd of

Prolog

pushing and shoving people swept her before them and she was pushed towards a rail car. Hands reached out from the rail car and grabbed hers and pulled her up. Her mother wasn't on that rail car, though. She must have gotten on a different car, another car stuffed with people like this one. She had looked around pensively and she clutched her doll tightly.

"You hold on tight to me," she admonished the doll, smoothing its bright yellow hair and imagining that she was the doll and her mother was clutching tightly on to her.

When the train finally came to a stop, everyone jumped out of the cars. There were dogs barking and men shouting and the little girl was forced to line up with the hundreds of other people from the train.

"Mother! Mooootheeeerrrrr!" She called over and over. But the noise of the other people shouting and wailing, and of the dogs barking, and the train puffing was too loud. Even if her mother had been close, she wouldn't have been able to hear her.

She couldn't see her mother, either, because she was so short and so small, and all those people around her were so tall and pressed so close; she could barely see a few feet in any direction. The crowd was moving forward in a huge line, several people wide, and the little girl and her doll were pushed along with the others.

It wasn't until she reached what appeared to be the front of the line that she met the nice old woman who was holding her hand now. She couldn't see what was happening until the people in front of her were told to move to the left and follow the long trail of others heading towards the large brick buildings.

When they moved away, she could finally see that she was at the front of the huge line. Before her was a man in a white lab coat and several soldiers. The soldiers were assisting him by prodding, poking, and shoving people in one of two directions. Most of the people were headed to the left towards one of the two large brick buildings down at the end of the railroad track. A few people, at the nod of the man in the white lab coat, were sent to the right towards a gate in the fence.

One of the soldiers took the girl's arm and pushed her to the left with most of the other people. He said something loud in a language she didn't understand. It was then that the nice old woman took her hand. She said something back to the soldier, who then continued on to the next person in line.

"Where is your mother?" the woman asked as they walked.

"I don't know. She was on the train… somewhere," the girl replied.

"Then you'll see her soon," the woman said with confidence, and the two walked together with the other people heading towards the brick building.

The gentle woman walked slowly and with a slight limp. She was stooped over and reminded the girl of her own grandmother, who had died some time ago. She wished it had been her mother who had taken her hand. The girl craned her neck looking around to see if she could see her mother. But there were so many people she couldn't find her in the crowd.

"Stay close to me," the girl sternly said to her doll, clutching its hand.

Now they were beginning to descend the staircase into the darkness of the brick building. She took one long glance back at the path they had come down. The man she had asked the question of was still standing there; in fact he was still looking shocked and staring back at the girl. She looked around one last time to see if she could see her mother outside the building.

Descending the stairs reminded her of a distant memory of a time, long ago, when she and her mother had lived in Budapest. They had made their home in the basement of a building with a lot of other people, and her mother

Prolog

would tell her stories and play games with her. And they'd both play together with the doll she clutched so tightly now.

And then, one day, they were playing and men came down the stairs and told everyone down there that they had to leave. And so her mom had packed up what few things they owned and the two of them, along with everyone else in the basement room, had joined with a bunch of other people. They all took a train ride out to the countryside. There they lived on a farm while her mom helped grow food and care for the animals.

While mom worked, she and her doll had run through the fields of sunflowers and climbed the trees in the fruit orchards and ran along the rows of grapevines. They helped pick grapes for wine and fruit for juice and palinka. They also helped to harvest sunflowers, olives, and did whatever else she and her doll could help with.

During that time, things were good for the little girl and her mother. Though some people left and new people came, she and her mother stayed and stayed there until just two days ago, when they were again told it was time to leave. How sad her mother had been; she cried and cried. The girl and her doll had tried to comfort her mother.

"Dolly says it will be a fun adventure!" she had told her mom, who, upon hearing that, tried to smile while the tears flowed down her cheek.

"She's right," her mother had said between snuffles, wiping away her tears.

And then the awful day at the train station with crowds of people from her farm and other farms and villages nearby. More and more people gathered and crowded together, and though the girl had managed to hang on to her doll, she had gotten separated from her mother at the train station.

Now they had reached the bottom of the stairs and were told to find a place to hang up all of their things and undress so they could take a shower.

Melting Point

The women were sent to one side of the large room and the men to the other, but it was all one big room. And the room was very warm and muggy, and smelled of sweat. The old woman and the girl found a spot where there was an unused hook on the wall that they could hang their clothes from.

A large, stern woman in uniform said, "Leave your shoes and belongings here, they'll be here when you return,".

The old woman and the girl undressed, and the girl thought it was a bit funny because there were men and boys in the room too even though they were on the other side. She wasn't used to having naked men and boys around and she shielded her eyes. It was embarrassing to her, especially because she was getting naked too.

"Just don't look at them," she told her doll. "Especially their *things*."

She and the woman started moving towards the showers as the crowd was being urged to do. One of the women in uniform pointed at the doll and said brusquely, "Leave that here."

The girl did not leave it. It was her doll, after all. She turned as if she were going to put it down, and the woman in uniform went on to chide others, so the girl quickly returned to the old woman's side, clutching tightly to her precious doll.

The old woman and the girl and the doll, hand in hand in hand, walked with all of the other people into the shower room. There were more people in that room than the girl had ever seen in one room before. Hundreds and hundreds of people all together in one room to take a shower!

And the noise! The room was concrete with no coverings on the walls, so the noise echoed loudly around the room. It seemed to the girl that people were afraid of the showers, because they screamed and wailed and clung on to each other as if in pain.

Prolog

"It's just a little water..." she said quietly to her doll. "Nothing to worry about."

The room began to get warmer and warmer with all those people in it, and there were so many people that they were all pushed together. The woman guided herself and the girl over to the concrete wall so that the girl wouldn't be pressed in on all sides by naked torsos. There was no place to sit here, but at least they could lean against the wall.

And then, from the center of the room began more noise; more shrieks and squeals and screams. The girl thought that the water must be either very cold or very hot for them to scream that way. She clutched her doll tighter.

And then she could smell it. A faint almond smell. At almost the same time, she became aware of a burning in her throat. Other people in the room were pushing in all directions to escape. Panicking, they began climbing on top of each other, diving down to the floor, clawing at the door, the walls, anything to escape the burning.

The girl felt thirsty. Her eyes burned. Her ears were becoming deaf from all the noise. She swallowed hard to try to stop the burning sensations in her throat and lungs. Nothing helped.

It takes as long as twenty minutes to die from the blue Hydrogen Cyanide gas. When the room is ventilated free of the gas and the doors are finally opened, the dead bodies will be untangled by many people. The girl will be found with her doll still tightly clutched in her hands. She, and her doll, will travel with others up the elevator and down a trough until they again meet the man of whom she asked the question. And, in death, she will change his life.

But all that is in the future. Right now, the girl is having a hard time keeping her eyes open, a hard time taking in breaths of air. She climbs above the bodies that threaten to crush her. The noise has started to quiet down as more and more people succumb to the gas and the pain.

Melting Point

And then…. recognition.

With the very last bit of her strength, the very last gasps of air, she throws one arm around her mother's lifeless body.

"See, everything *is* all right," the girl imagined telling the doll.

Her face showing relief, she died happy.

The Promise

Novato, California, 2004

I pushed the lancet into the end of its pen-like holder and took the cap off. Just a quarter-inch of the shiny needle was exposed. I pulled back on the spring mechanism at the other end of the pen, and pushed the button. The tip of the needle came out in a blur and retracted again. I again pulled back on the spring mechanism, and it was ready to go.

Our gray and white cockatiel, Rudy, was running around the top of the desk at which I sat. She stopped to nibble on a piece of paper, taking a tiny chunk out of it, and then dashed over to the lamp and nibbled at the cord. I shooed her away from the cord and she ran over to my lancet holder.

"Mine," I muttered, snatching it up.

Rudy made an indignant chirp, and ran to another piece of paper. The tuft of feathers on the top of her head lifted up, as they always did when she got excited or annoyed or angry or afraid.

I turned on the palm-sized glucose monitor and watched as it cycled through its self-test and asked for the test strip. I inserted the little plastic strip with its dot at the top, and the device asked for the blood sample. It would wait

Melting Point

patiently for a minute or so, since it knew that this was the difficult part. This was the part I hated the most.

Which finger this time? Let's try the ring finger. I held the stick pen against the finger and - here's the part I hate - pushed the button on the end of the pen. As if receiving a small bee sting, my finger momentarily felt outraged. It slowly calmed down, until the sting was more of a dull ache. I milked the finger over the test strip's dot, and a small drop of blood fell onto it, slowly spreading to the dot's edges. By the time I grabbed a tissue and held it over the end of my finger, I no longer felt the pain from the needle.

The glucose monitor immediately noticed that I had done as it asked, and started its countdown of 45 seconds until it could tell me the bad news. I suppose that's being pessimistic, but it was rarely good news. Even though it is just a machine, I imagined it with a disapproving frown, my mechanical nurse.

Rudy was scalloping the edge of the phone bill. My eyes flickered over at her and then looked out the window at the garden. The weeds were really getting out of hand, now half way up the old garden shed at the back of our small yard. I was never much of a gardener. Gardening was more Etta's department. Lately, though, she had been really slowing down. All of the stooping and bending made her dizzy, and so she had taken to just watering the plants rather than weeding or pruning or anything else that demanded hard work. I suppose I should encourage her to call a gardener. We can afford it.

My eyes flickered over to the photographs on my desk, arranged from most recent to ancient. First was the Christmas card from Amanda, Magda's daughter - my granddaughter. It showed her and her husband Tony, with two adorable infants on their laps, both dressed in snowsuits.

"Great-grandchildren." *How did I ever get to be so old?*

The Promise

Next to the Christmas picture was an old picture of Magda, graduating from college, with a cap and gown. It was one of those formal black and white oval pictures, now yellowed and faded with age.

Next to that was a copy of an older picture of Etta and Magda, leaning against the rail of a ship, the Statue of Liberty in the background. Etta was looking over towards Magda and smiling, and Magda, about three years old, was holding Etta's hand and beaming at the camera.

Draped over the picture frame was a small tarnished silver chain and locket. On the back, worn from years of fingers playing over the inscription, read: *To my lovely Mary, from your adoring Carl – love forever.*

The last picture, on the far right, was a tiny coppery-colored photo of my parents, set in a 4x5 frame, against a black felt background, taken back at a time when we were one happy family. When my brother still lived at home, and I, a couple of years older, was off at the University. When my aunt and uncle were still poor but happy farmers in Poland. Before Amanda was born; before Magda was born; before Etta and I had met; before all of the horrors of the war.

It was odd that a fading old photo of two pleasant-looking people could make me think of my whole life and the people who meant so much to me. This innocent-looking picture conjured up tremendous sadness in me, as if the couple staring out from the photo were telling me that this was the way they should have remained forever. As if they were the ones that should have lived to be in their '80s, and not me. So, my sadness included a lot of guilt, I suppose. Yes, it definitely included guilt.

The monitor let out a chime to tell me it was through deciding my condition. *160. Ugh. Neither super high, nor really low. 120 would be much better. I'll walk this afternoon. There, now stop nagging at me.* "Damned machines," I muttered.

Melting Point

A loud thump made me look up. Rudy looked up from her latest demolition project and warbled with concern, her head tuft rising to full sail. The noise had come from down the hall, in the direction of our bedroom. It sounded like a muffled door slam. I decided to investigate. Placing my index finger out for Rudy to hop on, I stood up. Rudy obligingly got on my finger, looking forward to some new adventure. I had just straightened up, an effort that was getting more and more difficult with age, when I heard a muffled cry from down the hall.

I hustled to the door of the room, pausing just long enough to leave Rudy on a bookshelf. She chirped with indignation, but I wasn't paying attention to her anymore. I walked as fast as my old legs would carry me down the hallway, my limp more pronounced without my special shoes.

As I reached our bedroom door, I heard Etta call from the bathroom, "Albert! Help me! Oh. . . "

"Etta! I'm here!" I called, becoming very alarmed. I reached the bathroom just a moment later, and saw Etta sprawled sideways on the tile floor. Blood was dripping from her nose onto the tiles, and her face was scrunched up with pain.

"Albert! I can't get up! Help me!"

"Etta," I said in a high pitch, my throat constricting with fear and dread, "hang on, I'll call 9-1-1. You just lie still." I moved to the phone by the bed and dialed 911.

A woman answered, "9-1-1; what is your emergency?" Calm and pleasant.

As rapidly as I could I said, "My name is Albert Stohl. My wife fell and hit her head on the bathroom floor."

The Promise

Still calm, still pleasant; "OK, sir, please calm down. Is your wife conscious?" Her calmness annoyed me.

"Yes, yes. Her nose is bleeding." I realized that this could take a while.

Over the next several minutes, a time that seemed to stretch out forever, the operator asked about Etta's condition, age, and history. After telling me that I should go make Etta comfortable as we waited for the ambulance, I hung up the phone and headed back to the bathroom.

"They'll be here soon, Etta. You just rest," I said, wadding up a towel and placing it under her head.

"Oh, Albert, my head hurts. My hips hurt," Etta said. She looked pale and unfocused.

"I'm sorry it hurts, Etta." A tear welled up in my eye. "I don't like to see you in pain." I stroked her forehead.

"I got dizzy, and then my legs just turned into rubber. Age is starting to be unkind to us."

She was right, of course. I suddenly realized how old we had become; how little time we had left; how much we had been through together. I knew this wasn't a good time, but seeing her hurt like this I had to let her know how I felt. What she means to me.

"Etta, dearest," I started haltingly, "I've always loved you. From the very beginning, the first time I met you. And I've always respected, trusted, and needed you. You were the candle that saved me from darkness. You still are."

"I know, Albert," she said weakly. "I'm sure it will be all right." Now she was telling **me** it would be all right! Etta was always so strong.

"Yes, Etta, but I still want you to know how much I care for you. How much I need you. How much I've enjoyed being with you these last sixty years," I said. I suddenly had the sniffles and watery eyes.

Melting Point

"Okay, Albert, Okay," she said softly, closing her eyes hard against the pain. After that I just stroked her face, softly.

After what seemed like hours, but was probably only five minutes, the paramedics pounded on the front door, and I left Etta, hobbling as fast as I could to open it. Two paramedics, a bald man and a tall woman, came in and I escorted them back to the bathroom. The next several minutes were a blur while they worked on Etta and placed her on a gurney.

I asked the woman, whose nametag read *Dianne Zimmerman*, "May I ride along with you?"

"Sure," she said. "Do you need to lock up the house, turn off the stove, anything like that?"

"Uh, yes, I, uh, I'll look," I said, struggling to think. Make a list. I muttered, "Check the stove, check the doors, and check on Rudy. Where did I leave Rudy?"

As if waiting for the question, Rudy loudly chirped from the back room where I had left her. I went to the room, offered her a finger, and ferried her to her cage in the kitchen. "Daddy's got to go now, my big bird," I said as I stroked her back. "Momma's hurt, and I have to take her to the . . . " My voice faltered and I looked down at the floor and took a large breath so I wouldn't lose all control. I kissed the bird and placed her in her cage. She warbled as I left her.

List; think about the list. "Stove? Check. Doors? Check. Rudy? Check. Keys?" *I need my keys and wallet.* I walked back into the bedroom just as Etta was being wheeled out. I grabbed my wallet and keys. Check.

"All set, sir?" asked Ms. Zimmerman.

The Promise

"All set," I answered, following the gurney out the front door. I closed and locked the front door, more out of habit than clear thinking. Then I followed the two paramedics and Etta.

Ms. Zimmerman said with concern, "Did you hurt your leg? You're limping."

I shook my head and waved my hand, "Birth defect." She nodded curtly, perhaps a bit embarrassed.

"What happened?" It was my next door neighbor, June, standing on the sidewalk, the concern evident on her face.

"She fell in the bathroom," I said, not stopping to talk.

"Don't worry about the house," June offered. "I'll keep an eye on it." She knew where we hid the key.

"Thanks," I said as I got in the back of the ambulance truck, with help from Ms. Zimmerman. Just before the doors closed, I yelled out to June, "Please feed Rudy if I'm not back soon!"

"I will, and don't worry," June called back, waving goodbye half-heartedly.

"Saint," I muttered, looking out the back window as my neighbor receded into the distance, the ambulance bouncing along the road, its siren wailing.

"What's that sir?" Ms. Zimmerman asked.

"Oh, nothing," I said, turning to look at Etta on the gurney. "How is Etta?" To Etta I said loudly, "Etta, how are you?"

"We gave her some pain medication," Ms. Zimmerman said, avoiding my question. I took that as a bad sign.

From the gurney Etta said weakly, "It hurts, but I'll be okay, Albert."

Melting Point

I took her cold hand in mine and rubbed my thumb against the back of her pale yellow fingers. I looked at her face, etched with wrinkles and mottled with brown spots. Her gray hair was thin and wispy. I suppose I'm not the same handsome man she knew all those years before, either. Still, she has those thin, curved lips I always liked, and her nose is, though bigger, still in the cute ski-jump shape. And her eyes, those eyes that were always alive with determination and life, they . . . well, actually, they were looking pretty defeated.

Ms. Zimmerman started checking Etta's body more thoroughly, I guess for bruises and cuts. She rolled up Etta's sleeves to check her arms, but stopped abruptly when she saw Etta's uncovered left forearm. In a faded purple and blue was a blurry tattoo of a six-digit number, 421750. With a worried expression, her mouth slightly open, Ms. Zimmerman looked up at me, an unspoken question in her eyes. *Old Polish woman, old enough to have been through the Holocaust, tattoo on her arm. Could she have been a concentration camp survivor?*

"Auschwitz," I quietly answered the unspoken question.

Ms. Zimmerman looked back down at the tattoo with a mixture of fear and compassion. Then, in what I took to be a non-professional, but entirely genuine, display of concern, she stroked Etta's cheeks softly with the back of her hand. Ms. Zimmerman's eyes blinked several times, and her eyes flickered back to me.

I sighed and looked sadly down at Etta's face. Ms. Zimmerman regained her professional detachment and continued looking for bruises and other injuries she may have missed earlier.

#

The ambulance pulled up at the hospital, and the driver ran around to the back and opened the door. Then he and Ms. Zimmerman wheeled the gurney out the back door of the ambulance and into the hospital's Emergency

Department. I followed them into the lobby and Ms. Zimmerman said to me, "Check in here. We'll be back out in a few minutes to talk with you."

There was a young man at the counter wearing several small earrings up the side of his right ear. His hair was a couple of different shades of red. He had a small ring through his lower lip.

"Fill this out," the young man said without emotion, handing me a clipboard with what appeared to be a thick stack of forms clipped to it.

"May I borrow a pen?" I asked.

The redhead stared at me for a moment, as if he didn't understand me. Then, with a heavy sigh, he looked behind the counter and found a chewed-up-stub of a pencil. Handing it to me, he said, "I **need** this back."

I was tense and nervous. I was filled with dread for what may be wrong with Etta. This young man's lack of concern made me angry. I fantasized about reaching across the counter and grabbing him by his neck. I smiled pleasantly at him as I imagined him dead, lying across the counter, his hair splayed on the desk, with just the pink tip of the pencil's eraser sticking out the back of his neck.

"Thank you," I said, and took a seat in the small waiting area. Redhead went back to work.

I filled out the forms and returned them to Redhead along with my insurance card. He impassively took it, not even looking at me. He started to look through the forms, not to see if they contained useful information, but just to make sure I had filled out all the fields.

"Have a seat," he said without emotion.

As I took my seat I could visualize the pink nub of the chewed eraser sticking out the back of his neck. I smiled and enjoyed my daydream, until a

Melting Point

ghostly young girl came over and looked at the dead Redhead and then at me and said, "You killed us."

My eyes widened and I shook my head and said to the girl, "No, not me. I just . . . I didn't."

"Please," Redhead said with concern. "The doctor will come out and talk to you as soon as she can."

The girl melted away, and I turned towards my chair, feeling shaken. I felt the old guilt in my stomach, churning and twisting my insides. I quickly looked around for a magazine. There was a faded old one that asked, "Are you prepared for Y2K?" I picked it up.

I stared at the pages of the magazine, as my hands flipped through them. My eyes didn't focus on any of the pages, though my hands didn't seem to notice. My brain was busy thinking about what I had just seen. *That girl. It was the same one from my old dreams. Long, dark, curly hair; sad expression; pale, white skin; dirty, gray coat, and big eyes.* The dreams hadn't come for years. I thought they were behind me. Usually in the dreams the girl would hold a small doll by her hand, dangling limp. She usually asked me a question, but this time . . .

"Mr. Stohl?" It was Ms. Zimmerman.

"Yes," I said, coming to my feet.

"Mr. Stohl, your wife is still being attended to by the doctors, but I think the immediate danger is over. Her bleeding has stopped, and her vital signs look good. The doctor will be out soon to talk with you."

"Oh, thank goodness she's all right," I said.

"Well, she's not out of the woods yet," she said. "But you've done the right things so far. We're going to go back to the station." She paused, and added, "Will you be all right?"

I thought about that question for a moment, and replied, "As long as Etta is OK, I'm all right. Thank you for your concern. Yes, I should be fine."

"All right, then. We'll be on our way," she said, gesturing towards her partner who had just taken the gurney back out the door to the ambulance. She added, "If you need a ride home, the desk clerk can arrange for a cab."

She smiled and shrugged and looked like she was going to leave, but kept stalling. Like an awkward teenager on a first date, I thought. She wants to say something more.

Ms. Zimmerman cleared her throat, and quietly asked, "Were you, ah, in Auschwitz, too?"

My old instincts would be to quickly deny anything like that, but I was emotionally drained, and realized that I could truthfully answer her question without telling her anything at all.

"Yes," I said in a whisper. It was a good thing I had a long sleeve shirt on, so she wouldn't notice that I had no tattoo.

She looked down at the floor and grimaced. Then she said, "I'm sorry," and left.

When the automatic door slid shut behind her I said quietly, "I'm sorry too."

#

The doctor's news wasn't good. Etta had a broken hip. She needed surgery to replace the hip. Only there was a catch. On the one hand, she needs the surgery to repair the damage and replace her hip. On the other hand, at her age the surgery could kill her. Some catch. After the surgery they would try to figure out why she gets dizzy, so she won't fall anymore.

"What'll we do?" I paced the floor and looked at Etta.

Melting Point

"I'm sure I'll be fine, Albert, quit worrying so," Etta said. "Let's just get the surgery over with so I can go home."

"But what if you, I mean, what if there's a problem?"

"There won't be any problems, and we don't have any choices. I'm getting a new hip so I don't have to spend what little time I have left in bed," Etta said with finality.

I stopped pacing, nodded at her, and said, "All right. You know best, of course."

Etta said, "You'd better call Magda. I want to see her before the surgery, just in case."

I looked at her in alarm.

Etta said, as if explaining to a child, "Well, we must be prepared for it, after all, right, Albert?"

Etta was right, and I excused myself to go call Magda. I walked out to the lobby where there was a pay phone. I stuck some quarters in the slot and dialed her number.

An abrupt voice grunted, "'Lo?"

I said, "Is this Tom?" Tom is Magda's husband. Second husband, that is.

"Yeah. That you, Pop?" Tom always called me Pop, because Magda called me Poppa. It rankled me a little, because Tom is not my son, but I'd learned to accept it in the spirit it was offered.

"Yes, is Magda there? May I speak to her?"

"Nope, sorry," Tom said. "Magda's out shopping somewhere. I'll tell her you called," sounding like he was ready to hang up.

The Promise

I decided to tell Tom the news, and maybe he could get a hold of Magda. "Tom, I'm at the hospital. Etta's fallen and broken her hip. She needs surgery, and the doctor says she might not survive it. Etta would like Magda to come see her before the surgery."

It was as if a different person had taken the phone on the other end. Tom said, "Oh, dear, I'm so sorry to hear that, Albert. I'll drive down to the mall and find Magda and get her there to the hospital. Which one are you at?"

"Community," I said. "Etta's in room 207."

"I'll get her there as fast as I possibly can. Don't worry, Albert, I'll get her there."

"Thank you, Tom. I'll see you then. Goodbye."

"Goodbye, Albert," Tom said. He almost never called me Albert.

I returned to the room. "Tom is going to go find Magda. She's shopping or something."

Etta nodded at me and smiled. The pain medication made her comfortable, but a little quiet. The two of us just looked at each other awhile. Then Etta spoke, slowly and clearly. "If I don't make it, I want you to promise me something."

I took her hand in mine, and said, "Of course, Etta, anything."

Etta looked at me a moment and I saw the fire return to her eyes briefly as she said, "Tell her the truth, Albert. Tell her the whole truth."

My face melted into a mask of dismay and fear. I said, "I, I can't do that to her. It will crush her; and me."

"Albert, she is sixty years old. She deserves to know who she is; who **we** are. I know it will be painful for you, and for her, but we owe her the truth. If I don't make it, you will be the only one who knows, and you must share it with her."

Melting Point

I pleaded with her, "But, Etta, it will hurt her. It will make her hate me. Can't I just live my last few years as the man she thinks I am?"

Etta lost her temper at me. "Albert! She is a grown woman. She has lived all these years not knowing the full story of her past." Etta calmed down and took a more maternal tone as she said, "I had always intended to tell her one day, and I still will if I can. But, if I don't have a chance before the end, you **must** do it. Please promise me this, Albert."

Now, not only was I in danger of losing Etta, but I could lose my daughter as well. But Etta was right. Etta was always right about such things. As I had done for sixty years, I gave in to her will. "Yes, Etta, you are right. I'll do as you ask."

"The **whole** truth," Etta admonished me, like I was a four-year-old boy.

I smiled at her, having accepted my fate, and said, "Yes, Etta, the whole truth. Now you just make it through that surgery so you can tell Magda long after I'm gone."

The argument over, she smiled at me. "Fine. Now, let me sleep."

I pulled up a chair and sat next to her and watched her breathe until she was asleep, then tried to figure out what to do. Go home? Not yet, I don't know when Magda will get here. Take a nap? Not in a hospital, I hate hospitals. Eat? I didn't bring my insulin, so that would be difficult. I'll have to deal with that sooner or later, but I can put that off a while. Coffee? Yes, coffee. I liked good coffee, and it would give me something to do.

The cafeteria was almost deserted as I filled up the Styrofoam cup with the black acid they labeled coffee. I flicked at the cup and felt satisfied to see the bubbles rise to the top, as if I had freed some of the bitter taste. The staff was in the back cleaning or something, one older man visible through the kitchen opening. I waved my two quarters in the air as I approached the cash register, and plunked them down by the register. The man waved at me and smiled.

I sat at one of the many empty tables and sniffed at the coffee. *I suppose the way to face the dream girl is to start with a list.* "That's it," I mumbled. "What do we know about her? When does she show up, and what does she mean or want? What are the facts of the case? Make a list. One, she shows up in my dreams. Two, she hasn't shown up for years. Three, I just saw her. Four, I, uh, what is number four?"

I guess I saw her today because of the stress of Etta being hurt. Etta is my moral shield, my link to what is good in life. Etta is hurt and may, uh, not make it, so I start to see the girl again. But who is she?

It's been so many years since I last saw her in a dream. I don't recall much about the dreams or her. I remember that she always wore a dirty coat; stained, maybe. She held a small doll's hand in hers, the rest of the doll hanging down, swinging as the girl walked. Yes, she was walking, always walking. I don't remember where she was going.

Her eyes would look at me with almost a pleading look, but with defeat and sadness. How do eyes convey that much emotional information? They looked right at me, and my heart felt chills.

Her hair was unkempt and curly, cascading down over her shoulders, in shades of deep mahogany. Her skin was very pale, more gray and ashen than pink. I don't think she wore shoes.

She used to ask me something; I don't recall now what it was. It was always the same thing though, a simple question directed at me. She would walk by me, almost in slow motion; with her mouth moving and words coming out, words that were a question, words that would make me want to scream. I would try to shout, and then I would wake up making not so much a scream as a loud moan. Usually Etta would comfort me for a moment and then go back to sleep, and I would lie awake for a long time, not wanting to go back to sleep and resume the dream. Eventually I would doze off from exhaustion, and dream of other things.

I sipped the coffee and tried to remember the question that she would ask me. Some parts of the dream remain vivid, yet what she said to me is long forgotten. Just as well. What did she say today? *You killed us.* Great. I suppose she means the redhead receptionist and her, but I don't recall killing her in my dreams. I would wake up right after she asked the question, so I didn't have time to kill her in the dream.

I was sipping some more coffee when I saw Magda and Tom passing by through the glass that separated the cafeteria from the hallway. I got up and hurried after them. I didn't catch up to them until I reached room 207. They were looking at Etta with quiet concern. They both turned towards me as I approached.

"Papa. . ." Magda whispered, and gave me a hug.

I wrapped my arms around her and hugged her tightly. Tom came over and placed his hand on my shoulder. I motioned that we should talk outside.

"What happened?" Magda said as we got outside the room.

"Well, when she was in the bathroom, she fell and broke her hip," I summarized. "They want to replace the hip, and then figure out why she's been getting dizzy spells, so that she doesn't fall again."

"How risky is the surgery?" Tom asked.

"They didn't say, which I take to mean that it is very risky," I said somberly.

"Magda, honey, is that you?" Etta asked weakly from inside the room.

We all walked back into the room and around the bed.

"Momma, how are you feeling?" Magda asked with concern.

The Promise

"Not too good, Honey," Etta said, managing a small smile. "But I'm going to be better just as soon as the doctors fix me up."

We pulled up chairs and after some brief chatting a nurse came in. Surgery was scheduled for that evening. In the meantime we would stay with Etta to keep her spirits up. After some more chatting, there was a pause.

Tom, trying to start a new thread of conversation, said, "Say, we've been planning a cruise to Alaska."

Etta smiled weakly. "The last ship ride I took was when we came to America." She pointed at me and said, "Albert, tell them that story."

I smiled at the memory and felt relieved to talk about something. "We came to America from Cuba. I have a picture of you and Etta in front of the Statue of Liberty that I took on that ship," I said to Magda.

Magda had heard this story a hundred times before. Bless her; she knew her part to play in this little farce. She acted like it was news to her. "Cuba? How did you get there?"

"We; how did **we** get there, you mean," I said, with a twinkle in my eye. I warmed to my task and said, "After the war, we decided we should leave Europe, because it was no place for a family such as ours. It seemed like the whole continent was in rubble. Of course, everyone wanted to get out. Ships were full, and foreign countries were full. Cuba was one of the few places that wanted people. So, we took a ship from Bilbao, Spain. It took a while to get to Cuba, and by chance it stopped first in New York, but that time we weren't allowed to get off. The difference between New York and Havana was startling. New York was reaching to the sky, and was bustling with industry and activity. And the Statue of Liberty! From what we had been through, it was a thrilling sight, to see the torch of liberty shining from that enormous statue! Havana had tremendous night life and culture, but it was just the hub of an

Melting Point

agricultural country, and there was no Lady Liberty and no Empire State Building. We stayed in Cuba for, what Etta, two years?" I asked.

Etta nodded and said, "We celebrated Magda's third birthday on the day before we left."

"On the ship from Spain to Cuba we were in third class, but on our way to America we traveled first class. This was before Castro, you understand, and Cuba was booming. Times were good to us," I said, seeing the ship again in my mind. "You had been pretty seasick on the trip because it was so stormy. The day we pulled into New York, though, there was some blue sky peeking through the dark clouds, and you were feeling much better. The sun was breaking through here and there, and hit the water in a few large pools. I'll never forget it; a beam of sunlight came through the clouds and lit up the Statue of Liberty in a blaze of light, with everything around it in shadow. It was breathtaking."

I gazed into the past and said, "And the smells in that morning air. Fish, ocean, the ship's exhaust, and garlic from some restaurant. In the harbor there were dozens of large ships; mountains of supplies and materials on the docks; the sounds of car horns, men shouting, ships' whistles. Opportunity. This was more magnificent than I'd ever dreamt of."

Etta said, "We stayed in New York for only a few days before your father got a job with a company in Philadelphia, U.S. Steel."

"Biggest steel mills in the world, and they wanted me to work on their new blast furnaces. Really state-of-the-art," I said.

Tom asked, "How did you get to Spain after the war? Weren't there any problems with you being German and all?"

I frowned and breathed deeply. "I think I've told you the story of the three of us fleeing the Russians, didn't I? Well, it was a long year from that time until we got on the boat in Spain. You don't want to hear about it."

The Promise

Magda said, "I do, Papa. I was born just before you guys left Poland, right? I'd love to hear about my first year of life. We've got lots of time." She gave me a slightly pleading look that Etta couldn't see, as if to say that we need to fill up the time with conversation.

I sighed and said, "OK. Etta, jump in wherever I falter."

"Albert, you are the family storyteller, you'll do fine," Etta said, perhaps with a meaning that Tom and Magda would not have understood.

"Mmm, flattery; you must be feeling better," I said. I looked up at a spot above the bed and collected my thoughts. Then I began. "Soon after you were born, Magda, the Russians were making great headway in Poland. Etta and I were staying with my Aunt Mary and Uncle Carl on their little farm. One wintry night, the Russians arrived with a vengeance. You, your mother, and I hid in the root cellar under the barn, but Mary and Carl stayed in the farmhouse. The Russians killed them. They came looking for us, too. Your crying almost gave us away, but we had a small goat that would bleat just like a baby. Oh, yes, and you filled your diaper while the Russians were above us in the barn. That almost made me jump out of the cellar just to get away from the smell! But the Russians soon left, and we left too. The three of us walked westward all evening and morning, finally catching up with some other refugees. We hitched a ride with them and eventually got to a railway station.

"I had some papers that said I was an important worker, so we were able to get on a train out of there. It was probably one of the last trains. It would travel a short way and then stop while they cleared the tracks or figured a way around bomb damage. All this took a long time. Food was scarce. It was winter, so there was plenty of water, if you didn't mind eating snow. There was a lot of chaos, too. People were on the edge of panic because of the Russians coming. We certainly knew first hand what they were capable of!

Melting Point

"We made it back to Germany, and I figured I should go back to where my job was and wait there for instructions, so we took trains until we got back to Erfurt, which is about midway between France and Poland, on the eastern side of Germany. I worked, and Etta raised you, until the end of the war. The Americans came to Erfurt, and for us the war was over.

"They questioned me, of course, but I had never been in the army or in government, and wasn't a member of the Nazi party, so they decided not to intern me with the other men who **had** been in the army or government or the party. For a little while, we just stayed put. But the Americans were going to turn over Erfurt to the Russians, and we decided that we'd had enough of the Russians. We headed out with the Americans to see if we could find a better place to raise you."

"What about your parents, or Etta's?" Tom asked.

Etta said, "My parents had been killed a couple of years before. They went up the chimney." Etta made a spiraling gesture with her hand, her index finger pointing up.

I winced and quickly added, "My parents didn't make it either. We had no one but each other."

I started up the story again. "Just as my papers helped us during the war, Etta's status as a former camp inmate made her an official Displaced Person, or DP. And as her family, we were DP's too. That was kind of cheating, I know, but we wanted to leave, and that small subterfuge let us leave."

Magda asked, "What do you mean subterfuge?"

Etta said, "He was German, and Germans were allowed to go back to Germany but were not usually allowed in the DP camps or offered help to leave. Most German men of Albert's age were locked up in prison camps for a

30

couple of years to make sure they didn't start another war. We hid the fact that Albert was German when we needed to."

I added, "By that time I spoke enough Polish to get by, and I had learned some English in school. The Allies could understand when someone was speaking German, so I tried to only speak Polish or English."

The nurse came in and told us it was time to get Etta ready for surgery. We all wished her good luck and kissed her, and she was wheeled away to Pre-Op. Now we had to wait several hours for the surgery to be complete before we could see her again.

#

Tom, Magda, and I decided to go out and get some food. We stopped by my house to pick up my insulin, and I checked on Rudy. We stopped by their house and they fed their dogs. Then we drove to a local diner.

We were pretty quiet during dinner, mostly making small talk. We talked about news, my grandkids and great-grandkids. We talked about their upcoming cruise. We talked about Rudy and coffee. We avoided any discussion of Etta or her surgery. Magda brought me up to date on the situation with Amanda's efforts to adopt a child.

"Amanda has the twins; she certainly doesn't need another child. Especially not now, and especially not one from another country," Magda said with exasperation.

Tom added, as if arguing a case in court, "You can't get any guarantees that the kid won't have AIDS or other problems. It's just a crapshoot."

"Imagine raising a kid from Rwanda," Magda said, raising her hands in frustration. "I'm not sure if it's a Hutu or a Tutsi or what. She asked for a girl, but that's all you get to specify."

Melting Point

Tom added, "And just between you and me, Pop, I think white parents raising a black child will cause them some problems. Or some problems for the kid."

I thought about that a moment and frowned. "I don't see how color should matter. People will know that they adopted, but, so what?"

"Well, sure, but what about the kid's own culture?" Tom said, splaying his hands as if to ask for an answer. "Do you ignore it? Do you raise it as a Christian like us, or do you try to do something with the kid's native religion, or what?"

Magda chimed in, "I don't even know what kind of weird religion Tutus and Hutsis *have*?"

"Hutu and Tutsi, dear," Tom corrected gently.

"Whatever; you see my point?" Magda asked of me.

I began to feel uncomfortable about this line of talk, though I couldn't exactly put my finger on why. I decided to change the subject. "Well, I'm sure Amanda and Tony will figure it out; they're smart people." I paused, and then, to change the subject, "Say, how about some espresso?"

Magda said, "I think Amanda is looking for something to fulfill her life. Tony has his work, and they both have their babies, but I think Amanda wants to 'do-good' or something. I think that's fine, you know, but there are a lot of American babies that need homes, too, if you **have** to adopt."

"White, Christian babies," Tom added. "Not that I'm against anyone else, I'm just saying. . ."

I tried again to change the subject, "Well, keep me informed of how it goes. I think I'll order an espresso. Either of you want one?"

The Promise

It was late when we left the restaurant and headed back to the hospital. There was still another hour or so before the surgery would be over, but we couldn't figure out what to do other than go back to the hospital and wait.

When we arrived at the nurses' station, however, we could sense trouble. The nurse behind the desk made a quick call, and within a minute or two Etta's surgeon, the one who was supposed to be operating on her, came out to talk with us.

He looked grave as he said, "Etta was weaker than we knew, and did not respond well to the anesthesia."

He said many more words, probably sentences about what happened, but my ears had stopped relaying any information to my brain. Or maybe my brain wasn't paying attention. All I did was stare at the doctor's lips as they moved. I didn't need to hear the words. They didn't matter. They all added up to three words.

Etta was dead.

Melting Point

Lost

For some reason, I didn't feel grief at that moment. I just felt numb. Magda gasped and put her hand over her face, then began to cry. Tom and I helped her over to a couch and sat her down. I sat next to her, and reached around her. We hugged and I could feel and hear her sobbing. I stared at the yellow plaster wall behind her, not really seeing anything.

Disbelief, I suppose, was what I felt the most. I had been with Etta almost every day for sixty years. After all that time, it was unimaginable that she was gone. It was like losing an arm or a leg. How could Etta **not** be here? Unbelievable.

As I stared at the wall, trying to figure out what I was feeling, I felt a tear working its way out of my right eye and making its way down to my lip, leaving a moist wake where it had been. The tear itself was warm, but when it had gone it left only the cold.

Another tear worked its way down my left cheek. My body began to lurch, like tiny convulsions, or like a rapid series of hiccups, and I realized that I was crying. This, too, seemed unreal, as though I were watching this scene unfold from across the room in slow motion. I don't cry. I never cry.

Lost

I clutched tightly to Magda and we cried together for a few moments. Then we both fell silent for a while, just holding each other. Finally, I broke the silence. "I can't believe she's gone. What will we do without her?"

Magda broke from my grasp, looked into my eyes, and said, "We'll go on, Papa; like she would have wanted."

I sniffed and wiped my eyes, saying, "You are as strong as your mother." I supposed a part of Etta will live on in her. I smiled at that thought and nodded. Then I felt a pang of fear as I remembered that Etta also wanted me to tell Magda about my dark past. I didn't want to think about that.

"Why don't you spend tonight with us, Albert?" asked Tom.

"Yes, thank you. I'd like that."

Tom drove us to their house and they fixed up their spare room for me to sleep in. We stayed up late talking, mostly about Etta. When I finally went to bed it was past midnight.

I didn't go to sleep right away. My mind was finally dealing with the idea, the concept, that Etta was gone. Though it still seemed unreal, I was beginning to think of what that meant to me. I began to mutter a list of questions. "Should I stay in our house, or move? Move where? Here, with Tom and Magda, or into a retirement home, or just into an apartment? They'd have to allow birds. I can't leave Rudy."

My mind tumbled through the benefits of staying home, of getting an apartment, of moving in with Tom and Magda. I thought about coffee and pets and gardens and anything else except the fact that Etta was dead; except the fact that I had made a promise to Etta that will ruin my life. Finally I was just feeling ill and confused. It was all so unbelievable. *Can't I just start this day over again? I could stop Etta from falling. We could be together again.* When I looked at the clock, it was three A.M.

Melting Point

The next morning I slept in, and had strange dreams. Dreams where I was a spectator, as if watching the dreams on T.V. I dreamt that the girl with curly hair, holding a doll, was sitting in Etta's lap. Etta was sitting in a stiff-backed chair, brushing the hair of the girl. Her hair had always been unkempt and bedraggled looking, but Etta was making it shiny and pretty. There was a kind of mahogany sheen that picked up the light. The girl's dress was dirty and torn, but she had taken off her coat, and her doll sat in her lap. The girl looked happy, too. Etta was talking to her as she brushed her hair, but I couldn't hear what she was saying. The doll was a rag doll, about eight inches tall, with different colors of fabric for the eyes and mouth, and a tuft of bright yellow yarn for the hair. It looked homemade, with large stitches and uneven cuts. Some stuffing was poking out one side. The doll had been well loved over the years, but was clean and in good condition. Maybe it had even been her mother's doll too.

In my dream I thought to myself that I might finally get a good look at this curly-haired girl. In my other dreams she just walked by and asked a question I couldn't hear. Now she was sitting still and I could get a good look at her. Maddeningly, dreams have a frustrating way of not being clear just when you want them to be. I tried to stare hard at her dress to see what it looked like, but it was as if a fog enshrouded it. The dress, though only a couple of feet from me, was indistinct.

I looked up at her face, and that was clearer. She had large brown eyes with wispy eyebrows. She was pale, almost alabaster white. Her nose was small and her cheeks had slight dimples. Her ears were completely hidden by her hair, which was thick and curly and full, cascading half way down her back. Now that Etta had brushed it, it was really striking. The light caught the hair in places, and it was almost like a sunset shining through a glass of red wine.

Lost

The girl was chatting with Etta and smiling, her dimples showing on both sides. When she looked at me, her smile faded. "You promised to tell Magda," she whispered.

Then she looked away and talked with Etta some more. I promised. Yes, I had promised Etta I would tell Magda the truth. I woke up for a moment, sweating, and then fell back asleep.

Then I dreamt I was inside the ambulance with the paramedic, Ms. Zimmerman. The ambulance was bouncing over the road, its siren wailing. She was examining my arm. "Where is **your** tattoo?"

I looked at my arm and then back up at Ms. Zimmerman. For the first time I noticed my mother sitting next to her. "Yes, you should have a number," my mother said with disappointment.

I woke up in a pool of sweat and blinked a couple of times, rolled over, and then faded off to sleep again.

I was outside in a park. I heard an orchestra playing waltzes quietly in the background. I was standing in a grove of trees, and the smell of pine was really distinct. I stood next to a path, and I could see Etta walking slowly on the path next to the girl with curly hair. Etta was stooped over and wore a shawl, so I couldn't see her face, but I somehow knew it was her. The girl was between Etta and me, and was wearing her coat again. She and Etta held hands, and with her other hand the girl tightly clutched the doll's hand. The doll hung limply, slowly swaying back and forth. The girl's bare feet were filthy. As they walked past me on the path, the girl turned and saw me. She looked apprehensive, afraid. Her brow was crinkled and her nose was running. She asked me something, but I couldn't hear her. When I didn't answer, she looked up at Etta, and they continued down the path away from me, hand in hand. I woke up then, sweating. It was my old dream.

Melting Point

By this time the dreams had become too disturbing, so I got up. I showered and shaved and dressed and went downstairs.

#

After breakfast, Magda and I went back to the hospital to get the death certificate and claim Etta's body, so it could be sent to a funeral home. There was more paperwork. We went to the funeral home and talked with them about the funeral arrangements. Still more paperwork.

The man from the funeral home asked tactfully, "Have you decided upon a casket, or were you leaning towards cremation?"

I became agitated and said, "No cremation! That's a horrible thing to do to a body!"

A better funeral director would have moved on, but this one said, "Certainly, sir, but it is a respectful way to treat a loved one."

I looked the man in the eye and said, "There is nothing respectful about burning bodies. She escaped that once, I won't have her go that way now!"

The man quickly apologized, and we talked about caskets. Then I asked Magda to take me home.

"Do you want me to stay with you today, Papa?"

"No, honey, I think I'll be fine. I need to face home sooner or later; it may as well be now."

The two of us opened up the house, and then Magda gave me a long hug. "Can you come over for dinner tonight, Papa?"

"I'd love to," I said.

"It's noon now, so I'll pick you up about four, all right?"

"Fine; thanks, honey." And with one last hug, she turned and left. I closed the door and stared at it a moment. I took a deep breath. I wasn't sure I was ready for this.

Rudy chirped, and I went to her cage and let her out. I put her on my shoulder and headed to the kitchen to get her some food. I put Rudy on the kitchen table along with a small dish of noodles. Vermicelli is her favorite. She grabbed a noodle from the tangle and pulled at it like pulling a worm from the ground. She loved it. Soon she had four or five "worms" lying on the table next to the dish.

As much as Etta said she didn't like the bird, she cooked Rudy noodles for breakfast and rice for dinner. She would loudly complain about the mess Rudy made, even as she would toast some stale bread for her, and then watch with a big smile as Rudy snapped up pieces of the crust and tossed them over the side of her cage.

"We're both going to miss her, eh?" I said to Rudy.

Rudy warbled in concern, and then grabbed a noodle and pulled it over to the edge of the table and watched it with a critical eye as it fell to the floor below. She skittered back to the noodle dish.

I needed to go to the bathroom, and out of habit walked in to the bedroom to put down my wallet and keys and use our bathroom. I stopped short just inside the door. The tub was still full of water, waiting for Etta to take her bath. There was a small pool of dried blood on the floor where she had fallen. There were scattered wrappers and plastic packaging from the supplies the paramedics had used.

"Oh, Etta," I said quietly, a tear coming to my eye. I sniffed and my eyes became bleary, making it hard to see. I rinsed my face off in the sink. I picked up the garbage and used some wet tissues to clean up the blood. I let

Melting Point

the water out of the tub. Then I had to leave the room. I was drenched in sweat from emotion.

I used our other bathroom, and then I went back to the kitchen and got Rudy and put her on my shoulder. I moved into the living room to sit down. As I entered the room, I slowed down, feeling like a movie in slow motion. Halfway between the entryway and my easy chair, I came to a complete stop and looked all around the room.

Everywhere I looked, there were reminders of Etta: her magazines, her knitting, her favorite chair, and her paintings. All around me were her cat statues, her nesting dolls, and the old cards on the mantle from friends and family. Yesterday it was all clutter and junk. Today it was Etta. Yesterday I put up with the stuff because I loved her. Today I loved the stuff because it was all that was left of her. With all this great **stuff** in the room, it was as if Etta had just stepped out. Perhaps she was in the kitchen, cooking borscht for lunch. Or maybe she was out in the garden, pruning her roses. I smiled at the thought, and then frowned, another tear welling up.

I sat down in my chair and looked carefully around the room at all of the wonderful things. "Now, what shall we do today, Rudy?"

That was a tough one. There was no one to talk to, no one to set the table for, no one to watch TV with, and no one to share the paper with. Hardly any reason to do anything, really - what could I do?

"List, must make a list," I mumbled sadly.

But no list came.

For the first time I could remember, my mind had nothing to list. Everything I thought of involved Etta. Read with Etta? No. Talk with Etta? No. Watch TV with Etta? No. Hide the remote control from Etta? No. Compliment Etta on her aromatherapy fragrance of the day? Tell Etta how much I love her? Have Etta show me her roses? Ask Etta what's for lunch? Make her some espresso? Damn it.

"What do **you** want to do today, Rudy?" I asked, stroking her soft back.

Rudy warbled.

"Eat seeds, eh? What else? . . . Yeah, that's what I thought. Me neither."

After a couple of minutes of looking around the room, I decided I would give Rudy a bath, if only to give me something else to think about. I took her into the kitchen and ran the water a moment until it was warm. Then I filled a small bowl with the warm water. Rudy was getting more and more excited as she realized what was going on, her head feathers slowly rising to full sail. When I placed her on the counter, she ran to the bowl and hopped up on its edge.

Rudy stepped into the water. Standing knee-deep, she first took a long drink of the warm water and then proceeded to shake her head around and flap her wings to splash water all over herself. More water made it onto the counter than onto her, but that's a bird for you.

I said, "Papa's been gone a lot lately, hasn't he?"

Rudy flapped and shook, spraying water everywhere. Then she hopped up onto the edge of the bowl and shook and flapped everything, like a dog fresh out of a lake.

"You really like baths, don't you? I'll be around more often for a while, and I'll give you lots of baths. I promise. And I always keep my promises, you know," I said.

"Promises. Damn," I muttered.

Melting Point

I'd made a promise to Etta, hadn't I? Well, if I didn't keep it, no one would know. No, that's not true. I'd know. And it would torture me if I didn't keep that promise.

I somehow have to tell Magda about my past, about her past. It was something I had dreaded from the moment that Etta mentioned it. But I had to do it. Probably the sooner, the better. I may as well completely ruin my life. "In for a penny, in for a pound," I muttered miserably.

I spent the afternoon cleaning Rudy's cage and thinking of what I would tell Magda. Do I just say something like, "Oh, by the way, Magda, I worked at Auschwitz – could you pass the potatoes?" Or "Hey, speaking of baking, guess what I did during the war?"

I decided that I couldn't tell it in a few sentences. I couldn't even tell it in an hour. It would be too foreign, too out-of-the-blue. I need to lay the groundwork. I need to put her in the right frame of mind, to help her see things through my eyes at the time, not through her 21st century eyes.

The doorbell rang. I looked at the clock, and it was too early for Magda to be picking me up for dinner. I put Rudy back on her perch and went to the door and opened it. It was June, my neighbor.

I think she wanted to ask me how Etta was, but when she saw my face, she just put her hand over her mouth, and said, "Oh, no!" I must have looked pretty miserable.

We hugged and she said, "I'm so sorry, she was such a wonderful woman."

"I know she enjoyed your friendship," I said awkwardly. *I'll have to work on what to say to people: Thank you? I'm sorry too? What do they want to hear? What would I want to hear? Maybe I should try the truth, and just let go. Stop trying to figure things out. Stop analyzing everything.* "I'm sorry, I haven't even figured out what to say to people yet. Thank you for watching Rudy. I really appreciate it. Won't you come in for some coffee?"

"Well, I don't want to intrude . . . " June started.

"Oh, nonsense," I said, waving my hand. "I'd love the company. It's awfully quiet in the house now." I stepped back to let her in.

We walked into the kitchen and I put some water in the kettle and set it on the stove. June was in her seventies; her husband had been older but had died a few years ago. She and Etta had been friends since we moved into the neighborhood many years ago.

"There's still a lot of Etta in this house," I said, gesturing to some cat statuettes.

June looked out the window and said, "There's a lot of her in the yard, too. Those roses of hers are gorgeous."

"She really loved them," I said, turning on the coffee grinder. I had to raise my voice to be heard over it. "I suppose I did too. Actually, come to think of it, I liked the way they made her happy."

Over the noise of the grinder, June said, "How come you have a bird, but Etta has all these cat statues and figurines?"

The grinder stopped and I could say in a normal voice, "Well, we used to have cats back before the bird. In fact, Etta used to run a cat kennel about, oh, maybe thirty years ago now." As I talked, I put a coffee filter into the plastic cone and placed it onto the coffeepot. "But being around a couple of dozen cats every day for months took its toll and made Etta allergic to the little angels." I got out a quart-sized measuring cup and put the ground coffee into it. ". . . Every night she would sneeze and her nose would be all stuffed up. It got worse and worse, and so finally she had to give up the business." I got out cups and saucers and a large spoon. ". . . It broke her heart. We moved on to

Melting Point

try snakes and fish as pets for a while, and then birds, none of which bothered her. Rudy is actually Rudy the Third, but she seems to prefer just Rudy."

The kettle whistled and I took it off the stove.

"That's a real shame. I can see why she has, uh, had, all this cat stuff, then," June said.

I poured the water into the quart measuring cup up to the right line, set down the kettle, and then stirred the coffee and water together. As I stirred, I said, "We talked about getting a hairless cat and her getting shots and the like, but in the end we decided that statues were better for her than the real thing."

There was an awkward pause and then June said, "So, I suppose you could get a cat now."

I poured the coffee and water into the filter cone and watched it drip down into the pot. I said, "Maybe. I'm not sure Rudy would approve of that decision. In any case, it's going to take a while to get used to her not being here. And, cats were more her desire. My mother had a bird, so birds were more mine."

June nodded and said, "I know what you mean. After my Edward died, I kept getting all the magazines he liked for years before I realized that I never read any of them. Now I still have stacks of them in the garage." She laughed and added, "I guess I should toss them out someday." Her mood changed to be more somber, as she continued, "Somehow that seems so final, though. Like he's never coming back."

I paused and thought about that a moment. Etta is never coming back? My mouth twitched and I sniffed again, trying to hold back a tear. I nodded slowly, and said, "I'll probably keep Etta's stuff right where it is for a while. I don't like the thought that she's not coming back either."

Lost

I poured two small cups of coffee. I handed one to June and offered her cream and sugar, which she declined. We walked out into the living room and sat down. She sat in Etta's chair, which for some reason made me a little nervous, like it should be saved only for Etta or something. We both sipped our coffee while she looked around.

Seeing an old picture of Etta and me, June asked, "You're from Germany originally, aren't you?"

"Yes, I was. Etta was from Poland."

"Can I ask - what did you do during the war?" June stepped onto the thin ice, testing its strength. "I don't mean to pry, but my Edward was in the army in Germany in 1945. It sounded like it was horrible. Complete destruction. It must have been miserable for you."

"Well, I've always had this limp, because I was born with one of my legs shorter than the other, so the army wouldn't take me. I spent the war being an electrical engineering apprentice. Pretty dull stuff, mostly. I was never near any battles, except at the end when the Russians were after us. I stayed out of their way, though, and lived to tell about it."

June nodded, accepting that explanation, and then said, "Edward said that most of the Germans he met were pretty ordinary looking people, and none of the Master Race we had heard so much about."

I chuckled and said, "I suppose today it would be called marketing hype. We believed it at the time, though. We wanted to believe it. Growing up there as a kid was pretty hard. After the war, the Nazi ideals all seemed so grotesque, but when we were hungry and my father was out of work and anarchy reigned, well, it, uh, didn't seem that bad. It's kind of hard to explain."

I decided to lighten the tone a bit and said, "But I stayed away from all that, and got out of Germany as soon as I could. We moved to the good 'ol USA and I never looked back."

Melting Point

After that, we just chatted about nothing and drank our coffee. I could see that explaining things to Magda was going to be sensitive, because I wouldn't be able to just change the subject so easily. Well, one step at a time.

We spent a pleasant couple of hours talking and drinking our coffee. Then the doorbell rang, and this time it was Magda. Magda and June knew each other and greeted each other warmly. Then June said goodbye and thanked me for the coffee. I thanked her for the company. After she left, I cleaned up the small mess from having made coffee, put Rudy in her cage, grabbed my keys and insulin, and Magda and I left for her house.

Tom and Magda's house was up against a land preserve, so they had a nice view of the hills behind them. From every window there was a view of trees, and, if I squinted a bit, I could imagine that I was in the country, rather than at the edge of a city.

My granddaughter Amanda and her husband Tony were at the house with their baby twins, Mike and Sophie. All together it was quite a crowd, but it was fun to have four generations of family together. Amanda had long, dark, straight hair and was always dressed impeccably. Her husband Tony was a software engineer, and we often talked as engineer-to-engineer, even though software engineering and electrical engineering are pretty different from each other. Still, it was fun talking shop with someone. It helped me feel less like the old man that I have become.

Dinner was barbecued chicken, corn, peas, and sourdough bread with garlic butter. I went easy on the corn, being that it is all starch, but garlic sourdough bread is a real weakness of mine. Hell, I'm over eighty. I can eat what I want, right? Well, maybe I'll need a little more insulin tonight.

Eating with infants at the table is like watching a food fight in slow motion. Tony and Amanda were pretty busy keeping the food near the table, let alone getting it into the kids' mouths. I stayed safely away on the far side of the table. More than once someone would leap up to get a towel or sponge from the kitchen.

I liked this family life, and I felt fear again that this might all be over once I tell Magda the truth about who she is and who I am. Etta was right, though, Magda deserves the truth. I owe her that after all I've done.

Sensing that things were too calm, Magda decided it was time to pick a fight. "Amanda, I don't see how you could manage another infant, let alone one from Rwanda."

Amanda rolled her eyes in exasperation. They had clearly had this conversation before. "Mom, I just feel like I need to do something good for the world. Saving a desperate orphan seems like a good thing to do. It's not like we can't afford it," Amanda said.

"I think your mother is just concerned for your sanity, that's all," Tom added helpfully.

"Well, if it gets to be a problem, we can hire some help for her," Tony said in Amanda's defense.

"But why Rwanda? Why not adopt a kid from right here?" Magda persisted.

Amanda was trying hard not to get angry, but she sounded exasperated. She said, "Kids here have a lot of opportunities, even poor orphaned kids. In Rwanda people are being killed just for being born into the wrong kind of family, not because of anything they did. Sometimes parents are killed, leaving behind their orphan children. Those children have no future. They'll probably be killed just like their parents. I can save one of them. Maybe that's not much, but it's something."

Just then, Mike vomited all over the place. People sprang into action to clean up. Ugh. After getting things cleaned up, they settled in to eat again. I

Melting Point

was happy the argument was over; I hated arguments. Soon, I need to ask Magda when would be a good time to tell her our life story. It would be nice to talk to her in private about this, but it didn't seem like I ever saw just her alone. With the chaos around cleaning up the mess going on, I thought maybe all the distractions would give us a kind of privacy.

I cleared my throat and said softly, "Uh, Magda, your mother made me promise her something before she died."

Magda looked up from the sponge in her hands and stopped wiping the table. "What's that?" she asked.

I took a breath and made the plunge. I said, "She made me promise to tell you what happened to us during the war. About what I did, how we met, that sort of thing. The whole story."

Magda raised here eyebrows and said, "OK. When do you want to do this, now?"

"Well, it's not always a pretty story, and I want to tell you enough that you can see your past through my eyes, so I thought I'd tell you, uh, sort of my life story. I think I'd need several hours to do it," I said.

Amanda stopped wiping the mouth of her son with a washcloth and said, "I'd love to hear how you and grandma got together, could I hear this too?"

Tony put down a tiny spoon halfway to his daughter's mouth and said, "Hey, me too. I want to hear what the 'great engineer' was doing back then."

I winced briefly. There went my chance at privacy. I should have waited. Outwardly, I smiled and said, "I'll only have the strength to tell this once, so anyone who wants to hear it should do so. If that's OK with you, Magda."

Lost

"Fine by me; I've always been curious as to how a Polish woman and a German man got together in the middle of the war. The ending is happy, so how bad could the rest be?" Magda said lightly.

I frowned and looked at her hard and said, "We never told you this, because it is something that will hurt me deeply to tell. I'm ashamed of what I did, and I worry that you will be ashamed of me when you hear it. I still have nightmares about that time. But, yes, it does have a happy ending, and that is thanks to you and Etta."

The mood at the table was somber for a moment, and that wasn't my intention, so I said, "Actually the ending is very happy, because of you and your mother, and Amanda and the twins, your husbands, the whole kit and caboodle." I always tried to avoid unpleasant situations.

Amanda said, "Tony's mom could probably watch the kids on Saturday. Would that work for everyone else?"

There was general nodding. Saturday it was.

Tony said, "How about if we do it out at Bodega?" Tony and Amanda owned a summer house out at Bodega Bay, overlooking the ocean. It would be quiet and peaceful there.

There was more general agreement, and it was set for 11 A.M., which gave us all time to get out there. Tom and Magda would drive me, and Tony and Amanda would come out when Tony's mom had settled with the kids. Magda would coordinate getting food so we could have lunch, snacks, and dinner.

#

So, Saturday was to be it. After all these years, would it be a load off my chest, or a tombstone over my head? Would I be relieved to have the truth finally out, or be devastated by losing Magda's love? Will the girl with curly hair

Melting Point

leave me alone after this confession? Maybe I'll end up answering as many of my own questions as Magda's.

Once home, I said to the living room, "Etta, I'm afraid of what is going to happen. I'm afraid of what they will think of me. But you wanted me to tell her the whole story, and for your memory, that is what I will do."

Promise Kept

Bodega Bay is located on the Pacific Ocean about forty miles north of San Francisco. Alfred Hitchcock's movie <u>The Birds</u> was filmed there and in the nearby inland town of Bodega. The area around the town is typical of the northern California coastline – steep cliffs, rolling hills, and winding roads. Part tourist attraction, part 60s hippie hangout, part fishing village, the area offers breathtaking views, coldwater beaches, funky shopping, and peace and solitude.

Tony and Amanda had struck it rich in a Web startup back in 2000, and were able to buy a 'summer home' in Bodega Bay. Located on the edge of a hilltop golf course, it was one of a hundred or so modern homes in a development that was particular about the way homes were built and maintained. Spring and fall are the nicest times on the coast, and so it was really a 'whenever we can get away' home for them.

I stood on their rear deck, looking over the cliffs at the ocean. The surf could be heard crashing onto the rocks down below me. The barking of sea lions was mixed in with the sound of the surf and distant foghorns. In the distance to the north was Doran Beach with its mile of white sand, dotted here and there with people and dogs. The sky was overcast and dark, the noontime

Melting Point

sun well hidden behind clouds. There was a stiff cold breeze that made standing out on the porch a temporary pastime. The air was heavy and damp, the salt air mixing with the smell of fresh cut grass, a sure prelude to a storm.

Tony stepped out onto the deck and said, "It's getting pretty chilly, time to put on a jacket or go inside."

"Inside, I think," I said. "Smells like a storm, and I'm not sure how long a jacket alone would suffice." I grinned at Tony and turned from the railing towards the door.

"Right," Tony followed me after one last look at the ocean. "But it sure is beautiful. I never get tired of this view."

Amanda and Tony had arranged some comfortable furniture around the wood stove. Magda added a small oak log to the fire in the stove, which was just beginning to get hot. She left the door to the stove open to let out more heat. The fire crackled and spat, slowly embracing the log with its long fingers. I stopped and watched the log for a moment as the flames licked higher and higher around it. A long forgotten memory flickered through my mind, and I winced briefly in pain.

"Relax," I muttered to myself.

I went to the kitchen and poured myself a large mug of coffee from the pot that had just finished dripping. The coffee was too hot to drink just yet, but the warm mug felt good in my hands, driving away the cold from the deck and helping me to relax.

"Who wants some coffee?" I asked.

"Not that mud, no thanks, grandpa," said Amanda.

"Ha ha," I said, sarcastically. The family often joked that a spoon would stand up in a cup of my coffee.

"I can take it," said Tony. He gestured at Amanda with his thumb and said in an exaggerated whisper, "Wimp."

"Hey!" Amanda threw a couch pillow at him. Tony ducked and the pillow missed him but winged a lamp.

Magda said, "I'd take some with cream and sugar."

I poured Tony and Magda some coffee, leaving room in Magda's cup for the cream and sugar.

"Tom?" I asked.

"No thanks, I'm holding out for the beer later," he said. Then he added, "Maybe I'll have a Pepsi now, though."

Tony said, "I'll get it!" He grabbed a can from the refrigerator and tossed it gently to Tom, who then regarded the can as if it were now a grenade.

Magda smiled nervously and said to the group, "Well, are we all ready?"

We gathered in front of the wood stove and took our seats. I sat in an easy chair in the middle of the group, with Tony and Amanda on my left on a love seat and Tom and Magda on my right on a couch. Magda had placed bowls of popcorn and other munchies on the tables next to the seats. I had told her this wouldn't be as good as watching a movie, and we had chuckled at that.

I sniffed my coffee and took a tentative sip. It was still pretty hot for my tastes, so I held it in my hands and stared into it as I collected my thoughts and prepared to begin. I took a deep breath in and slowly let it out. It was time. I spoke directly to Magda.

"Magda, your mother asked me to tell you the full story of your past; the story of how your mother and I met; the story of what happened back in Poland at the end of the War, when you were born. I originally thought that I could tell you the story in a few minutes, but I realized that would just short-change us both. The more I thought about it, the more I realized that I want you to understand how it felt, how it was, how it happened. So I have to bring you back to the past. I have to try and make you see things as they seemed to **me** at the time.

"I think you will see me differently after this story, and I worry that you may not think much of me when I'm done. I begged your mother not to make me do this, but she insisted." I smiled in helplessness and added, "and when your mother makes up her mind . . ." I trailed off.

Magda interrupted, "Poppa, I love you and always have. Nothing you can say will change that. But, I have to admit; I'm a little worried, too, about what happened. You're scaring me a bit by this dramatic introduction."

Magda had a comic worried look on her face and we all laughed lightly in the face of the tension.

"Well, as you know," I said, "I am German and your mother is . . . I mean, was . . . not. We were on opposite sides of the war, on opposite sides of the Holocaust. I can't tell you everything that happened during that time, I can only tell you what I saw with my own eyes. I'm so very sorry that Etta isn't here to tell you what she saw, and I couldn't begin to tell you what she went through, so I'm afraid that part of the story will be brief."

A log snapped, sending a spark out towards the space between Tom and me. It startled me, and I stamped on it quickly, crushing the life out of the ember. I was feeling a bit on edge.

"So, let me start at the very beginning." I said.

#

I don't know whether my father wanted me or not. I was born in the last year of World War I, when Germany was being reduced to poverty by the other European nations. This was 1917, and Europe was still in the last agonizing throws of what was called 'The Great War'. Not so great for Germany, who would lose and go on to pay restitution to the other countries.

My father, Frank Stohl, was a soldier and had been an architect before that. Just before I was born he was wounded, losing his left thumb and forefinger to a sniper's bullet. After the war, he wasn't able to find much work. He'd spend his days trying to find enough labor to put food on the table, and spend his evenings drinking beer and complaining about his plight. There were few new buildings for him to design, and he said bitterly that what architecture work there was would tend to go to the **whole** men, as he bitterly called them.

So, with little money and little future, I was born into this family. Not only was I a burden to my father's wallet, but I was born with one leg shorter than the other, and my father would lament how the family now had two cripples to deal with. He was a man defined by his work, and it pained him that he couldn't provide well for his family. He would look down his hawkish nose at me with his piercing eyes, and tell me that I should at least learn to use my brain, so I could be of some use. I was determined to please him, and felt ashamed on those occasions when I didn't.

But where my father was bitter and angry, my mother was happy and loving. Happy to have a child, happy to have someone to shower with her love and affection, and I think happy to have something to do besides listen to my father. She was a big woman with rosy cheeks and long chestnut hair that she usually kept in a braided ponytail. She laughed a lot and smelled of caraway.

When I started to toddle around, my mother glued a section of an old bicycle tire to the bottom of my shoe to even up my legs. She wouldn't hear of any talk about being crippled. To her, I was just Albert. Whenever I was feeling bad, or had been taunted by the kids at school, she would wrap me up in her big arms and hug me until I felt warm and loved.

Melting Point

My mother took in laundry and sewing to help the family make ends meet. She never complained about not having much. Before the first war, when my father had been working as an architect, they had more money and a nicer house, even a maid. But I guess most of our neighbors were in the same boat. My mother would spend a part of each day chatting with some of the women of the neighborhood as they worked on a tiny plot of land that was a kind of community garden. But sometimes I'd wake up late at night and hear her softly crying. Today I would guess it was about her situation, about the toughness of her life. At the time, though, I thought she was crying in disappointment over me. I felt so bad that I had let them down.

My mother had a brother named Carl. He and his wife Mary were farmers up in Poland, and they would occasionally send us packages of food, mostly jars of preserved fruits and vegetables, and sometimes potatoes. Railroad service was too unreliable to send anything perishable. Every bit helped. In return, my mother would knit sweaters and socks and mittens for my aunt and uncle. Polish winters get awfully cold, and they needed all the warm clothes they could get.

I guess my parents must have decided that having a child wasn't all that bad, because when I was two years old I got a brother, Herman. The first thing my Father noticed about him was that he was **whole**. Well, it was the first thing I noticed about him, anyway. My parents just adored him. I expected that from my mother, but it was unusual to see my father happy about a child, and, well, it didn't make me feel too good. As we grew up together, though, I came to like Herman too, because he was always proud of his big brother. When he was little, he would sometimes imitate my limp, not to make fun of me, but to be like me. How could I not love that?

Herman was strong, good-looking, and even-lengthed, all the things I wasn't. He had bright blue eyes and blond hair and a strong jaw. My earliest memories of him were how my father beamed at him when he came trotting into the room. My only hope for attention was to do well in school, something Herman couldn't do. I remember one time when I was in seventh grade and Herman was in fifth. We brought our report cards home. My father praised my card, and then looked at Herman with a frown.

"Why can't you do as well in school as Albert?" He said, shaking his finger at Herman.

Herman was crushed.

I glowed.

My smile was so wide, my cheeks hurt. My father was proud of me for something! My celebration was short-lived, though, as Herman couldn't stay in my father's bad graces for long, just as I couldn't stay in his good graces for long. Soon life was back to normal, with Herman as the favorite son.

As we grew up, Herman and I developed a symbiotic relationship. He was big and strong, almost hulking, and would hang around with me on the playgrounds and any other places bullies might be tempted to pick on me. I helped him through his homework, and helped him prepare for tests. Together we made it through school. I suppose we each envied and respected the other's abilities.

When I was young, Germany was in chaos. The depression got worse and the government wasn't able to keep order. Riots broke out. Different factions wanted to take over the government – the extreme right, the extreme left, and everything in between. My father became, if possible, even more bitter about the government.

One night, though, after being at the local beer hall, my father came home late, his face flushed.

"They've invited us in!" He said to my mother. "They've invited **me** in!"

Melting Point

"Who? Who has invited you in?" asked my bewildered mother.

"They want us to join in, so we can help restore order in the town," my father explained, as if that answered my mother's question. He continued, "Most of them are ex-soldiers, like me. They need experienced men to help keep the order. The army can't do it. The police don't do it. So, they want **me**."

He was grinning from ear to ear. His cheeks were bright red, though that may have been from the beer. His eyes were ablaze. He was ecstatic.

Over the next couple of days, my mother put together a uniform for him, kind of a cross between a boy-scout uniform and a military uniform. Made of brown fabric, it had a black belt and was decorated with my father's war medals. My mother also took a pair of leather gloves and filled the left thumb and forefinger with wooden dowels, and my father would wear these gloves with his uniform, looking dashing and handsome. He went out almost every night after that, and he would come home all fired up about how he was helping to be a part of the solution to Germany's ills.

And that is how my father joined the brown-shirts, the forerunner of the Nazi Party.

Most of the brown-shirts were thugs - uneducated or working-class fellows who hated those in power and those that were trying to get into power. Being an educated man, my father stood out as someone who could help with organization and planning for the group, and he quickly rose in the ranks. It kept him off the streets, too, which is something that he says that he didn't like, but I think that secretly he was glad to avoid all the violence that the brown-shirts were involved in.

I like to think that my father didn't, at the time, understand the political stance of the group, other than that they were trying to keep order and keep the Russian socialists from taking over the government. My father seemed to think

Promise Kept

that was a serious threat. I know my father was bitter about the way he was treated after the war, but I don't think he was a hateful person.

As you know, Adolph Hitler became the leader of the Nazi party. My father took Herman and me to hear Hitler speak when I was thirteen. This was in September of 1930. By this time, the Nazis had many seats in Parliament, but Hitler was not yet Chancellor. We saw him in an auditorium, with professors from the local university on the stage with him. Quite a crowd had gathered to hear him speak. He started by speaking softly, almost intimately, about how the audience was composed of some of the best that Germany had to offer, and how proud he was to be there. Then his voice slowly rose in volume and speed as he talked about the people trying to ruin Germany. He worked up to a fever pitch, shouting at the top of his lungs. Then suddenly he halted and gazed out at the audience, looking at each of us in turn. Then he started talking softly again. He talked about how we, banding together, could make Germany great again, just as our ancestors had done. He alternately spoke fast and slow, loud and soft. He used a lot of alliteration, almost in a kind of hard-hitting poetry. It was mesmerizing.

Hitler said he wanted law and order. He wanted to put unemployed people like my father back to work, in well-paying jobs. He wanted to build, make Germany strong again, and reclaim past glory for the country. He wanted to expand the borders of the country, not just to get back what was taken from us after the end of the war, but to make the vast lands of the East become German farms with 'gentlemen farmers,' like those plantations of the old American South. He talked too about the recent victories in Parliament, where the Nazis now had more seats than ever before. I can still hear him telling us why these seats were needed…

"It is not for seats in Parliament that we fight," Hitler said quietly. "But we win seats in Parliament in order that one day we may be able to liberate

Melting Point

the German people." He looked at us with those piercing eyes. I felt him look at **me**. His voice boomed much louder, "Do not write on your banners the word **Victory**. Today that word shall be uttered for the last time. Strike through the word Victory and write once more in its place the word which suits us better; the word **Fight**."

I know, now it sounds terrible. Now we hear what he said and we read between the lines. Now when we hear Hitler talking of 'law and order,' we think of the Gestapo and how they turned that term upside down. When we hear about expanding borders, we think of the war. When we hear about 'gentlemen farmers,' we think of the slaves needed to make that work, and of the legal owners of the land who would be removed so that Germans could own it.

At the time, though, we were naive and in need of hope, and I must confess that I loved the idea that we could be prosperous, important, and free from turmoil. And we could be on par with other European governments, not just the-losers-of-the-war. And my father could have a good job that made money and made him happy. My father wanted these things; he wanted Hitler. I wanted all these things too. So, I wanted Hitler.

After the rally, my father took Herman and me for some sweets and he really beamed as he talked about Hitler and the National Socialists. He was really proud to be with them. Herman, too, was full of our father's enthusiasm for law and order, for German importance in the world. I suppose I was too, but there were a couple of things that nagged at me that night. Hitler had blamed all our problems, not on entire countries, but on a group of people in control of those countries. He blamed our own problems on the same group of people, who, he said, controlled the banks and the newspapers and other important parts of society. Hitler blamed the world's and Germany's problems on the Jews. I had a hard time believing that the kids I played with at school were part of some giant plot to keep Germany down.

Hitler had said some other things that disturbed me, too. It sounded to me like he wanted to invade other countries. My father and Herman just laughed, because no one was ready for war again.

Hitler had said, "England did not conquer India by the way of justice and of law; she conquered India without regard to the wishes, to the views of the natives, or to their formulations of justice, and, when necessary, she has upheld this supremacy with the most brutal ruthlessness. Just in the same way Cortez or Pizarro annexed Central America and the northern states of South America, not on the basis of any claim of right, but from the absolute inborn feeling of the superiority of the white race."

When I mentioned this to my father, he shrugged his shoulders and said, "Well, we should get back the land that belongs to us." But he stopped and looked at both Herman and me and said, "You boys won't have to fight a big war, though. I mean it. Hitler was in the Great War just as I was, and no one wants that again. I'm sure he means we'll just take what is rightfully ours. But not with a war." He looked off into space, as if trying to believe what he had just said.

In January of 1933, when I was still fifteen years old, Hitler was elected Chancellor. My father soon got work with the government and left active participation in the brown-shirts. It's good that he did because a year later Hitler had my father's old boss killed as a part of what became known as 'The Night of the Long Knives.' Eventually, my father worked in Albert Speer's construction department, working on the design and construction of new buildings in Berlin. All I knew at the time was that he was making good money, and he was happy. That was enough for me.

In school, there began to be more of an emphasis on physical fitness, which suited Herman, but not me. Not only did I have my uneven legs, but I was also clumsy. So, I worked harder at math and science to make up for my

Melting Point

failings on the playing field. Still, the 'Ideal German' was someone who was more like Herman than me.

#

The spring after my last year at the Gymnasium, which was what German grade schools were called, Herman and I visited our aunt and uncle in Poland. That was in late March of 1936. Several months earlier, the German Army had occupied the Saarland, which was a small strip of land along our French border. The Saarland had belonged to Germany before the last war, but was given to France as part of the punishment for Germany losing. Now Germany had taken it back. France hadn't put up much resistance, and Germans everywhere were celebrating. It was just as my father had said; we took land that was ours and we didn't start a big war!

It was all my Uncle Carl could talk about. Hitler had been saying he was going to reclaim lands that rightfully belonged to Germany. There were large ethnic German populations in the Saarland, as well as in many of the countries around Germany, including Poland.

"Boys, maybe Poland will be next," Uncle Carl said to Herman and me the first night we got there. "That would suit me just fine!"

"Hush, Carl!" Aunt Mary admonished. "Don't say that too loud or the police will visit us."

Carl just brushed that fear aside. I'm not sure when Carl and Mary moved to Poland; it was long before I was born. There wasn't a lot of available farmland in Germany, and so they moved out like so many other farmers had. I guess a lot of them really wanted to live in Germany.

"If we can't go live in Germany," Carl told us, "Maybe Germany can come to us."

Promise Kept

Carl and Mary were tough folks. They worked hard, and it showed in their lined faces and tanned skin. Winters in Poland are very cold and harsh, and spring and fall can be very wet and swampy, so you have to be tough survivors to live there. Carl was very stubborn about things, and Mary was very opinionated about everything and everyone. They were a perfect match.

Herman and I spent time helping out on the farm. It wasn't a large farm, being bordered on all sides by neighbors also trying to eke out a living from the land. Being a small farm, there wasn't a lot to do. But we fixed fences and dug drainage ditches and patched the barn roof. Mostly we just played. We spent time hiding in bushes and rolling in the grass. We had brought our bicycles, and we went for rides in the rolling marshy countryside.

Herman had taken a strong interest in horses. In the city there wasn't a lot of opportunity to be with them, but on the farm he could work with my uncle's horse. She was more of a work animal than a riding horse, but Herman liked her. He spent a lot of time grooming and caring for her.

One evening as we were finishing dinner, Uncle Carl said, "Well, Albert, what are you going to do with yourself now that you've graduated?"

I put down my beer. "Well, I start Labor Service next month. That will last six months, and then I'm off to the University to study engineering."

"Not the army?" Aunt Mary looked astonished. "I would think your father would want you to be in the army like he was."

"Well," I responded, "the army would love to have all of me except my feet. Unfortunately, wherever my feet go, I go, so if the army won't take my feet, they won't take me either." I turned to Herman. "Now Herman, I'm sure, they will love. In two years, when he graduates, he'll join up and become a general."

Melting Point

"No, not a general," Herman piped up. "I want to work with horses, so I'd like to be in the artillery. Horses pull the guns, they pull the ammo wagons, and they pull the food wagons. I want to work with the horses."

"Well, Herman," started Carl, "if you want to work with horses in the army, maybe you boys should go visit the Polish army unit that is about a dozen miles from here. They seem to have a lot of horses."

Mary added, "That's a great idea. Take a lunch and your bikes and make a day of it. Their camp is near a beautiful old town. It's lovely there."

So the next morning Herman and I packed up a lunch of goat cheese, dried meat, some brown bread, and some dried fruit, and took off on our bikes up the road. It was a beautiful day, with plenty of sun, and some cool spring breezes that kept us from sweating too much. The dirt road from Mary and Carl's farm was narrow, wet, and slightly rutted. After a few miles, which zipped by on our bikes, we turned east on a larger road that was gravelly and well traveled, but with potholes. We could ride side by side on this road, which was harder to do on the other road, but sometimes one of us would hit a pothole. By the time we reached the town we were tired and a little sore in the rear.

Just before the town we crossed over the large Vistula River, one of the main waterways in Poland, and went through a little hamlet known as Harmense, barely a few buildings. From there we were fast approaching the Sola River. We got to some railroad tracks and decided to ride along the tracks towards town, so we turned off the road and rode along the track bed, keeping watch for any trains that might come along.

We got to the town's rail yard, which was fairly large. This town was the junction between rail lines going north-south and east-west, so the rail yard had a lot of tracks and buildings to house trains and goods and such. From the rail yard we followed the road southeast, and then turned right on a road that went south across the Sola River and into the town itself. Prominent, as we crossed the old wooden bridge across the river, was the town hall's steeple. We used the steeple as a guide and rode towards it and the center of town.

Like many medieval towns, this one had been built with a castle and a church surrounding a market square. The buildings were mostly in long rows in case the town needed defending. Today, though, there wasn't much need to defend the town. The day was peaceful, the air clear, the breezes cool. Some farmers had wagons in the market square in front of the town hall, and were selling vegetables, breads, and other items.

Herman and I parked our bikes, sat on a bench, and ate our lunch as we watched the town life unfold. Some birds came down to see if they could steal breadcrumbs from us, and we tossed them bits of our crust. They would pick up pieces and dart into the air, sometimes with another bird close behind. The sun was as high as it was going to get in the sky, and the sunlight felt warm on our skin.

Some children were playing a game that seemed to involve a lot of running and squealing. A small group of Hasidic Jews in long black robes, black boots, and black puffy hats walked by the town hall involved in an animated discussion. An old woman in a shawl was haggling over the price of some sort of root vegetable. An army officer strode purposefully across the square.

An army officer! Herman jumped up and ran after him. I followed, leaving the remains of our lunch behind on the bench.

"Sir, excuse me, sir!" Herman ran after the officer shouting. "Do you speak German?"

The officer turned smartly and looked Herman up and down. Herman was puffing from his sudden burst of effort, and I was limping to catch up to them. The officer narrowed his eyes at us.

"German. A little," he said. He didn't look happy to see us.

Melting Point

"My name is Herman Stohl, and I'm interested in seeing your horses. I love horses," Herman said expectantly.

The officer seemed to think a moment, probably trying to translate what he had said.

"Horses? You want to see horses?"

"Yes, I, er, we, er, well, we like horses, and . . ." Herman started to see how silly this was, two German boys asking a Polish army officer to see his horses. He stammered and looked at the ground. I looked away.

Unexpectedly, though, the officer started to smile and spoke to us in thickly accented German. "We have many horses. Go across the river and take the first road to the left. Follow it about a mile to our barracks. Tell the guard at the gate what you told me."

We thanked the man and shook his hand. We watched him walk away for a moment, and then looked at each other excitedly. We headed back to the bench where our bikes and lunches were. However, instead of seeing a bench, we saw a mass of birds. They were tearing at every piece of food left.

"Lunch is over," I said.

"Who cares? Let's go see the barracks!"

We rode back across the wooden bridge that brought us into town. But instead of heading back to the train station, we turned left onto a side road immediately after going by the bridge gatehouses, part of the ancient defenses of the town. We rode parallel to the river for a while and came to a cluster of brick and wooden buildings.

We went up to the entrance and tried to explain what we wanted to the guard on duty. However, he didn't understand much German and we didn't understand much Polish. The guard was nice enough to go get an officer though, and the officer spoke some German.

"Horses? Why do you want to see horses?" The officer looked at us suspiciously.

"I like them," Herman said simply, a slight grin on his handsome face.

I nodded sagely.

"OK," the soldier said simply. He waved for us to follow him.

For the next few hours he showed us around the stables. Most of the rows and rows of wooden buildings were portable horse stables. They could be broken down and transported by train to another site and re-assembled. This was mostly an artillery post, and so the whole camp needed to be mobile. The brick buildings, we were told, were left over from a labor exchange that had once been there.

Herman and I split up for a while, so he could look at the magnificent horses, and I could look at the architecture of the buildings and the lush greenery. Well, actually we split up because I was tired of walking. The soldier who was with us said I was free to explore the grounds while he showed Herman the horses.

At this time of year with the lush green of the grasses, and the trees and bushes in bloom, contrasting with the bright red of the brickwork buildings, was breathtakingly beautiful. What a perfect day it was. The world was at peace, Germany had retaken the Saarland, my father was working at a good paying job, my mother could buy nice things again, and I was smelling spring flowers in Poland and basking in the sunshine.

I walked up and down the rows of buildings. The central part of the camp was mostly in a square, with three neat rows of twelve buildings, all brick and mostly two stories. They were about 30 feet wide and 100 feet long. Paths of gravel and dirt separated them from each other. Many of them had flowers in little pots hanging from the window ledges. Here and there was a tree or

Melting Point

bush, now in spring bloom. Most of the buildings looked like they were dormitories to house soldiers.

In the center at the front of the camp was a cluster of buildings and a large hall that seemed to be a kitchen and dining hall. While most of the buildings were oriented north-south, this one was oriented east-west. It was also the same width as the other buildings, but about twice as long. The other buildings around it were smaller than the rest of the buildings. There were a lot of soldiers there, and I didn't want to disturb anyone, so I kept away from that part.

Off to the north-east side of the camp, away from most of the rest of the camp, was an ammo bunker, half sunk into the ground. It had earth mounds around it to direct any accidental explosions up into the air rather than out at the surrounding buildings. Good thing, too, because there were what appeared to be officer's houses near the bunker. There wasn't much to see there without climbing over the dirt mounds, so I instead walked by the houses. Besides being different in appearance, these buildings had little yards with flowers planted in them.

I came to a good-sized tree in a small courtyard between two houses. It was quiet there, with no one around. Having toured the whole place for a while now, I was tired. I sat in the crook of some low branches and leaned against the trunk. In the distance I could hear horses whinnying, but right around me there were just some birds chirping and the occasional rustle of leaves in the breeze. I sat there and rested for a while, just enjoying the day. Out of idleness and a little boredom, I pulled out my pocketknife and carved my initials into the tree trunk, **A.S.**

After a little while, I headed back to the front of the camp to see how Herman was doing. He was just coming back to the front of the camp as well, animatedly talking with the soldier. He was excited and flushed and looked like he was ready to join the Polish army right then.

When he got to me he said, "This is fantastic! I've just **got** to do this when I join!"

We had a good time there, and were treated very well by our hosts. When we noticed what time it was, we had been there almost three hours. We thanked our host profusely, and I think he enjoyed showing off the beautiful camp.

Rather than head right home, we rode back into town to sit and have some tea. After some inquiry, we went to a small café in the lobby of the Hotel Herz. Herman regaled me with stories of what he saw and learned at the camp while we had some tea and cookies. When we were done, we each wrote a postcard home to our parents, and then left this beautiful, charming town. We rode back over the Sola, and rode out to the train station so we could retrace the tracks to the road that would take us home.

As we cycled back through the train station, I noticed the sign that announced the name of the town. It was a town I was destined to come back to.

Melting Point

Indians

The rain in Bodega Bay had just started to fall in large drops on the deck outside as I looked around at Tom and Magda, and then over at Tony and Amanda.

"The sign hanging from the train station read Oswiecim. In German, the town was called Auschwitz."

Outside, it started to pour.

We took a short break to let my voice rest and to stretch our legs. So far, nothing in the story was too bad, and the mood of my listeners was positive. The rain was coming down hard, and the loud thrumming hiss of the rain on the roof covered most other sounds.

As she poured me some more coffee, Amanda said, "I never thought about there being a **town** of Auschwitz. And I would certainly not have expected it to be pretty."

Tony added, "It probably looked just as pretty during the war, if you didn't know what was going on."

I nodded. "At that time, it was beautiful in all senses of the word. Later on, the trees and flowers and birds would still be there, but it was no longer a beautiful place."

Magda smiled a bit worriedly, like she wasn't sure what was going to come next. She presented me with a small plate of cookies.

"These were Mom's favorites," she announced wistfully.

I ate a cookie. It was shortbread, light and buttery; definitely not on my diet. I asked for another. Etta used to make these with very little sugar, and we both loved them. They weren't crunchy enough for Rudy.

Tom poured himself another Pepsi, and looked out the window at the rain. Magda came back from the direction of the bathroom, and we all took our seats again. I took a sip of coffee and continued my story.

#

So, in April of 1936, after leaving Aunt Mary and Uncle Carl's farm, I went into the Labor Service and Herman went back to Gymnasium. Labor Service was a cross between a roadwork crew and scout camp. It was mostly fun, and I met a lot of other boys. I suppose it was a dress rehearsal for the army. We did do a lot of good service for the betterment of the country. Because of my bad feet and good brains, I was assigned survey duty. My group spent the summer doing flood control work. We cleared streams of logs and debris, made drainage ditches alongside roads, put in culverts, and that sort of thing. I would go around with maps, a compass, and a slide rule and make elevation calculations and such. It was, truth be told, kind of fun. It was my first time away from my family for an extended period, and I learned how to rely on myself and my new-found friends.

After six months, I left the Labor Service and bade my new friends goodbye. Most of them went right into the army, but I was going to go off to the University. At that time, most young boys were going into the army, and

Melting Point

girls were being groomed to be mothers, so universities were poorly attended. It was just as well, because the faculty had been considerably reduced once the Jews weren't allowed to teach.

When I got home from the Service, I found that my mother had acquired a bird. My father complained about it when he was home, which wasn't often, as it created quite a mess, but my mother said it was good companionship since she was home alone so much. She would baby that bird the way she used to be able to baby us. At first I thought it was silly, but I kind of grew attached to the fluffy thing.

I won't bore you with details of my studies or the antics we used to inflict on the professors. Instead, I'll skip ahead two years to 1938. For me, there were four big events that year. The first was that Herman graduated from Gymnasium and went into the Labor Service and then the army. He got his wish by being assigned to artillery training. This made all of us so proud that Herman would serve the country. I was determined that I would do my part, somehow, to help the country too. I just figured that my path was to stay in school so I could get a good job.

The second big event that year was in March, when Germany invaded Austria. It was mostly peaceful, and helped reunite us with Hitler's birthplace. Many ethnic Germans were happy to rejoin their fatherland. I suppose many other Austrians were not so happy about it, but at the time we didn't hear about them. I was happy that this had happened. I got a postcard from my Uncle Carl that just said, "Maybe we'll be next!" I'm sure he had to sneak that by my aunt!

As if in answer to his postcard, the third big event was Germany invading Czechoslovakia. Again, it was mostly peaceful, though I think fewer Czechs wanted us than Austrians. Well, Germany was on a roll! With almost no loss of life we had made huge gains in territory. Hitler's promises seemed to be coming true, and the future looked great for us. People were at work, the depression was completely over, we had a booming economy, and the country was expanding in size. True, the French and English were screaming that we'd broken treaties and such, but they didn't do anything about it. At the time, it looked like it was all just for show, so they could claim that they had tried to aid countries when all they really did was talk. Most of the rest of Europe and America were still in a depression, so we all felt pretty smug.

The fourth and biggest event for me that year was the Evian Conference. This was a conference for other countries to discuss what to do with Germany's Jews. It was held in between the invasion of Austria and the invasion of Czechoslovakia. However, for me personally, it was to become a bigger deal than the other three events combined.

You see, for years Germany had been encouraging German Jews to leave the country. Many did leave. In the six years Hitler had been in power, about a quarter of our Jews had left the country to seek a better life elsewhere. But when we invaded Austria, we got more 'New Jews' into the expanded Germany than all of those that had left! So, Hitler was demanding that, if other countries were so Jew-friendly, they should be clear on how many Jews they were willing to take, and open their doors. He even promised to pay for sending them there!

America's President Roosevelt convened a conference of world leaders in Evian, France, to discuss setting quotas for Jewish immigrants. After some initial balking from various countries, Roosevelt said that countries would not be strong-armed into taking more Jews than they wanted. Otherwise, many countries were threatening to not even participate.

In what became a terrible spectacle, most countries refused to change existing policies that either didn't allow Jews at all, or only a very small number of Jews. Australia's representative even said, "We have no race problem now,

Melting Point

and we do not intend to import one." Canada, another democracy with huge amounts of land, also said no. In fact, most countries said no. It was a terrible international defeat for Roosevelt and a victory for Hitler.

Hitler made a lot of hay about this. He basically said, "See? No one wants them. Don't criticize Germany about the way it treats Jews if you don't want any yourself."

For me, this was a real eye-opener. I had heard general anti-Semitic comments growing up, much the way that one here in the U.S. might hear comments about people whose ancestors came from Africa, or the Middle East, or wherever. I just figured that people who made such remarks were uninformed, or hadn't met many Jews. When Hitler made it government policy to hate Jews, I was taken aback. But, I accepted this as a part of the 'total package.' You know, you take the good with the bad, and I really liked the good things Hitler was saying and doing, so I looked the other way at the bad things.

But as the government's policies became increasingly harsh, I became dismayed at what we were doing. By that time, though, I was fully invested in the other parts of Hitler's programs, and so I felt that, well, at least the Jews could go to another country. In retrospect, this sounds bad, but at the time, it was a way I could keep closing my eyes to what was going on. If they don't like it, they can always leave.

At the Evian Conference the world in essence said to Germany, "The Jews can't leave Germany; they are Germany's problem." A problem; a problem left to Hitler to solve. No one wants them, and so no one cares what we do to them. No one cares what becomes of them.

I remember that as a boy we had been taught in school how the Americans had killed the Indians. While most good citizens of America might not have wanted the natives murdered, they wanted them off their land. But

74

where could they go? So, the cavalry moved the natives onto reservations that were in climates unfamiliar to them and unsuited to their way of life. The cavalry let them freeze in the winter; starve in the summer; and die of disease. When the Indians rebelled, they were killed.

My teacher had said that this was why the Americans weren't as civilized as we Europeans. Yet, after the Evian Conference, I felt that the participating countries were like the ranchers who sympathized with the Indians' plight, but didn't want them on **their** land. Now, Hitler would have to play the role of the U.S. cavalry.

I remember vividly seeing that image of Indians displaced by cavalry in my mind when I read about the Evian conference. Part of me thought that this was far-fetched, that we were civilized Europeans, after all. But I couldn't deny all the privations and alienation from 'normal society' that we had already bestowed upon the Jews. I expected Hitler to make good on his claim that they would be removed from German soil and moved east. While it wasn't clear to me then that they were doomed, it was certainly unjust and unfair.

So, the obvious question is, what did I do about it? My answer is that I did nothing. I could have run around town screaming that the Jews were being treated unfairly, but that would only land me in the hands of the Gestapo. I could have left the country in protest, but where would I go? Had I known what was eventually to transpire, I would have left, I suppose. But, it was summer. I was on break from school. Life was good for me. Germany was enjoying a boom that I hadn't known my whole lifetime. If some things in your life depress you and other things fill you with joy, what do you do? You try hard to ignore the depressing things, of course. So, that is what I did.

Time passed at the University. The next year, 1939, was my third year at the University. My brother was in an artillery unit, my father was working for Albert Speer rebuilding Berlin, and the world continued spiraling towards global

Melting Point

war. In September, Germany invaded Poland from the west. Two weeks later, Russia invaded Poland from the east. World War II had officially started.

I've always felt the **world** war actually started three years earlier in 1936. That's when Germany invaded the Saarland, the Spanish Civil War started, and Japan invaded China. By 1939, over a half million people had been killed in Spain, hundreds of thousands in China, and Germany had begun the Holocaust. But, history says the war started in September of 1939, because that is when England and France officially joined the war. I say **officially,** because France and England declared war on us after we invaded Poland, yet they did nothing about it. They waited; for what I don't know. Waited for Germany, I suppose.

The Polish invasion campaign didn't last long, however, and my life at school was hardly even interrupted. Germany was now at war, and so young men were joining the army in record numbers. German industry was desperate for new workers. My university started an apprentice program with certain companies, so that we could start working sooner and still get school credit. I applied to the companies that interested me.

#

One day in late November the rain pelted down on my hat as I ran towards my rooming house. It was dark, and the streets were covered with water. In the inside pocket of my rain jacket were three letters, one from my brother Herman, one from my mother, and one from a heating company in Erfurt. I had decided to get to my rooming house before opening the letters, so I could savor them with my feet up in front of the fireplace. I didn't think anything of my gait, though a stranger may have thought I had hurt my foot from the way I limped slightly.

I got to my rooming house, and took off my boots, coat, and hat in the foyer and hung them to drip onto the stone floor. I took the letters from the inner pocket of my coat and headed into the main room. The old house was cold and damp, but there was a fire in the fireplace and a couple of my school chums were playing a game of chess in front of it.

"Boy it sure is wet out," I said to no one in particular as I plopped down into the only available chair, a deep low chair that was a bit hard to get out of.

"Shhhhh!" said Gregory, one of the chess players. Maybe 'chums' was overstating my relationship with Gregory and with Paul, the other player. Housemates may be a better term.

I took out the three letters and decided to read them in reverse order of pleasure. That meant I would read the one from the heating company first, then . . . well, I should have saved my mother's for last, but the truth was I saved Herman's for last. But I felt a little guilty about that.

The letter from the heating company was from a Mr. Prüfer, a senior engineer with the firm, informing me that I had been accepted as an apprentice with the company, and could start to spend time with them as soon as I was able. It was a position with a company that made sophisticated gas heating systems; state of the art, really. It would be a fine way to learn. The university encouraged apprenticing at companies, and you earned school credit from being there and from reporting on what you learned. It would help me become a part of the great renaissance that was happening all over Germany, and throughout our new territories.

Since the war with Poland had been won, Germany had quite a bit of new land - Austria, Czechoslovakia, half of Poland, and the Saarland. There was a huge need for engineers of all kinds, and I was excited to finally begin being a part of Germany's climb to greatness. Well, if my niche was to be as a designer and builder of state-of-the-art heating systems, so be it.

Feeling the cold in the room, I mumbled, "We could use a state-of-the-art heating system in this room."

Melting Point

"Shush, Stohl!" hissed Gregory. "I'm trying to think." I ignored him.

I carefully replaced the letter into its envelope for later, and took out my mother's letter. It was written on thin paper with tiny writing on it. I had to hold it towards the light to read it.

#

Dear Albert,

I hope you are doing well in school. In your last letter you mentioned that you are feeling a little lonely, and I must say I sometimes feel lonely too. With Herman off at army training, your father off at work, and you in school, it is awfully quiet here. If it weren't for the bird I'd go crazy! That is why I look forward to your letters – please keep writing. Let me tell you a little about what's going on with the rest of your family.

Your brother is doing well in the army. He is enthusiastic, though he does complain about some of the hardships of the training. He is getting high marks, though, and he is confident he will be selected for officer training. There is a huge demand for soldiers now, and so there is a big need for officers too. As you know, we are supposedly at war with England and France now. Even though nothing has happened yet, I'm hoping that when it does, your brother will perform gloriously at headquarters in Berlin, and not in some battlefield! I hope he wasn't involved in the Polish campaign, I haven't heard yet.

Your father got a promotion and is now working very closely with Albert Speer, Hitler's architect. They are designing the new city center of Berlin. Your father has been sent on expeditions all over looking for materials. He had been in Italy recently buying marble, and was amazed at how much the Italians want to be more like us Germans. Everyone treats him with great respect and asks him about the 'new

Germany'. He no longer feels his missing thumb and finger make him less of a man.

Your Aunt Mary and Uncle Carl are doing well. Their farm ended up on the German side of Poland. What a relief not to be on the Russian side! Germans in Poland are the new celebrities there. Anything they want, they can have. The new German authorities relocated the neighboring farmers around your aunt and uncle's farm so they could have more land. The authorities also helped them get some farmhands to work their new lands!

In October, Heinrich Himmler was made a Reich Commissioner and placed in charge of helping Germans in Poland, and he is apparently already delivering results. With the new lands, Carl can finally be the 'gentleman farmer' he always dreamed of being. They both ask about you and hope you can come visit them soon.

#

At this, I muttered, "Soon. Not during winter! Maybe when school is out for the summer next year."

"Shush, Stohl, please!" This time it was Paul.

#

Not much more to tell. Things are going well here at home. I was in the market place early one morning and saw the tailor and his family rounded up by the police and taken away towards the train station. They protested their innocence, but the police must have had their reasons. They had always seemed so nice; I wonder what they did? Later that same day there was a new owner of their shop, and with all the same merchandise! With typical German efficiency, a bad event was made good in record time. Please write soon.

Melting Point

#

I looked the letter over a second time. My mother hadn't said much about how she was doing besides being a little lonely, but I could imagine her enjoying a little time free, what with her husband in Italy and her sons away. I suppose she finally has time to do the things she really wants to do. Then another thought crossed my mind. What does she really want to do? All she's ever talked about were her husband and sons. I thought of her hobbies, knitting and cooking. These were things that helped the family, not her. Maybe caring for the bird would take up her time. "Well, she'll find something," I muttered.

Gregory lifted his head from his game, and said, "Stohl! Find somewhere else to talk, can't you?"

"What, do you need some help playing?" I said, smiling maliciously. "Is your brain as wet as the outdoors?"

"Harrumph. Like you could help." Gregory said, smiling slightly, as he looked back at the chessboard.

I thought again about Mother's letter. Herman is doing well, but his future could be rough if we fight France and England. Dad is having a great time. Mom, I'm not sure about, but I guess she's doing fine. Aunt and Uncle seem to have struck it rich, if not in money yet, then at least in opportunity. Only the tailor seems to have been doing poorly. I wasn't as naïve as my mother, or as she tried to sound. The tailor was probably Jewish, and Jews were being removed from Germany. They had their chance to leave by themselves, but now they were being removed by force. Well, that's just too bad, I told myself. But then I realized that that was a silly notion; they should be left alone. However, the government had practically outlawed being Jewish. I frowned at that, not quite sure how I felt about it. So many great things are happening, but there was this one ugly stain on our honor.

Then I thought again about my aunt and uncle. What had the letter said? Their neighbors had been removed so they could have more land. What happened to those farmers? I wonder if they were hustled off like the tailor. Then Carl and Mary can go from peasants to rich landowners, and another 'bad event was made good.' I shivered. That ugly stain again.

I placed this letter back into its envelope too. I had a folder with all the letters I had gotten while at school, and I intended to keep them all. I pulled the last letter, the one from Herman, out from its envelope. It was a little smudged and dirty, and creased in a number of places. I savored the moment, because I liked to hear about Herman's exploits.

"Checkmate!" Paul said to Gregory, smiling triumphantly.

"Oops. Too bad," I said quietly while grinning at Gregory's misfortune, but loud enough for both of them to hear. Gregory stood up, thanked Paul for the game, looked at me with a frown, and left the room.

"Play the winner?" Paul asked.

"Maybe later." I said. "I've got a letter from my brother in the army."

"Really?" Said Paul with envy. "Can I read it when you're done? I'd love to hear about what's going on. We're not allowed to listen to the radio in our rooms, and I don't buy many newspapers."

I realized that Paul was at the University rather than in the army, not because he had an infirmity like me, but because he was part Jewish. More and more restrictions were being put on the Jewish students, though, and they lived like recluses. I looked at my letter. I didn't want to part with it, but I could use another friend.

"Sure," I said. "But after I finish with it, and then I need to have it back. I save all of the letters I get here in school."

"Sure thing," Paul said happily.

Melting Point

I studied Paul closer, thinking that he didn't **look** Jewish, and that may be why he was still here. Maybe he was only a tiny part Jewish. He was thin and pale, but he smiled pleasantly and looked relieved to have survived the encounter with another student without insults. I read my letter.

#

Greetings from Poland!

I hope you are doing well, sitting indoors and sipping brandy while I sit in a freezing stone hut getting wet and eating canned brown bread! Well, the hut would be colder, but the horses we share the hut with provide some heat. Too bad they provide some smell, too! Still, I wouldn't have traded this experience for anything! I hear that we will soon be moving into some better quarters, and the food is getting steadily better as supplies reach us here at the border between the Russians and us.

My little adventure started with my unit hearing we were to be a rear artillery unit in the Polish campaign. Since most of us were new recruits, they didn't want us up front. So I started the war trying to convince horses to get into railroad cars. You would think that they would have remembered being on trains from our exercises, but, well, they're even dumber than I am, so they didn't. We spent two days loading our train, and then heard that the war had started already! We were all thinking we were going to miss the war, and were saying, "Oh, no!" But we got on the trains and rolled along for a couple of days and got to our kickoff point, which was just inside the Polish border. It takes a long time to move a train of horses, because you have to stop frequently to feed and water them, and to shovel out the crap.

Anyway, we got there and unloaded (another day lost!). The next morning we set off to catch up to the army. All the mechanized units were a couple of days in front of us. And they were moving at a good clip.

The theory was that they would get bogged down in fighting and then we would catch up to them. Well, put theory in one hand and horse dung in the other, and see which gets full first! We trudged for days along roads clogged with the litter of war, but we were not getting any closer to the front!

After a while, we met prisoners of war and wounded Germans coming back. There were lots more prisoners than wounded Germans, let me tell you. As we got closer to the battles, we could hear the sounds of war in the distance, like thunder from a storm. And the closer we got, the more debris there was. It was crazy looking. Trucks were standing on end, as if a farmer had planted them in the ground. Smoking tanks without turrets or treads - what had happened to the turrets and treads? Where do you hide a turret weighing thousands of kilos? Livestock, lying dead and bloated on their side, looked like some statues that kids had tipped over. I felt bad for the animals - this wasn't their war.

Have you ever thought about the sounds of a war? That's what gets me the most, the sounds. From far away you just hear a booming, like a big bass drum. But as you get closer, you're still too far to see anything, but the noise comes from all directions, bouncing off hills and clouds so you can't really tell where it's coming from. There are the large booms of bombs, thuds of artillery, snaps, zings, whispers, shrieks, and a sound that is like rain, probably bricks and rocks thudding back to earth from being kicked up. It is both beautiful and terrifying. In the evenings there are the light shows that go along with the sounds - flashes and glows of various colors. And still we walked along with our horses, trying to catch up to the war.

Horses have to stop every now and then to rest and eat and drink, and they lose shoes and develop rashes and bruises and chafes and

Melting Point

get sick. Caring for the horses is almost a full-time job, and our progress was no faster than a slow walk. We'd get close enough to the battles to see them in the distance, have to stop for the horses, and the battles would roll forward. When we caught up to where they had been, the battles would be in front of us still, and we'd plod through the litter and waste of the war. But as time went on, the waste got steadily greater. At first there had been just a few dead men here and there, but now we would find fields covered with dead Poles and animals - hundreds of rifles, thousands of men. Entire trains were in ruins, horses and carts were strewn about, planes were on fire in the trees, and artillery pieces were bent and twisted like they were made of soft clay.

I had mixed feelings about all this. I was nervous as to how I would do in a battle. Would I be afraid or freeze in fear? Everyone worried about that. I also felt elation at our success, and the fact that we did so well against the Polish army. I felt bad for all the animals being killed. Surely after the battles farmers will need them for food and work? I also felt bad for all the civilians. I probably shouldn't mention this, but the civilians, well, get in the way during battles. They should flee into the hills or something, but they don't always, and then they get killed - by the thousands.

There's also the problem of the prisoners. Entire army groups surrender to us, and have to be taken care of. They have to be de-armed, and sent to the rear (at least away from the active battles). This takes lots of our own men to do this, men who should be fighting new battles. Fortunately, there are Gestapo men available for the guarding duty, and we turn over prisoners to them. I wouldn't want their job, having to care for hundreds of thousands of prisoners of war.

Finally, late one night, my group caught up to a battle. We were attacking some city whose Polish name I can't pronounce, let alone spell (ha ha like that would surprise you). The main army units were going to bypass the town, and they left it to us to shell the town until the Polish soldiers in there gave up. So, I finally got to fire guns in battle. In our practices, we would fire a gun or two, but here we had some 25 guns, all firing at the same time. God almighty, was that ever loud! Each time a gun fires, the dirt around the gun for several meters kicks up, making a small cloud of dust. But with 25 guns firing, it seemed that the very ground we stood on was disintegrating. The ground kicks up at your feet, as if it is trying to push you off the earth. Soon your ears stop working, and you feel the pounding in your chest, in your lungs, even in your eyes. Your ears hurt, your teeth knock together, your eyes sting, your feet feel unsteady, and your stomach churns. Funny thing was, I felt fantastic! I felt like I was finally really giving it to the enemy!

The next dawn we stopped shelling the town, after having pounded it for hours. We were just about out of ammunition and had to wait for supplies to catch up to us, and some of the guns needed maintenance, and the poor horses needed a break from the noise. We all collapsed, too, since we had been shelling all night and running without sleep, and with only some cold soup and canned brown bread for food. I slumped down to take a quick nap, and looked in the direction we had been firing. I felt an odd feeling, and had to look around to make sure I had my bearings, because the town that had been there only yesterday had vanished. There were lots of pits and small fires and some smoke, but the town was gone. I don't remember seeing any prisoners from that town. I slept fitfully that morning, with dreams of long lines of men walking up towards heaven.

Well, before too much longer the war in Poland was just about over, and my group proceeded to the border between the Russians and us. We don't trust that they won't try to grab some of our land, so we sit here and wave at them, very friendly like, but keep our guns trained in their direction. Sometimes a small group of Russians will come over to trade food. We trade our crummy rations for their crummy rations, just for a change of pace. The men seem healthy and strong, but their equipment looks pretty old and out of date. We don't speak much Russian, and they don't speak much German, so we mostly smile and gesture. It breaks up the days.

It's October, and already the rains have turned the ground into mush. Horses get around all right, but the wagon wheels get bogged down in mud, and a man is in danger of leaving his boots behind if he doesn't pick his feet up just right. At night it gets really cold, and sometimes the rain turns to hail or snow, but not long enough to freeze the ground. The horses don't like the cold any more than we do, so we try to keep them warm in old farmhouses and whatever other shelter we can find. We have tents, which keep you somewhat dry, but the buildings with horses in them are warmer, so we tend to spend time in there.

What I wouldn't give for those old tents we had in the Labor Service, with their wooden floors and bunk beds and down comforters. Here, a wool uniform and blanket is about our only concession to the cold. All the more reason to find a warm girl to spend time with. We go out in 'raiding parties' into the local village for friendly girls. With food almost non-existent, there are plenty of girls who will be your friend for a small can of brown bread, something we seem to have an abundance of. Some of the guys like different girls each time, but I'm kind of stuck on one in particular, real thin with curly black hair and some missing teeth. But she giggles a lot and is fun, and calls me 'her protector' in broken German.

Last week some of us were in the village on a social call. I'd picked some of the last wildflowers of the season and was going to deliver them to my girl. A bunch of Gestapo men were going door-to-door with *some local Polish official and rounding up Jews. The local officials would point out the houses of the Jews, and the Gestapo men would round up the families and take them away. We chatted with one of the Gestapo men, and he turned out to be a policeman from near our hometown! He said that groups of police were helping out as Gestapo men to make the villages Jew-free. I asked him where the Jews were going to be sent to live. Another man in my unit joked, "yeah, tell us, because we don't want to go there." The policeman just told him that he was right; he didn't want to go there. But he didn't say where that was. He did say that we could help ourselves to anything in their houses before the bankers came to claim them. Some men did that, but it didn't seem right to me, so I didn't.*

My girl wasn't at our pre-arranged meeting place. Since that day, I haven't seen my girl at all. I didn't think she was Jewish, but maybe she was, and was one of the families taken to live somewhere else. I've looked for her, but no one seems to know what happened to her. For all the times we were together, I never did know exactly where she lived or who her family was. I hope I see her again. I feel bad now about the people being taken away, and hope they are sent somewhere that's not too bad. Some 'protector' I turned out to be!

Well, I hear the truck coming that takes our mail. Learn lots in that university of yours, and write to me of your exploits.

Fondly, Herman

#

I looked over the letter again and re-read some parts of it to savor the feeling. Then I handed the letter to Paul, who thanked me and began to read. I felt glad to be living in the old rooming house, and not out in the mud or in a horse stable. As cold and damp as the old boarding house was, it was probably a palace compared to that.

Melting Point

I again thought of the thread of the letters from my mother and Herman about the Jews. Apparently, there was a well-organized effort to move Jews from wherever they were to somewhere else. Hitler had talked about sending them **east**, but you couldn't go much farther east than Poland, and Herman was already on the eastern border of Germany's side of Poland, so where were the Jews going that were in that village of his? And the ugly part of all this seemed that wherever the Jews were going, they weren't allowed to take their possessions with them. Maybe a suitcase or two, but having to leave a house or shop or farm behind, you would lose so much of personal value. That just seemed wrong. Maybe Hitler doesn't know that the Gestapo is doing that. Maybe the bankers come to collect the stuff to pay off debts. Maybe the bankers sell the places and forward the money to the families. There must be more to this than I know.

I looked at Paul, who had just finished the letter. Paul was ghost-white and trembling. I said, "I'm sure they are all right, wherever they are moved to."

"This is a bad time to be Jewish," Paul said sadly. "I don't know what's to become of us. I don't know how much more we can take."

I felt very awkward. "I'm sure it will be all right. Just weather the storm. Have you thought of leaving the country?"

Paul had a momentary flash of anger on his face, but returned to his sad look as he replied, "My family tried. There's nowhere to go. I had hoped that here, in a university, I would at least be away from the street thugs. But it's become government policy to hate Jews, so there's no escaping it." Paul handed me the letter and stood to leave.

"I'm sorry, I . . ." I said, at a loss for words.

"Thanks for letting me read the letter. I'll see you around." Paul turned and left the room.

Indians

I folded my letter from Herman, placed it back into its envelope, and sighed. I never saw Paul again. I didn't stay at school much longer, so he could have remained there. But, I doubt it. Like an American Indian of the old West, he was probably moved.

Topf

The rain had subsided somewhat, and Tom and I looked out the windows at the dark sky. In the distance a few fishing boats' lights could be seen in the bay. Closer to us were a few lights from neighboring houses.

"You don't think of the German army as being horse-drawn," Tom said. "In the movies, all you see are trucks and tanks and motorcycles."

I looked out over the bay. "We became more motorized later in the war, but at first there were the spearhead groups that were motorized, and everyone else had to catch up."

Magda came over and touched my arm. "How are you holding up?"

"So far, I'm doing just fine. But I need these breaks to rest my throat. The coffee has helped keep me going, too. Though, I don't want to get too jittery so maybe it's time to stop drinking it."

Amanda came over with Tony and said, "Grandpa, you are a great storyteller! It all seems so vivid and clear."

"You know, I've spent a lot of years trying not to think of those days," I said with a small smile. "But as I'm telling it, it comes back to me so vividly, it's like it was just a few months ago."

Tony said, "I agree with Amanda, I think you are doing a great job. This is really interesting stuff."

I laughed, "You don't have to be so kind to me! I haven't told stories this long since Magda was a little tyke." I excused myself and went to get rid of the coffee I'd been drinking all afternoon. So far the story had gone well, but now the story was about to take a dark turn. In the next couple of hours, Magda would learn the awful truth about me. I couldn't stop telling the story, but I wish I didn't have to go on. My nerves were on edge, making my stomach a little upset. When I came back from the bathroom, I decided to switch from coffee to water. That wouldn't stop me from having to relieve my bladder, but I didn't want to get any more jumpy than I already was.

When I got back to the living room, Magda said, "Are you ready to go on, or do you need to take a longer break?"

"No, let's keep going." No point in delaying the inevitable. And so we took our seats and I resumed my story. "Now we'll jump ahead a few months to the late spring of 1940. I was on my way to an apprenticeship with the heating company in Erfurt."

And so I began again.

#

I walked slowly along the old cobblestone street as it wound its way alongside ancient buildings. I periodically compared my map with the street signs. With my slight limp, my hips started to hurt after walking a ways from the train station. I came to a break in the buildings on my right and saw the river that bisects the town. The cloudless sky made for a spectacular view, and the cool breeze made the walk a little more pleasant. In the distance I could see

Melting Point

the spires of the medieval castle over the roofs of the old buildings. If Hansel and Gretel had lived in a big town, it would have looked like Erfurt.

I was about a mile away from the town center, along Weimarische Strasse, when I came to a compound with several large brick buildings surrounded by fencing. An iron plaque on the ornate gate announced the company as **Topf**. The carving looked a little like a cross section of a teapot without a handle, and with the name spelled as **TopF** inside it. The **T** and **F** had their bottom tails joined, with the **op** cradled between them. This was sort of a play on words, because Topf means 'pot' in German.

I entered the building closest to the street and announced myself to the pretty, freckled woman behind the entrance desk, who asked me to sit and wait while she paged someone. While waiting, my eyes feasted on her. She was wearing a low-cut blouse and her breasts were in danger of spilling out at any moment. I was smitten.

I waited too briefly before standing to greet a middle-aged jovial man in a white lab coat with a large smile.

"You must be Stohl. I'm Prüfer, Kurt Prüfer, one of the chief engineers here. It's a pleasure to meet you," Mr. Prüfer said, extending his hand.

"Albert Stohl, at your service," I said, bowing slightly and then shaking Mr. Prüfer's hand. He was completely bald, and wore dark-rimmed glasses. A little overweight, he looked like someone you could trust, like a close uncle, perhaps.

"You've met Gitta, here, she guards the door," Kurt Prüfer said, gesturing towards the plump, freckled woman. Well, girl really. I was beginning to think I was in love with her.

"Don't ever cross her, she bites. Come to think of it, she bites even if you **don't** cross her. Let me show you around." And with that, my hopes of getting closer to the curvy Gitta seemed dashed.

Gitta stuck out her tongue at Mr. Prüfer good naturedly and muttered, "Joker."

Mr. Prüfer showed me around the old buildings, going up and down narrow corridors. The floors were mostly made of old brick and stone, worn smooth from nearly a century of people walking over their surface. Stepping into one room, Kurt motioned towards a thin man with a lined face hunched over a tall workbench covered with wires, electric motors, and fan blades. "This is Karl Schultze, our ventilation expert. Karl, this is our new apprentice, Albert Stohl."

I extended my hand to shake Mr. Schultze's, but he just frowned and remarked grumpily, "Try not to get in my way, boy. I like my coffee black with sugar. Remember that, and we'll get along fine."

Mr. Prüfer laughed good naturedly and said, "Albert's all the help we're getting this year, Karl, and we need him. He's in the top of his class, and comes highly recommended. Try to treat him like an engineer and not as your personal servant."

"Right," Mr. Schultze said with disdain, going back to his drawings. I hoped I wouldn't have to work much with him.

"Right," I muttered under my breath. Kurt Prüfer appeared to be much nicer than Karl Schultze.

Continuing into another building, Mr. Prüfer led me into a large room with several men working busily over drafting tables. Each man sat on a stool, but the man in the center of the room had a taller draft table, and a taller stool, than the rest. "This is Paul Erdmann. Paul, Albert Stohl, the new apprentice," Kurt said, gesturing to the plump blond haired man on the tallest stool.

Mr. Erdmann said, "Welcome, Albert. Are you a good draftsman?"

Melting Point

I winced slightly. "I do all right, but the truth is that I'm much better at calculations and planning. My lines aren't as neat as they should be. . ."

"Hmm, that's too bad. Well, Schultze can probably use you. How are you with managing construction crews? Field work?"

I brightened a bit. "I'm a good organizer, and get along well with people. I read plans well, of course, and can translate them into reality." I then lost a little steam, realizing that I had never really done much of this for real. The most organizing I did was in the Labor Service. I added, "Well, I think I can, anyway. But I'm here to learn, and will try anything."

Kurt Prüfer slapped me on the back and laughed, "That's our boy. You'll do fine! Let me show you the crematorium."

"Uh, crematorium?" I said, with a little trepidation, as Mr. Prüfer took me to another building and down the stairs to the basement. "I thought Topf made furnaces and blowers, things like that."

Kurt laughed, "Ha! Furnaces, incinerators, crematoriums, they're mostly the same. The main difference is in how much you care about the ashes. Topf and Sons make the finest furnaces, incinerators, and crematoriums in the world! But right now, my department is working on crematoriums. That means *you* are working on crematoriums."

Mr. Prüfer took me into a large room off to the left down a dingy basement hallway. Where as the hallway was small and dark, the room was large and well lit. Against one wall of the room was a large brick structure that looked like a huge baker's oven. On the front were two large iron doors about three feet high and two and one-half feet wide. Some small gas pipes ran from the back of the oven around to the front and ended in a small valve. A narrow metal chimney extended from the rear of the brickwork. The Topf logo, like the one outside the factory, was proudly displayed on the iron of the furnace doors.

Patting the brick structure, Mr. Prüfer explained, "This is a crematorium, with two sides, or *muffles*. It's a duplicate of one we built for the government last year. You can incinerate two bodies an hour, one in each side. Here at Topf we've built incinerators big and small, but this was the biggest crematorium we'd ever built. It burns oil so it is really clean, has low exhaust, is mobile, and is cheap to make and run . . . a real beauty."

"Mobile?" I raised an eyebrow.

"Yes, mobile. We build it here and ship it, rather than building it at the customer site. They can move it, too, if they want. Things are on the move, Albert. The war has changed everything, you know," Kurt said with a big grin, spreading his arms to indicate motion. "Although, to be fair, we built a mobile crematorium before the war started. Hey – it's what the customer wanted!"

"The dead people?" I asked densely, a puzzled look on my face.

"No, the government! These high-capacity crematoriums go for use in prisons. The prisons grow and prison populations move, so they want their crematoriums to be able to move too."

I poked around the crematorium. It really did look like a large brick baker's oven, designed for two enormous loaves of bread.

"Why do prisons need these?" I asked, touching one of the iron doors gingerly.

"Well, I imagine that prisoners *die*, Albert," Mr. Prüfer said just a bit sarcastically. "Before they had their own, they used to have to cart the bodies to the local town morgue and crematorium. I'm sure that was unpleasant. I figure that in any population of a few thousand people, someone's going to die sooner or later. And in a prison, they probably die sooner."

"Sounds gruesome," I said with a frown.

Melting Point

"Sounds like money to me, Albert. Never forget that we are running a business here. You may not like the fact that prisoners die, but they do. And with the war, there are more and more prisoners. For Topf and sons, that means more and more business."

I blanched and said, "My brother's in the army and said that there were a lot of killed enemy soldiers and civilians in Poland. Maybe they'll need crematoriums for that."

Kurt nodded and said, "As it so happens, I just got some inquiries for a crematorium to be installed up in Poland, a place near Krakow. Maybe I can take you up there with me if we go to install it."

I brightened at that and said, "Great! I have an aunt and uncle who have a farm near Krakow; I've been up in that area before."

"Now, this baby here is due for a prison camp at Flossenburg. It is exactly the same as one we built for the government last year."

"Where was *that* one?" I asked.

"That one is a ways away in a place called Dachau. That was a great sales job," Mr. Prüfer said with evident pride. "I'll have to tell you about it some day. Another one we recently finished is in the prison at Buchenwald. That oven was a little cheaper than this one."

Mr. Prüfer glanced at his pocket watch. "Well, I've got a meeting soon, so why don't I show you where you'll be working?" He turned back towards the door.

He took me back upstairs, into the front building, and showed me to a small work area that was, in truth, just a nook in the hallway. He got a devilish gleam in his eye as he said, "Well, it's Karl Schultze who needs the most help right now, so why not get settled here and then ask him how you can help. See Gitta for supplies."

Topf

I remembered the cold reception Mr. Schultze had given me before and said quietly, "Yes, sir."

"Call me Kurt. Old Shultze isn't so bad once you get to know him." Kurt turned and walked a few feet away, then turned around to look at me. "You're going to make a real difference here, Albert. Remember that."

Kurt walked off towards the rear of the building. I took off my jacket and placed it over the wooden chair that sat in front of the tiny desk. If I pulled the chair out very far, it would be in the hallway. Still, I had a desk. I walked back up to the front to see Gitta and get some supplies.

Gitta handed me a pad of paper, a mechanical pencil, an eraser, and a protractor. *Her eyebrows were impossibly thin.* Next came an assortment of rubber stamps. *And her lashes were very long.* She handed me a stamp pad. *She smelled of bratwurst.* She stared at me. *Her breasts . . .*

"Anything else, Mr. Stohl?" Gitta asked impatiently.

"Oh, ah," I said, waking from my daydream, trying to think fast, "is there a coffee pot about?"

"Haven't even started and you're ready for a coffee break, eh?" Gitta batted her huge eyelashes at me, causing a small breeze, and added sarcastically, "You act like you've been here for years. You should fit in well."

"Sorry," I said, and then added, "but it's not for me, it's for Mr. Schultze. I'm hoping it will stop him from biting my head off."

Gitta laughed and said, "Karl? He acts gruff, but he . . . no, he *is* gruff! Good luck to you!" When she laughed she looked radiant. Her hair, which was in two braids and pulled forward over her large chest, bounced around. Still, she mostly had an icy, stay-away look. "Oh, and the coffee is just around the corner here, since I'm the one that has to make it," she added with a hint of disgust in her voice, bringing the conversation to a close.

Melting Point

I headed off in the direction Gitta had indicated for the coffee. I thought to myself, "Black, with sugar. I wonder how much sugar? Start with a teaspoon; I can always add more, but can't take any away." A few moments later, I knocked on Karl Schultze's door. "Mr. Schultze? Mr. Prüfer said I should come and help you."

Karl smiled wickedly and asked, "What makes you think *you* can help *me*?"

I tried to pull my foot out of my mouth by saying, "Well, I don't think Mr. Prüfer meant it that way, and I should have said that he asked me to come and learn from you." I tried to look innocent. I held out the cup and said, smiling hopefully, "I brought you coffee, with sugar."

Karl paused and narrowed his eyes at me, then accepted the cup of coffee and sipped at it, swishing the hot sweet liquid around in his mouth. "Good. Next time just a little more sugar. And remind me to show you how to brew a real cup of coffee, not this stuff that that beer hall maid at the front desk makes."

Beer hall maid? Gitta? The way he said it seemed to imply that he thought that was a bad thing, but it piqued my interest. Beer hall maids were usually fun and, ah, outgoing. Well, at least they seemed so after a few pints of beer. Maybe I shouldn't write Gitta off so soon. "I'd like to learn how to make great coffee," I said, trying not to sound too insincere.

He smiled a genuine smile and said, "I think you'll work out fine, boy. Now, did Kurt show you the body burner downstairs?"

Body burner. Ugh, that must be furnace humor. "The crematorium? Yes, and he said we may be working on another one soon."

Karl raised his eyebrows and said, "We?" Then he relented and said, "Well, I suppose it is *we*, now, isn't it? Yes, there may be another one for some place up in Poland."

"He said that the crematorium you sold last year to, er, Dachau, was it? Mr. Prüfer said that was a great sale, but he didn't say why."

Karl sat on his stool facing away from the workbench and leaned back, tipping the stool up on its hind legs a bit. He again narrowed his eyes at me as if to try and judge if I knew anything. Maybe it was an act. It was a good one.

"How much do you know about crematoriums, boy?" asked Karl.

Not knowing how this related to my question, I answered, "Not much. I would imagine that you just burn up the stuff inside the oven and then take out the ashes."

"Yes, I can see you lack education," Karl said with a mean smile. I briefly thought about defending my education but before I could Mr. Schultze said imperiously, "Sit down and learn, boy."

I took a seat. Karl's stool was tall and the only other chair in the room was lower, so I was looking up at him like a child at his father. I wasn't really enjoying this, but I was curious about the furnaces.

Karl looked like a professor lecturing his students, which, actually, was not far from the case. "As Kurt Prüfer is fond of saying, the only difference between an incinerator and a crematorium is what you do with the ashes. In a crematorium, job number one is not losing the ashes, and not mixing one person's ashes with another's, or with coal or wood ash, or whatnot. We use oil in our stoves, and that makes them clean burning. The problem is: how much oil? It takes a lot of heat to burn a body. Bodies have a lot of water in them, you know." Karl took another sip of coffee and muttered, "Yes, a little more sugar would be nice."

I nodded, and said quietly, "Sorry."

Karl waved my apology aside with his hand and continued his lecture. "Kurt Prüfer is a bit of a genius with crematoriums, and a bit of a legend

Melting Point

around here. Back twelve years ago, in 1928, some clever guys figured out how to use a heat exchanger to save on the amount of fuel it takes to cremate a body. The idea was to save money on fuel oil by recycling some of the heat from the burning body. But, their contraption was bulky and complicated. Kurt Prüfer comes along and takes some ideas from blast furnaces, which Topf and Sons also makes, and applies them to crematoriums. His idea was to use compressed air to feed the fire, kind of like blowing on the flames in a wood stove. In this way, a body can partly burn itself. The fatter the body, the better it burns."

I shuddered at the thought of a fat body burning. Karl Schultze chuckled at me.

"Get used to it. It sounds gruesome at first, but it is a sanitary and respectable way to take care of the deceased," Karl said. He continued, "Kurt Prüfer put Topf and Sons into the crematorium business, and sold several gas-fired units around Germany using compressed air. Took all the wind out of the sails, so to speak, of the heat exchanger guys."

"Is that what you do with all these fans," I asked, gesturing to the motors, fanblades, and wires littering the workbenches, "Supply the compressed air?"

"Yes, that and exhaust fans for the chimneys to help push out the smoke. We draw the smoke through scrubbing chambers to clean the soot from the air some, and that impedes the draft. Fans help. Anyway, if I may continue with my story," said Karl looking slightly annoyed at me for interrupting, "Three years ago the SS wanted a crematorium at their Dachau prison. They asked for bids. Well, the company that had built heating systems for the local SS barracks figured they could capitalize on their inside track and proposed a copy of one of Kurt Prüfer's designs! Their bid was a little over 9,000 Reichmarks for a single-muffle crematorium."

"Single-muffle?" I asked. I didn't want to make him mad, but I wanted to understand what it was. Kurt Prüfer had mentioned something about muffles, too.

"A muffle is a chamber," Karl said. He didn't sound impatient with me this time. In fact, he was beginning to thaw out a little, I think. He must have wanted a student for a while. "The oven you saw downstairs had two openings and two chambers, so it is a double-muffle furnace. A single-muffle furnace has only one chamber. Sometimes the chambers are called crucibles, but around here we just call them muffles.

"Kurt was livid about them stealing his ideas, but he didn't have the inside track like they did. As it turned out, the SS dragged their heels. A year and a half later, they were back asking for new bids, and Kurt Prüfer decided he was going to get this contract if it was the last thing he did."

Karl's eyes were sparkling as he retold the story. "The other company, Allach, had proposed this fancy furnace like the kind you would build for a public morgue. It had a marble-looking Grecian façade on it, as if it was in ancient Rome. And the brickwork! It was built to last forever. But what the SS wanted was capacity. And this was for a prison, so it didn't have to be fancy. It takes almost an hour to burn a body in a muffle, and there's not a whole lot you can do to change that. So Kurt figures you can build two muffles side-by-side, and they can be heated by the same gas jets. Now you have double the capacity of the crematorium but you don't double the amount of gas you need. Then, Kurt strips off the façade, reduces the amount of brickwork, makes it cheaper all around, and makes it *mobile*." Karl was laughing now. "Can you imagine? A mobile furnace with twice the capacity of Allach's, and the price was 500 Reichmarks cheaper than their furnace!" Karl slapped his knee. "You should have seen the look on the face of Walter Müller, the Allach designer. He went white!"

Melting Point

In spite of the fact that I had only been at the company an hour, I felt pride. Kurt Prüfer was not only a nice man, but also a genius to boot. Maybe this job could be fun after all.

After calming down a bit, Karl Schultze continued, "Well, we delivered that crema on time and on budget."

"Crema? As in crematorium?" I asked.

Karl stared at me with one eyebrow raised as if to say, *How could you be so dense?* He nodded slowly. "Yes," he said exaggeratedly, as if explaining to a small child. Then he smiled, like I was now in on a joke. In a normal tone, he continued, "A short time later we built another one for the Buchenwald camp. That one was even cheaper. The SS like cheap. Actually," he looked around the room conspiratorially and said quietly to me, "the SS *are* cheap."

"So, the one at Buchenwald was built on a budget. It wasn't mobile, which means it had to be constructed right at the camp. Normally, that would be more expensive, because we'd have to send workmen to the site rather than building it here and shipping it. However, Buchenwald is a prison camp, and so they had prison labor that could do some of the simple construction work for free. Also, the SS supplied the cement, lime, sand, and bricks without us having to pay for them. Total cost was under 8,000 Reichmarks.

"The body burner you saw downstairs is like the Dachau model and is mobile, so it will cost more and we build it here. I hear the Auschwitz oven will be the same."

What? "Auschwitz?" I said. "Oswiecim? I've been there! My aunt and uncle live near there."

"Well, maybe you can go for a nice visit if we install the oven there," Karl said coolly. "In any case, we're always on the lookout to save money in building these things, what with the competition and all."

"Competition?" I asked.

"Well, Allach is still selling heating systems and they may be trying to sell crematoriums too. They stole from us once and they could again. But our biggest competitor right now is the Kori Company. They just got a bid from the Mauthausen prison camp for a single-muffle job. Kurt is meeting with SS folks right now about a bid for the Sachsenhausen prison camp, but it looks like those Kori bastards will get that one too. You see, it's partly price and partly whom you know. The SS is an old-boys club, and being chummy with them has its advantages. Like getting orders."

Turning professorial again, Karl continued, "Now the odd thing about the Kori furnace in Mauthausen is that it will burn coal. Coke, actually."

Coke is to coal like charcoal is to wood. It burns very hot without sulfur gasses, and so can be used for both cooking and blast furnaces.

"Those fools!" Karl chuckled and rubbed his hands together. "Coke is dirty and adds all kinds of problems to the furnace. Particularly the problems with mixing ashes. Coke has its own ash, and you'd have to worry about mixing the human ash with the coal ash. Also, coke makes a lot of smoke and would need much better venting and chimney systems. All around, coke is a messy, dirty business. Alas, in some places it's easier to get coal than oil."

Karl smiled at me and said, "So, we all try to come up with better ideas, and hope Kurt can keep making those sales. These days he's more salesman than engineer. But, the more he sells, the more Topf makes, and the more *he* makes. And he takes care of his friends." He said this last part in a conspiratorial tone.

"How do you mean?" I asked innocently.

"Well, Kurt makes a commission on each sale. He is a generous man, so he spreads some of it amongst us peons who do the real work," he said with a smile.

Melting Point

Just at that moment, there was a brief knock and Karl's door opened. An older man in a fine suit poked his head in the door.

"Karl, have you seen . . . oh, is this the new man?" he asked.

Karl introduced us. "Ludwig Topf, Albert Stohl. Mr. Topf is the senior owner of Topf and Sons."

"Ah, welcome, son. I hope you will enjoy your stay here at my company. Kurt needs all the help he can get implementing his wild ideas," he said with a wink and sparkle in his eye.

"Thank you, sir, it's good to be here," I said. I winced briefly because I felt I should have thought of something better to say.

"Well, I just wanted to stop by and welcome you to our family here. I won't keep you. Take good care of him, Karl. With the war on there may not be many more newcomers for a while. 'Bye now," and with that he shook my hand and left.

Karl said, "Now that was the *nice* Topf. His younger brother, Ernst-Wolfgang Topf, is completely full of himself," Karl looked at me sharply, "Though you didn't hear that from me."

"I didn't hear that from you," I agreed, smiling and nodding, glad to be in Karl Schultze's confidence.

"He's married, where Ludwig is not, and he's arrogant, pushy, and thinks he's better than everyone that works for him. I think he secretly imagines himself a Teutonic Knight. Most of the staff dislikes him," Karl said with evident distaste. Then he added, "In a way, it makes Ludwig seem all the better, by comparison. The important thing to know is that Kurt Prüfer gets along well with Ludwig, but not Ernst-Wolfgang."

#

And so I tried to settle in to my new life. I learned about the ins-and-outs of crematoriums, oil burners, ventilation systems, and the like. But after only a couple of weeks, everything changed. It was on May 10, 1940. Germany invaded France. We were all pretty nervous. Poland had been easy, but the Polish had been ready to fight a nineteenth century war. The British supported the French, and together they were the best the world had to offer. I worried about my brother Herman, not knowing what his unit was doing all this time.

By the end of the month, things were going well for Germany, but the fighting was far from over. We had pushed the British to the shores of Dunkirk, and the French were in retreat, but we still had a ways to go. For us at Topf and sons, the biggest problem we faced was the oil shortage. This oil shortage was something that was to plague Germany for the rest of the war. For us it meant, at that time, that the crematoriums we had delivered to Dachau and Buchenwald had been shut down due to the lack of fuel oil.

Kurt Prüfer was in a panic. The SS building offices at Dachau and Buchenwald were screaming at us as if it were our fault that there was no fuel. The SS building offices at Flossenburg and Auschwitz were thinking of canceling their orders for crematoriums. This could be a real disaster for us.

We were all irritated that the one crematorium that continued to work was Kori's coke-fired Mauthausen oven. As much as we all despised the idea of coke furnaces for cremation, the SS became hot on the idea. The SS had coal works run by their own prison labor, and so could get the coal for almost nothing. By the end of May, the SS gave Kurt an ultimatum. Convert the ovens to coal, or lose the contracts.

Fritz Sander and Paul Erdmann, the department heads, called a meeting that we all attended. After some pleasantries and discussions of how well Germany was doing in the war, they mentioned the fuel shortage, and then turned the discussion over to Kurt Prüfer.

Melting Point

Kurt looked around the room, and said, "We can't use oil. We've got to use coke. Sooty, dirty, messy, bulky coke." Kurt shook his head sadly. "Using coke changes everything," Kurt said, ticking off the items on his fingers. "First, you can't just turn on and off the heat; it takes time to get the coke going and more time to snuff it out. Second, it takes a lot of coke to get the oven up to temperature, but then not much to keep it going, so you want to run the oven for long bursts. But that makes the brickwork much hotter, so you need more bricks and better insulation. Third, the coke is really sooty, and the byproducts are very hot, so you need a large chimney to handle the heat and volume of exhaust. Fourth, you need to force air over the coke to keep it burning hot, and you need better chimney drafting, so that means more fans and more electricity. Fifth," here Kurt looks sternly at us, "coke means ash and soot, but we have to keep the bodies' remains separate from the coke ash, so we are going to use coke-fired superheated-gas generators. This keeps the coke ash separate from the contents of the muffle. Thus the body's ashes can be handled with the proper respect." Kurt nodded solemnly, and continued, "We'll convert the nearby Buchenwald furnaces first, as a test. That way we can work out the kinks close to home."

"Now for some good news," said Kurt, brightening. "Paul and some of his boys have figured out a clever trick to double the number of bodies we cook without increasing the number of muffles. Paul?"

Paul Erdmann got up and cleared his throat. I still was uncomfortable with terms like *bodies cooking*. I wished they would keep the language clinical.

Paul looked around the room and then focused on Kurt. He said, "Yes, well, with the move to coal, our customers will probably want to save up several bodies to be cremated in one burst of effort, rather than starting and stopping the oven as you would with our oil furnaces. As Kurt said, the cost of firing the ovens is higher, but the ovens should stay hot longer with little added coal. Now, as you all know, it takes about an hour to fully cremate a body. We can make the ovens a little hotter, but that would only save a few minutes, and there is a diminishing return on the fuel required. What you may not know is that in about half the time, all of the water and tissues in the body are gone."

This discussion was making me queasy. The bratwurst I had for lunch wasn't sitting well in my stomach.

Mr. Erdmann continued, "What you have left at the halfway point is mostly bones and some ash. The rest of the cremating time breaks down the remaining bones into ash."

I considered whether I should make a run for the bathroom, but decided to just take deep breaths of air. I thought to myself *Think of this as an engineering problem. These bodies aren't people, just part of a process.*

Paul called on a couple of his draftsmen to hold up a sketch of the internal view of his proposed new crematorium muffle. At the back end, away from where the bodies enter the muffle, on the floor of the muffle, was a grate. Under the grate was a small chamber, extending to the front under the main muffle. It had its own opening at the front of the furnace below the main muffle door. The bottom of the main door was at waist level, and this smaller door was at the ankle-to-knee level.

Paul, using a meter stick as a pointer, showed off the features of this new design. "When the body is half done, we can open the muffle door and, using a pushing tool, move the ashes and broken-up bones back to the rear of the muffle, where they fall down this grating, ending up below the main chamber."

Paul took a marker and drew the direction of the ashes on the side view, showing how they end up in the smaller chamber below the main one. "From here, the body will finish cremating for a second half hour, and then the ashes can be removed from the small door on the front, here," Paul said, pointing out the door on the front, below the main door. "Meanwhile, another

Melting Point

body can be in the upper chamber doing its first half hour. With this method," Paul said triumphantly, his eyes gleaming, "We keep the ashes totally separate, and yet each muffle has double the capacity. Our double-muffle crematorium can now handle a total of four bodies per hour."

And with that, we doubled the number of bodies the prison camps could burn. Using coal rather than oil, and using slave labor for some of the construction. The ovens needed some down-time each day to clean them, but Paul estimated that we could handle around 70 to 80 bodies per day in this crematorium. That seemed like a lot, but the SS had apparently asked for about a one-percent-cremated-per-day peak capacity, and the Auschwitz camp was to house ten thousand prisoners, so they needed around one hundred bodies a day capacity. This would come close enough for the SS.

I felt that we had somehow lost some of the dignity of cremation. Burning so many bodies, and burning them so close together, just seemed to be disrespectful of the dead. Yes, we were keeping the ashes separate from each other and separate from the coal ash, but it was very, I don't know, *factory oriented*. I thought about my earlier queasiness at the discussions, when I had wanted to think in industrial terms. Yet, in reflection, thinking in industrial terms isn't right for dealing with human remains. I had no legal objections to what they were proposing. And I had no real moral objections, either, because we were preserving the integrity of the ashes so they could be handled properly and with respect. It just somehow seemed wrong.

Kurt Prüfer managed to keep the contracts for both Auschwitz and Flossenburg, using this new high-capacity crematorium. We weren't sure, yet, what to do with the mobile oven in the basement. That was lower capacity and oil burning. Kurt was trying to see if anyone wanted it. Eventually, he sold it to the SS to be installed at a sub-camp of Mauthausen, at Gusen. They would even pay to convert it to coal. Kurt had pulled off another coup, because Mauthausen was Kori territory. We all celebrated this victory.

On June 10, 1940, Italy invaded France. Just in time, too, because eleven days later France surrendered. There was euphoria everywhere in Germany and no less so in our offices in Erfurt. We danced in the streets, we got drunk, and I even got to kiss Gitta; just the once, though, and only on the cheek. Imagine; I was 23 then, and still so unsure about women.

In early July, Wilhelm Koch and I went up to Poland to inspect the site where we were to install our new coke-burning oven. I had an odd feeling as the train rolled into the Oswiecim train station. Things mostly looked the same as when my brother and I had bicycled there those few years earlier, but there were scars of war here and there. At first I wasn't sure where the prison camp would be, but when we started walking towards the old Polish army barracks, which had earlier been a labor exchange, I knew that the barracks now had a third job.

Sure enough, when we got to the old camp entrance, the place had definitely been turned into a prison. A wrought iron banner over the main gate read **Arbeit Macht Frei**, literally **Work Makes Free**, or **Work will set you free**. Barbed wire fencing surrounded the whole area. There seemed to be construction going on everywhere, with prisoners in striped suits digging and bricklaying and scurrying around.

We were let into the camp and given green armbands, which signified us as civilian workers. We were told to keep our distance from the prisoners, as lice were beginning to be a problem in the camp. So much so, that the camp had started to fumigate clothes and other fabrics using prussic acid, a lethal gas that would take care of lice and any other vermin.

We were led by a guard past the rows of red brick buildings I had admired before, and over to the old ammo bunker off to the far left in the camp. Prisoners and civilians were working side by side converting the old ammo bunker into a couple of morgues and a room for our crematorium.

Melting Point

The outside looked much the same as when I had been at the camp before, with earthen embankments up against the walls in case of an ammo explosion. In the back of the building the embankment had been partly removed to make way for a chimney that was being built by the center of the back wall. Window openings were being cut into the solid walls next to where the chimney would be, and an underground tunnel led from the chimney base inside the building.

On one side of the building was the entrance. Since the entrance didn't have the blast-protecting embankment, there was instead a solid wall many feet in front of the main door, forming a natural courtyard. Prisoners had planted flowers in the dirt around the entrance and walls, making the whole thing quite attractive.

I had not been inside the ammo bunker when I was at the camp before, so I wasn't sure what was new and what was original. The rooms were still being modified when we got there. The building was being divided into two large rooms and several smaller ones. One of the large rooms - a long, narrow room along one side of the building - was to be used as a morgue to hold the bodies waiting for cremation. Next to it was the furnace room. This room was large and square, with openings being cut out of the back wall to provide windows for ventilation. Also in the floor by the back wall was the underground flue for the chimney. Our crematorium would vent down, under the floor, through the wall, and into the chimney.

The smaller rooms included a storehouse for the coke, an autopsy room, and some other storage areas and workspaces. I asked Wilhelm what reason the SS would have to autopsy a body in a prison. It wasn't likely that they had many mysterious deaths here. He just shrugged.

Wilhelm and I paced out the room for the furnace, and then measured everything. The room was just not really situated right for us, but there wasn't much we could do about it at this point. The oven itself was more or less square, but then there were the coke heat generators at the rear. The space behind that was needed to feed coke into the ovens. In front, space was needed for the cart the bodies would be on. All in all, the room wasn't wide enough to have the chimney at the rear of the oven and have the bodies slide in from the front of the room closest to the morgue. We figured out that the problem was that whoever had given the dimensions to the SS had been quoting the dimensions of the ovens using oil, and they had forgotten to include the space needed for the coal loading area and burners.

So Wilhelm and I decided to have the oven face sideways and run the underground flue a little farther from the center of the back wall where it came in from the chimney. The flue came up from under the wall about where the front of the oven would now be, and would need to be routed around to the rear of the oven. The cart that carried the bodies up to the oven would have to be loaded some distance from the morgue entrance, and so we may need a supplemental cart or something. Nothing too difficult.

Our measurements taken, our job done, we went home to Erfurt. I didn't get a chance to visit my aunt and uncle on that trip, so I promised myself that I would on the next trip. We had expected that Kurt Prüfer would be happy with our decision to rotate the furnace, because if we hadn't rotated it, the furnace wouldn't have fit. But he was upset with us. Rotating the furnace may have been the only reasonable option, but it made the underground flue longer. We, that is, Topf, had committed to building the underground flue, whereas someone else was building the chimney. This was going to make the oven more expensive. The SS wasn't going to be happy with us, and we had barely gotten the contract as it was.

By the end of July, the furnace had been built and the bunker was finished with its conversion, with the one exception of the chimney, which

Melting Point

wasn't due to be finished until the middle of August. The furnace ended up costing about 25% more than we had planned, but Topf absorbed the cost overrun to keep the SS happy. Maybe then they would ask us to do more work for them at Auschwitz in the future.

I wasn't present for the trial runs in the middle of August. I think Kurt Prüfer was still somehow mad at Wilhelm and me for the cost overruns, and also he wanted to see the place for himself. They tinkered with the system for a month before it was finally turned over to the camp officials.

In October, Kurt went to Mauthausen and managed to sell them a second Topf system for the sub-camp in Gusen, one just like the Auschwitz oven. I wondered why they needed a second oven, since they already had on order the lower capacity mobile oven, recently converted to coal, that I'd seen on my first day at Topf. Now they would have a capacity for around 120 bodies per day, an astounding number. I flinched when I heard that.

But as winter fell, I got an even more amazing jolt. In mid-November, Kurt Prüfer was asked to go to Auschwitz to discuss a second oven, with the same capacity as the first! The prison at Auschwitz hadn't seemed that big to me when it was a Polish Army barracks, and I didn't think it had grown much in size since Germany took it over for a prison, yet here we were proposing enough cremation capacity to incinerate 160 people a day! What was going on there?

Karl Schultze got a phone call late in November, asking him to make plans for ventilation of the morgue and autopsy room. The autopsy room made sense, but I wasn't sure why they wanted to vent the morgue, since it had seemed pretty cool in there, being surrounded on two sides by the earthen embankments as it was. Perhaps the bodies stayed too long in the room. But with the furnace capacity they had, you would think the bodies wouldn't spend much time waiting.

Kurt Prüfer also wanted Karl Schultze to vent the furnace room, since it would be too hot for the windows in the room to cool it down with both furnaces running. I spent a lot of time fetching Karl coffee. Black, two sugars. All the while, I wondered what on earth was going on in these prisons.

The second furnace was to share the same chimney and some of the same underground flues and fans with the first, so it would be cheaper than the first oven, which was about 9,000 Reichmarks. This one was to be around 7,800 Reichmarks. However, the venting work was another 1,800 or so Reichmarks, bringing the total cost up to more than the first system. But that was to be expected, and I think the SS was happy with Kurt for making a good deal for them.

At the end of 1940, August Willing, another of our installers, went to Gusen to finish setting up the mobile furnace I had seen in the basement on my first day at Topf, which was now equipped for coal. At the beginning of 1941 he added side coke burners to the oil ovens at Dachau. Each of these modifications was made at additional cost, of course. Topf and Sons would make around 2,000 Reichmarks for each system converted.

Topf had made a lot of money on crematoriums in 1940. Kurt Prüfer had made some nice commissions. And, true to what Karl Schultze had told me, Kurt was a generous man. We all lived well that year, and our future looked bright. But the sheer numbers of bodies we were planning capacity for haunted my dreams.

Melting Point

I looked around at my family in Bodega Bay. I frowned and said with sadness, "So, by the end of 1940, we had just about converted everything to coal, and Topf crematoriums were burning bodies at an incredible rate. We had become the premier supplier of crematoriums to the SS prison camp system. But what came along in 1941 would dwarf the capacity of the systems we had sold and installed thus far. With the war on there were a lot of bodies to cremate. And there was a lot of money to be made disposing of those bodies."

The rain had stopped for the moment, and the house at Bodega Bay was silent. Tony said quietly, "Maybe this would be a good time for a quick break."

There was general agreement on this, so Tony got up and stretched, and Magda stood up with her lips pursed, but there wasn't the bustle of activity that there had been before. Tom added a log to the fireplace, whose embers had been glowing and becoming dimmer as time passed.

Telling the story was difficult, as it brought back a flood of memories best forgotten. But worse was the knowledge that my family was beginning to see me for who I was, and for what I did, and not for the nice old man I appeared to be. It must be like the feeling you get when you find out that an old school friend is a criminal. Or, as in this case, when you find out that your father is a criminal.

Melting Point

"Actually, Poppa, it's getting kind of late. Do you want to break for dinner?" Amanda asked with concern on her face.

"I can keep going, but if you would rather stop for food, we can," I said, looking around at my family.

Tom said, "Well, that all depends – what's for dinner?"

Tony laughed and Amanda smiled. That lightened the mood a bit.

"Well, in honor of Mom, I have bratwurst and sauerkraut," said Magda.

"I think that Karl Schultze sounds like a sour-Kraut," said Tom with a grin.

Tony screwed up his face and moved his hands as if hitting drums, saying, "ba-dum bump."

Amanda groaned and even Magda smiled a bit. I just nodded. "He sounded gruff and treated me like a servant at first, but he warmed up to me a bit. He did show me how to make good coffee," I said lightly.

Amanda excused herself and went to the bathroom. Magda went to the kitchen and pulled the bratwurst and sauerkraut from the refrigerator. I went into the kitchen to offer help.

"Well, you could get out the mustards. Tom, could you set the table?" Magda said as she set a pan on the electric burner and turned on the stove.

Tony joined Tom in setting the table while I rummaged through the refrigerator for various kinds of mustards. Yellow, Dijon, deli brown, honey mustard, there were several kinds to choose from.

While the sausages and sauerkraut started heating, I came back into the kitchen to find something else to do. Magda came over and hugged me for a long moment.

"What's that for?" I asked.

Melting Point

"That's for not being a Nazi guard or one of those horrible doctors or something. You had me scared for a while there."

"I'm not proud of what I did, and there's more to come in the story," I said, not wanting to be too reassuring.

"Well, I never knew any of this, and I can see why you couldn't talk about it. But I'm grateful you are telling us. I just don't see how Mom comes into this picture – is she already at Auschwitz at this point?" Magda asked.

"I don't think so, though she didn't talk much about when she got to the camp. I didn't meet her until a few years after this part of the story. We'll get there," I said.

Magda narrowed her eyes at me and made a pretend scowl. "You weren't mean to her, were you?"

I laughed lightly and said, "Oh, no, I could never be mean to Etta." But then I turned more serious and said, "Though, no one who was at Auschwitz could have had anything remotely like a *good time*."

Amanda returned and we moved on to lighter topics. When dinner was served, we all sat around the dining room table and ate our sausages and sauerkraut. I tried a few different kinds of mustard, though Etta had trained me over the years to prefer simple yellow mustard. It was her favorite, and she saw to it that it became mine.

After I had started eating, I casually leaned down as if to pick up my napkin from the floor and stuck myself with my insulin pen. I had gotten good at doing this quickly, so I wouldn't get questions from concerned onlookers. As I popped back up, I brought my napkin up in one hand and dabbed at my mouth to complete my deception, pocketing the pen with my other hand. Smooth. No one was the wiser.

"How's your diabetes coming, Poppa?"

Argh.

After dinner we cleaned off the plates and put them into the dishwasher. The wind outside had picked up and the rain was starting up again, so Tom had stoked up the fire and we sat back down in our places with topped-off drinks. Tom and Tony had switched to beer, something black with a thick head, maybe Guinness. I didn't ask, as I couldn't drink with my diabetes, and I'd just rather not know what wonderful stuff they were drinking. The fire flared up, making a roaring sound as the flames were fed by the draft of the stove and the wind blowing over the chimney.

Tony, sipping his beer, asked, "How much was a Reichmark worth?"

"Something around eighty cents U.S. back then, or maybe ten dollars in today's money."

I took a deep breath. "Shall we continue?" *Get through this. Just get through this. It's what Etta wanted.* And so I began again.

\#

We left off at the end of 1940. I was 23 by then, and Topf had successfully converted most of its crematoriums to coal. August Willing was in Dachau converting the last of our oil burning furnaces. Meanwhile, Germany had taken over France, attacked Britain from the air, and controlled Norway, Denmark, half of Poland, Austria, Czechoslovakia, Luxembourg; basically dominating Europe. Russia was our ally, America was neutral, and only England still held out against us. Of course, all that was to change in 1941. For us at Topf, business was picking up.

Early in January, Kurt Prüfer got a panicked call from Auschwitz. The crematorium had developed some problems and was no longer operable. Kurt asked Wilhelm Koch and me to go to the camp to see what was wrong and determine what was needed to fix it. Down in the basement of our building in Erfurt, the pieces for the second oven were almost together, and there was

Melting Point

some hope we could send out the repair parts when the second oven was ready to ship.

So, I traveled back to Auschwitz for the third time. The train rolled past fields of snow, the icy wind blowing through the cracks between the window and the sill. The sky was a silvery-blue, so the scenery rolling by had an almost ethereal beauty to it. The town of Oswiecim/Auschwitz itself, with its dusting of snow on the roofs and clean white boulevards looked almost magical.

The prison camp of Auschwitz, however, had a much more foreboding appearance. The red brick buildings were dusted with an inch of white snow, and might have looked pleasant, if not for the rows of barbed wire obstructing their view. The paths inside the camp were dirty and slushy, and the camp prisoners looked stooped and cold. They wore thin striped outfits that made them look all the more downtrodden and miserable. The guards wore their heavy gray coats and black boots. Despite my heavy coat, I shivered at the thought of being locked up in this place.

The guard at the gate gave us our green armbands and asked us if we had heard about the lice problem. I had but Wilhelm said that he hadn't.

"Well, we have a nasty lice problem here," the guard started. "Don't touch any prisoner, and don't touch any fabric a prisoner may have touched. Those lice are resistant little bastards – once you get them they're almost impossible to get rid of!"

"Why can't you just fumigate the place and be done with them?" asked Wilhelm.

The guard shook his head. "Nah. We've been using some really nasty stuff to kill them on clothes and bedding, but it is so lethal it would kill you long before it kills the little pests. We've got to control them, though, or we'll have a typhus epidemic on our hands. We've been delousing the prisoners by shaving their heads and by using some strong pesticides. But it is the one battle in this great war that Germany seems to be losing," said the guard with a wry smile.

"We'll be careful," I promised.

The guard let us find our way back to the old ammo bunker unescorted. We turned left at the end of the first building after the *Work Makes Free* gate and walked past the four rows of brick buildings to the gate separating the camp proper from the outlying buildings. Just in front of us was the old ammo bunker, now the crematorium and morgue. With its dusting of snow and oblong shape, it looked almost like one of the big barges floating down the Rhine, only with a huge chimney on one side. It was quiet in this part of the camp, and the air smelled of pine and campfires. Just beyond the crematorium building was another brick building used by the camp administration and beyond that was the courtyard with the tree that I had carved my initials in a few years before.

When we walked into the crematorium building and found the furnace room deserted, Wilhelm and I set about looking over the crematorium furnace to see what was wrong with it. It was cold from having been out of commission for several days.

Wilhelm gestured at the oven opening. "Do you want the privilege?"

I shuddered at the thought of being inside the oven, even when cold. "Uh, no thanks. I get claustrophobia. I'll inspect outside and you can have the fun of being inside."

Wilhelm crawled inside the oven opening to inspect the interior parts, while I walked around the outside, examining all the external fittings, wiring, and ducting. There was a sooty, dusty smell about the room. There was also just a hint of sweet decay, like you smell at a garbage dump.

Looking over the outside of the oven, I called to Wilhelm, inside the oven, "The fabric insulation on these electric wires is all burnt off!"

Melting Point

Wilhelm called from inside, "The mortar between the bricks is cracked in here. It must have been damn hot!"

"I'll say," I called back. "Some of the iron fittings are bent over here. The sheet metal is warped. The electric wires are thinner where they run against the back of the oven. Something is really wrong."

Wilhelm crawled back out of the muffle and dusted himself off. "This oven has been in use, what, four months now? It looks in worse condition than the civilian crematoria I've seen that have been in use for many years."

After discussing this a bit, we decided that we should get a better understanding of how they operate the system, to see what was going wrong. We decided to find someone and ask him if we could speak to the men that operated the oven. There were some sounds of activity coming from the morgue room next door, so Wilhelm and I went to the door separating the two rooms and opened it.

The first thing that hit us was the stench. An incredibly strong, horrible, putrid smell was in the room. And the room's air was heavy and humid. Like stepping into a sauna of dead, rotting animals.

The second thing to hit us was the sight. Along one entire wall were corpses piled up neatly like cordwood, some with their heads against the wall and their feet facing into the room, others laid the opposite way. The pile was four or five high. There must have been 300 or 400 dead bodies stacked on one side of the long room. On the other side of the room was a small and more haphazard pile of bodies, only one or two deep. The center of the room had a drain in it, and there was a wash of blood and other fluids going to the drain from the piles of bodies.

Also in the room were two men in prison-striped garb, carrying a body from the small disheveled pile to the large neat pile. They both looked thin and gaunt, and were struggling with the load. They looked up when we opened the door.

I immediately backed away from the doorway, the sight and smell too much for me. Wilhelm gagged a moment, but took out his handkerchief and held it over his mouth, then managed to ask the men where a guard was. They pointed to the only other door in the room, and Wilhelm thanked them, backed out of the room, and closed the door. We both took deep breaths of the cleaner air of the furnace room.

What was this? Why were there hundreds of dead bodies there? I breathed heavily for a moment and tried to gather my thoughts. Well, the crematorium had been stopped for several days, so I suppose that the morgue backs up. If the crematorium can handle one body in each muffle every half hour, with some downtime for cleaning and such you could manage some eighty bodies a day. A week's backup would be as much as five hundred bodies. But that was at peak capacity, which we hadn't thought would be typical. Apparently it *was* typical.

"Typical. Ugh," I mumbled. Wilhelm paid me no attention, apparently lost in his own thoughts.

So that solved that mystery. But something had bothered me from the beginning about this. The camp held 10,000 men. We can cremate close to one percent per day. But, in a typical city you expect maybe a one to two percent death rate per year. Here we have almost that per day! And here we are, getting ready to double their cremation capacity with a second oven! There was a lot going on behind these prison walls that I didn't want to see.

Fortunately we didn't have to go through the morgue to get to the room on the other side of that door. We could go around from the other side, and we did. A guard was in that room, supervising some prisoners cleaning the floor.

Melting Point

Wilhelm introduced us to the guards and asked, "We'd like to talk to the men who run the furnace. We'd like to see how they operate it."

"I'm one of the supervisors," the guard said. "I'll go fetch one of the teams. I'll meet you back in the furnace room in five minutes."

Wilhelm and I walked back into the furnace room, and this time the sickly-sweet garbage smell was more pronounced. It reminded me of the smell from the morgue, and I wrinkled my nose at it.

Wilhelm threw the switch to turn on the forced draft fans, but nothing happened. "Well, damn, I was hoping I could vent some of that smell. I bet the wires for the fans melted too."

I followed the wires for the fans. "No, not melted. Shorted here by the oven where the insulation burned off. Looks like the ducts for the fans are warped enough that they would leak a lot of smoke."

Wilhelm pulled out a notebook. "I'll make a list of the stuff we need to fix. Let's see, mortar, wiring, ducts, some fittings . . . "

A group of prisoners and the guard came into the room. There were seven prisoners in all, wearing thin striped prison garb. The guard motioned for one man to come forward. He bowed and introduced himself as the leader of the team, called Sonderkommandos, or *special team*. Like the prisoners working in the morgue, these men were all gaunt, their skin looking weathered and aged. The leader of the team looked like he was 70 years old, though he was probably in his thirties.

"I speak German, the others don't," said the leader of the Sonderkommandos, gesturing to the other six men.

Wilhelm said, "We are trying to figure out what went wrong with the crematorium. Would you show us how you would operate it?"

The leader nodded, then turned and said a few words in Polish to the group, and they leapt into action. They moved quicker than I would have believed possible given their appearance. Two men ran around to the back.

"Those men would feed the coal," the leader said.

"Shouldn't need much after things get going," Wilhelm said to no one in particular, a puzzled look on his face. He turned to me. "Why were two men needed to feed tiny amounts of coal? The oven was supposed to partly fuel itself from the burning bodies."

Another two men ran into the morgue, returning in seconds with a body. They set it on the ground near the morgue door, and fetched a wood plank that was leaning against the wall. They laid the plank next to the body, and then lifted the body onto the plank. I didn't see the necessity of using real bodies for this demonstration, especially given the putrid smell, but for the moment the Sonderkommandos were in charge.

Meanwhile, another man ran to the trolley, a pushcart on a track. The track ran from the door of the oven straight out about eight feet to a wooden turntable. On the turntable, the trolley could be switched to another set of tracks, leading to the spot where the next oven was to be installed. The top of the pushcart was sheet metal with high sides. On the side of the pushcart away from the oven was an iron bar for pushing the cart and a moveable sheet metal end piece that could be slid towards the front.

The men with the body picked up the plank and quickly dumped their body onto the cart. Apparently in their haste, they had placed the body on its side on the far side of the cart. Then the men ran back to the morgue. The trolley man held the trolley steady.

The leader said, "When it is time to change, we first empty the ashes." He gestured to the remaining man who was holding a long-handled shovel.

Melting Point

    The leader took a metal hook, like a long crowbar, and opened the bottom metal door, while the shovel-man pushed the shovel inside and pantomimed removing ashes and shoveling them into a pail. He did four quick shovels, taking maybe eight seconds in all.

    "Next we move the ashes from the top to the bottom," the leader continued.

    The shovel-man set the shovel down on the floor and moved the pail aside while the leader with the door hook closed the bottom door and then opened the top door. The shovel-man now picked up a tool that looked like a long-handled hoe and pantomimed scraping ashes from the front of the oven towards the back grate. He made three pushes, and then removed the hoe. He took the hoe, shovel, and ash pail and moved to the exit door. Total time, maybe another eight seconds.

    While this had been happening, the two men who put the body onto the trolley had come running back with a second body. They placed it on the wood plank, picked up the plank with the body on it, and quickly tossed the body onto the trolley next to the first one. My mouth fell open in shock.

    "Then we add new bodies," said the leader

    What I had earlier thought was just carelessness was actually careful planning. Both bodies were on their side, one head-first and one feet-first. Together, they would just barely fit into the opening of the oven door. The two body-men moved to the sides of the trolley closest to the oven. With the trolley-man in the rear, they pushed the trolley up to the oven. The front and side edges of the trolley fit inside the oven opening. Then the two body-men and the trolley-man pushed the bodies into the oven using the sheet metal partition at the back that slides towards the oven, pushing the bodies in with it.

    The bodies in, the trolley-man pulled back on the trolley to free it from the oven while the body-men used poles to hold the bodies in, keeping them from sliding back with the trolley. When the trolley was free, the leader closed the door. The trolley-man took a pail of murky water and poured it over the surface of the trolley to cool it down and clean it.

The time for inserting the bodies was about twelve seconds. Total time for the whole operation was about thirty seconds.

"We wait ten minutes, and then do the next oven," the leader said, pointing to the other muffle. All the men stopped, most panting from the effort. I closed my mouth and tried to swallow, but my mouth was dry.

"This is all wrong." Wilhelm had his mouth open in bewilderment. He said, "Twenty minutes on the top, twenty on the bottom? Two bodies? All wrong."

The leader looked nervous and stared at the floor. The guard looked alarmed. Wilhelm tried to absorb what he had seen.

"So, you put a *pair* of bodies into each muffle every twenty minutes?" Wilhelm's voice rose in pitch and volume. Not in anger, more like disbelief. "It's supposed to have *one* body every 30 minutes! You managed twelve bodies an hour instead of the specified capacity of four?"

The leader stared at the floor and nodded.

"We ran it the way you say it should be run for a while," The guard said. "Then we discovered we could run it a little faster with careful timing and some extra coal. Recently we had a big backlog, and we were ordered to clear it. That's when we started doing two at a time. Everything went fine for a while, but the oven got so hot the men were getting burned from being close to it. The door glowed white hot."

"White . . . hot," I whispered in awe.

Wilhelm nodded slowly and said softly, "The door glows white when the inside of the oven reaches 1,100 degrees centigrade. The iron pieces inside

Melting Point

get so hot they soften, bend, and even melt. Bricks crack. Wire insulation burns, copper wires melt. The oven is not designed to handle this load."

1,100 degrees. *Melting point.*

Wilhelm was still talking. "You should run it closer to the rated capacity."

The guard nodded and said impatiently, "Then we need more capacity."

Wilhelm nodded too, splaying his hands, "It's coming. It's coming. Be patient."

Two bodies at a time violated one of the big rules of cremation – keeping the ashes separate. They were mingling the ashes of the dead, a definite breaking of established rules of conduct. Second, if it took an hour to fully cremate a body, how were they doing it in forty minutes?

"Are the ashes completely burned when you take them out?" I asked.

"No," the leader shook his head. "The ashes and bones are taken outside where some men use mortars and pestles to crush the remaining bones."

"So, the bodies aren't completely burned and the ashes are commingled." I shook my head. "This is disrespectful of the dead. This is not good at all."

The guard screwed up his face and looked incredulously at me. "They're prisoners - Poles, Jews, and criminals. Their ashes don't deserve much thought." He straightened his jaw and said, "We have backlogs to clear, that is what is important."

#

Wilhelm and I stayed at the camp only a short time longer. We completed a list of replacement parts needed, and we made some final measurements for the second furnace, which was to be installed next to the first in a few weeks. Then we headed back to the town. We spent the night at the Hotel Herz before starting the long train ride back. After dinner, we sat in the café of the hotel, sipping coffee. Coffee was generally no longer available to the locals, but we had no problem getting it. One of the pleasures of being the victors, I suppose.

"I can't get that morgue out of my mind," I said, nibbling on a cookie.

"You heard the guard," said Wilhelm, taking a gulp of coffee. "*A backlog*, he called it. Gruesome." He ate large mouthfuls of cookies and chased it with more coffee.

I paused, my cup at my lips. "Imagine stuffing two bodies in an oven built for one. Well, actually, I suppose they're *all* built for one, aren't they?" *Was this a first?*

"Violates morality, I say," Wilhelm grumbled, stuffing another cookie in his mouth.

Nodding, I added, "It Violates Kurt Prüfer's rule number one: handle ashes with respect and dignity."

"And Prüfer's rule number two: Don't mix or lose the ashes," Wilhelm added, downing the rest of his coffee in a last gulp. "Still, like the guard said, these people are criminals."

"And Poles and Jews," I said in a low voice, so as not to be overheard. "We may have won the war, but they are still humans worthy of dignity and respect."

Wilhelm stared at me a moment with wide eyes, then leaned over the table and said, also in a low voice, "You may believe that, Albert, and I don't deny what you say, but you should be careful who you say that to. Especially around the SS in the camp. In their view, Poles and Jews are *worse* than criminals. It wouldn't do for you to appear too sympathetic to their plight. You saw the way that guard looked at you."

I felt like my face had been slapped. Of course Wilhelm was right. It wouldn't do to be too sympathetic to the enemies of the state. I felt resigned and nodded slowly. "You're right; I'll be careful what I say. But, it takes getting used to, to have a crematorium that is, well, just an incinerator. Kurt told me on my first day that the only difference between an incinerator and a crematorium is how you treat the ashes. It seems like we just crossed over some line in that camp," I said, cocking my head in the general direction of the camp.

"Yes, well, we will tell Kurt all that we learned, and let him make the next move." With that, Wilhelm got up, bid me good night, and went up to his room.

Not yet sleepy, I went outside into the wintry night air and walked around the town's central square. There was the bench that Herman and I had sat at on that wonderful day in 1936. So much had changed. Herman was in the army, literally galloping around foreign lands, and here I was serving the Fatherland back in Poland. But it was a different Poland. It was a Poland where the Poles themselves were treated like criminals. We had heard stories about the Russian zone, and how the Poles were being treated much worse than on our side. Hard to believe, really.

#

Wilhelm and I discussed the needed repairs on the long train journey back home. Back in Erfurt, we briefed Kurt Prüfer and the others on what we had seen there. In a private moment, I asked Kurt about the practice of cremating bodies together.

"Well, you are right, Albert, it is distasteful," Kurt said, looking thoughtful. "However, it would be efficient. I hadn't realized that the SS would

Melting Point

consider putting bodies together. If that is what the SS wants, we should think about designing a crematorium with that in mind."

I must have looked alarmed, because Kurt snapped out of his thinking and laughed at me. "Relax, Albert, it's just a thought. The systems installed now handle one body and one body only. The second oven going to Auschwitz is the same as the first. One body at a time. Period."

Soon after our trip, we sent a boxcar-load of materials to Poland for the second furnace and replacement parts for the first furnace. I didn't go this time. Construction work in Auschwitz continued well into February. Meanwhile, I was in Erfurt helping Karl Schultze revise plans for the ventilation systems. The camp wanted ventilation exhaust in the furnace room, and also in the morgue and autopsy room.

For some reason, we kept getting conflicting signals from the building office at Auschwitz. They kept changing their minds on how much exhaust they wanted, where they wanted it, and how much it should cost. We (well, Karl) would put together a plan, and send it to them, and they would think about it for a day. Then the phone calls would start. Can you move this vent? Can you increase this fan capacity? Can you route the exhaust through these existing holes in the walls? Can you make it cheaper? And so Karl would redesign the system and send it to them again.

The Auschwitz building office finally accepted our ventilation plans in March. Sheet metal was becoming difficult to get unless you had some kind of war priority, and so we only had some of the parts we needed for the furnace room, and almost none of the parts for the other rooms. We even borrowed parts from another company that was installing ventilation for the guard's barracks. I hoped the guards didn't find out, or we might not be welcome there anymore! The other rooms had to wait a while for us to scrounge up the parts.

Melting Point

There was bad news, too, from Wilhelm and the men installing the second furnace. During trials, they found that the furnace didn't draft well. We thought that the chimney should be raised to make a better draft. We argued with the Auschwitz building office over this for a while, because they thought we should increase the fan capacity. But, eventually they agreed to raise the chimney. It was to be increased to 60 feet tall!

#

This is how my spring passed. I wrote to my mother and Herman often. My father was always off doing errands for Albert Speer, so I just added notes to my father in my mother's letters, rather than trying to have the post office track him down.

Then on June 22, 1941, three million German soldiers, my brother included, invaded Eastern Poland and Russia. The largest invasion of all time. They quickly pushed east in another lightning attack that looked as promising as the invasion of France. However, Russia is so damn big that it took longer. As it would turn out, a lot longer. Our rapid progress netted us hundreds of thousands of Russian prisoners of war, lots more Poles, and of course lots more Jews. For our camp in Poland, it meant that they had plenty of need for the added capacity of the second furnace.

#

While the army had its hands full making huge gains of land from the Russians, we were battling more mundane problems. We had finally rigged the ventilation systems according to the approved designs, but the new height of the chimney had changed things. The heat and exhaust from the two double-muffle furnaces was so great, and the new chimney so tall, that the ventilators in the morgue and autopsy room actually ended up *adding* heat to their rooms rather than venting them. The SS men who used those rooms found them intolerable and demanded changes in the ventilator system, changes that

130

ironically were much like those of Karl Schultze's original, more expensive, proposal.

Karl Schultze was livid. He blamed the problem on the new taller chimney. He called the building office up there all kinds of names, but of course there was not much that could be done. He and I set out to figure out how to salvage most of the existing parts and wiring, yet improve the ventilation.

Meanwhile, the day after the invasion of Russia, some cracks appeared in the new bricks of the taller chimney from the stresses of the heat. The furnaces were shut down for a few days while metal bands were put around the chimney for support. It sounded precarious to me, but the furnaces were fired up again before the end of the month.

"See? More proof of their incompetence up there," said Karl Schultze. "They should have asked us to build the chimney for them. Then we would have done it properly, and corrected the venting problems all in one go. Fools."

At least he wasn't mad at me. That was a nice change.

Kurt Prüfer also had his problems. In Erfurt we had been building a new Auschwitz-style double muffle furnace for the Gusen sub-camp of Mauthausen, when the contract was abruptly cancelled. Apparently the Kori Company had re-asserted itself in Mauthausen, and Topf was no longer in favor there. Kurt applied his charms, but to no avail. He was pretty upset about it. I think he took it as a personal slap in the face that they didn't want *his* furnace. Well, there was also the commission to think about.

Kurt made a lot of noise around various SS offices, and I think he made some enemies of the SS men in Mauthausen, which was not a wise thing to do. I believe, though I have no proof of this, that they were determined to get revenge on our company. With the SS, it was always important to have some powerful friends, and avoid powerful enemies.

Melting Point

Kurt did have a genius for turning lemons into lemonade, though, and by the end of the summer the need for a third furnace arose in Auschwitz. They needed it immediately. Well, Kurt just happened to have one ready to go – the cancelled Gusen furnace!

As if psychic, as soon as the ink was dry on the order for a third Auschwitz furnace, the original furnace at Gusen fizzled out. August Willing went back to Gusen to fix it, only eight or nine months after converting it to coal. Apparently, they were overusing their furnace there as well. I was beginning to wonder if anyone would be left in Poland when this war was over.

There wasn't any space in the current furnace room to place a third oven, so some changes were needed of the building so the rooms could accommodate the new furnace. And, of course, the ventilation we at Topf had been working so hard on was going to be all wrong again. That made Karl Schultze very frustrated.

"What we need up there is someone who knows how to build, how to plan," Schultze complained to Kurt Prüfer. "A professional, rather than those circus clowns they have now."

"Calm down, Karl," Prüfer said, putting his arm around Karl's shoulders. "I hear there is a new man being assigned some large building plans up there, I'm going up there to meet with him and see what he's like. If he's no good, I'll suggest they hire us or another firm as general overseers."

Kurt Prüfer went to Auschwitz to meet the new man in charge of a large new building project up there, Karl Bischoff. When he came back, he gathered us all together.

"What I'm about to tell you is to be kept to yourself. No one outside our firm is to hear about this," Kurt began mysteriously. There was a murmur in the room.

Melting Point

"The camp up in Poland is expanding," he continued, with a widening smile. "The camp is about to triple in size, *and* they are building a whole new camp a couple of miles from the existing one, called Birkenau." Kurt Prüfer looked around the room from man to man. "The new camp is to be twelve times the size of the current camp! There will be about 150,000 prisoners altogether in the two camps!" Kurt said with flair.

Some gasps went around the room. Mine was one of them; 150,000 people! Today there were 10,000, with four, and soon to be six, muffles. Surely they won't need as many muffles per prisoner as we need now.

As if reading my mind, Kurt said, "And, in keeping with the SS's planned one-percent-per-day capacity, we'll need to be able to cremate some 1,500 bodies per day. If we continued using our existing technology, we would need almost 40 muffles. And, given the history up there, one percent is not enough, so we probably would need 80 to a 100 muffles, a ridiculous number."

By now, most people in the group listening to Kurt looked shocked. This was a staggering number of crematoriums, and of bodies. There could be nothing like it elsewhere on earth. Most of the towns in Germany had fewer than 150,000 people. And they weren't losing one or two percent of their population a day.

"Normally, I would say this was impossible. However, Albert here gave me the answer."

All eyes turned to look at me. *What? Me? What answer?* I was about to ask, when Kurt smiled at me and continued.

"Albert said that the SS didn't mind cremating more than one body at a time in the same muffle. It is a tremendous idea for efficiency. If we make our muffles big enough to handle two people at a time, then we get increased efficiency. If we make the ovens bigger and stronger, we can run them hotter. With those two changes, we could probably increase capacity to close to five or

Melting Point

six bodies per hour per muffle. It's what they tried doing with the original oven up there, but it just wasn't able to handle the load. We've also been tinkering with the idea of increasing the ovens to three muffles each, and so then you'd really have something. Five of these triple-muffle ovens should just do the trick." Kurt beamed at the small crowd.

We were silent except for a few gasps. Most were trying to absorb what he had said. I was shaking my head, because I hadn't suggested that we cremate two bodies at a time – quite the opposite! Now here he was, pinning these monster ovens on me! I couldn't let this go on.

"Mr. Prüfer," I began, "I'm *against* cremating two bodies at a time, and that was why I told you about the SS's actions, so you could stop them, not imitate them."

I had stepped over the line. Kurt lost his smile and said directly to me, "Mr. Stohl, it would be too expensive to continue to build ovens the way we have in the past for operations on this scale. Our customer is our government, and we are at war. We will strive to satisfy their needs so as to remain in business. We have competitors who would be happy to take our contracts away from us. If any of this doesn't make sense to you, perhaps you should not be here."

"I . . . I'm sorry, Mr. Prüfer, you're right of course." I said, turning bright red. "It just takes some getting used to, that's all."

Kurt softened and smiled again. He said, "I don't like the idea either, Albert, but these are prisons, not our normal customers. We're at war, and that demands action. I'm sure we will be victorious over Britain and Russia, and soon Topf and sons will be back to making civilian furnaces. For now, though, we must make our money by helping the Fatherland. It's really not a bad way to make a profit."

Melting Point

The meeting continued with some discussions on how to implement these new furnaces. I sat silent, staring at the chair in front of me, not wanting to look at any of my co-workers. Surely no one had ever built a three-muffle crematorium before, and no one had ever needed five of those. This is insane. With this kind of cremation power, the SS could turn the camp population over every 100 days or so. Almost a half a *million* people a year. Why did they need that much capacity?

After the meeting, at the end of that day, when most of the others had left to go home, I went to see Mr. Prüfer in his office. The building was quiet, the sun outside going down. Rays of orange light lit up the brickwork on his walls, illuminating his diploma, which was hanging framed on the wall.

"Mr. Prüfer?" I began tentatively.

"Call me Kurt, Albert."

"Uh, Kurt, well, I'm uneasy about what's going on at Auschwitz," I said, trying not to provoke him.

"About the plans to cremate more than one body at a time? I sympathize, Albert, really I do. But this is a huge wartime undertaking, and it would simply be impractical to build 50 of those ovens like we've been building them."

I thought a moment, nodding slowly. But this wasn't the real problem. "Well, besides that, I'm concerned with the sheer numbers of deaths. A town of 150,000 people would lose maybe two or three thousand people a year. We're proposing handling almost 200 times as many as that."

Kurt looked at me somberly for a moment. Then he said softly, "Albert, when we invaded France, we lost some 27,000 men. The allies lost some 90,000. Now, in Russia, we're losing more and more men each day. The Russians are losing hundreds of thousands. Death happens in wartime, Albert. I'm sure the prisoners who make it to Auschwitz are near death already. And

Melting Point

the new camp is to be a work camp, where prisoners are made to work to help the war effort. There will even be a huge synthetic rubber plant built there, and they'll use prison labor to build and run it. That's got to be miserable, backbreaking work. I heard that almost 9,000 Russian prisoners died in October alone!"

Kurt put his hand on my shoulder and almost whispered, "I wish we were at peace, Albert. I wish your brother didn't have to risk his life in the army. I wish we didn't have to make money building ovens that dispose of people who died because of the war. But we are at war, and our country needs us to do this job. If we didn't, what would the SS do with the bodies? They would have to bury them in mass graves. That isn't a good thing, either, Albert."

Kurt put his hands in his lap and stared at them as he said, "Now, I've met this new building director up there, Karl Bischoff. He's in charge of the Birkenau building projects. He's a good man with a lot going for him. He and I hit it off right away. Unlike some of those SS goons, Karl Bischoff is a professional builder. He's brought in a top-notch architect, an old buddy of his, to work on the plans with him. Bischoff seems like a real hard worker, and got his position through hard work rather than connections. I think I can work with him. He and I seem a lot alike in some ways."

Kurt cleared his throat and looked at me again. "Anyway, I think some of the confusion up there will calm down; the work will be hectic, but at least they'll be clearer on what they want. I'm hoping that things up there will be more, well, professional."

Kurt stood up, signaling that our conversation was about over. "The war effort needs us every bit as much as it needs your brother, Albert. I'm sure your brother has to deal with unpleasant things every day. Stick this out, and soon the war will be over and things will be back to normal. Okay, Albert?"

Melting Point

What could I say to that? *Gee, Kurt, I'm going to leave the country because I don't like death? Gee, Kurt, I'd rather be in the army with Russians shooting at me? Gee, Kurt, I'd rather be on the inside of Auschwitz than the outside?*

"Thank you, Mr. Pru . . . I mean, Kurt. Of course I'll do my utmost for the war effort. I guess we're all being asked to do things that are, well, unusual, and sometimes unpleasant. I'll try not to complain any more. And the technology is fantastic," I said, trying to end on a positive note.

So, once again, I caved in. Did nothing. Raised feeble objections and allowed myself to be beaten down. All the while, it was our *moral* temperature that was rising to the melting point.

#

In late November, I went to Auschwitz with some others to help install the third oven, and to look over the plans for the big crematorium at the new camp. The furnace room had been changed since I was last there. For one thing, the second oven had been installed to the right, further from the windows, of the original furnace. For another, the wall that was at your back when you faced the first oven had been removed. Behind that wall had been the autopsy room. It looks like I had been right in thinking that autopsies were not a big deal in a prison camp, and they had designated that room to become part of the furnace room, and to be the place for the third furnace.

The old morgue area that had housed bodies awaiting cremation had new doors that sealed the room better. On the door from the furnace room was painted a skull with the word *Lethal* on it. I much later found out that in September the camp had starting having prisoners *walk* into the morgue area and used the same stuff they killed lice with to poison the prisoners. At the time, though, I didn't know that and thought the sealed door was because of the smell of the bodies.

Melting Point

At this point we were just starting the foundation work, and I was mostly figuring out the practical aspects of how to convert the current venting setup to the new improved plan. Karl Schultze and I had worked on various blueprints, but you really needed someone on the site to tell what could be done. For one thing, we wanted to salvage as much as we could of the existing systems so we wouldn't have to try to get more sheet metal than absolutely necessary. For another, fuses and heavy-gage wire were getting harder and harder to get, so we had to be careful of overloading the electric circuits.

I also got my first look at the blueprints for the big new cremation facility. It was ambitious. There was a building with a furnace room holding the five triple-muffle furnaces. To the right of the furnaces there was a storage room for coke, and to the left was an autopsy room and some rooms for handling bodies just about to be cremated. I smiled ruefully to myself as I wondered how long it would be before that autopsy room was converted into something else. Behind the furnaces, close to the center of the building, was a small annex with a trash furnace and the huge chimney. All six furnaces, the trash furnace and five triple muffle crematoriums, would share one tall brick chimney.

An elevator at the far left of the building went down a flight to the morgue cellars, which were mostly underground. This would keep them cool in the summer, which was important. One cellar, called the Leichenkeller, or *morgue cellar*, was the large *receiving morgue*, where bodies would be lowered in by chute to be prepared for cremation. Once prepared, the bodies were to be moved to a storage area, called the Belüfteterkeller, or *aerated cellar*. From there they would be moved upstairs by elevator on demand.

Above the furnace room was an attic that could be used for storage or for living quarters for the Sonderkommandos. It would be plenty warm in winter, but probably too hot for living up there in the summer.

Most of the building would be built with prison labor and prisoner-made materials like bricks, so costs were reasonable. Our parts were the furnaces and ventilation system. The venting system was being designed by Karl Schultze, and I'd see his plans when I got back to Erfurt.

A few of us decided to walk over the site to see where the new camp's buildings were going to be. The new camp, Birkenau, was on the other side of the railway station from the original camp. When we got to the site, there was a lot of construction going on by tens of thousands of Russian prisoners, and the site was immense. It was about a half-mile wide by a quarter-mile deep. A long walk took us to the area where the new crematoria and morgue were to be built. Just beyond that site were some trees and beyond them the Vistula river.

Arnold Mahr, one of our construction overseers, whistled. "Ground's pretty wet here; we'll have to dig late spring at the earliest." He shook his head. "Gotta let it dry."

I had noticed some wooden barracks on the site. "I saw those barracks, before the war. They were portable Polish Calvary stables for their horses."

"And now they house Russians," Mahr said with a laugh. "Fitting."

"Kurt Prüfer told me 9,000 Russians died here last month," I said, gazing over at the old stables.

Mahr just gave a low whistle.

#

It was cold, so we didn't stay long. Instead of heading right home to Erfurt, though, I went to visit my aunt and uncle's farm. They had expanded it to encompass the land of some of their old neighbors, and had a few Polish men and women to help work the farm and keep the house going. One

Melting Point

neighbor's old farmhouse had been converted into living quarters for the ranch hands. Another neighbor's house had been burned down.

"We never liked them, anyway," Aunt Mary said, spitting on the floor. "We're going to replace their house with a flower garden."

"Where did they take them?" I asked.

"Who cares?" she said, throwing up her arms.

I looked surprised at her, and she explained, "Well, they always needled us about not being Polish, and when the war started they were openly hostile to us. Many times we almost came to blows! Carl and I were happy when the Gestapo came and took them away."

I only stayed that one day, and then went back to Erfurt.

#

"Well, you missed the excitement," said Karl Schultze what I got back.

"What happened?" I asked.

"Those idiots at Mauthausen," Karl sneered, "probably pulled some strings out of spite. They got old Ludwig Topf drafted into a construction battalion."

"Ludwig Topf, the owner of the company, drafted? Are you sure it was the Mauthausen people?"

"Well, we're not completely positive, but we did annoy some people up there trying to horn in on Kori's territory. I wouldn't put it past them. Besides, don't you see the irony of being assigned to a *construction battalion*?" Karl asked.

"I thought leaders of industry could get deferments," I said with a frown.

Karl Schultze shrugged. "Only if they are indispensable to the war effort."

140

"Does that mean that his younger brother is being drafted too?" I asked.

"Ernst-Wolfgang Topf?" asked Karl, his nose up in the air and imitating Ernst-Wolfgang's pompous voice. "That pompous fool is married, so he's immune. The worst of it is that he'll be our new boss."

Usually Ernst-Wolfgang Topf spent his time away from the day-to-day operations of the company. That was just fine with us, because when he did come in, he acted like the Pharaoh amongst his people.

"Poor Ludwig. What are we going to do?" I asked.

"Prüfer has been talking with his new best friend in the SS, Karl Bischoff. We'll just have to see where that goes," said Karl Schultze with resignation.

A few days later, I happened to be in a meeting with Kurt Prüfer and Karl Schultze, discussing ventilation for the new crematorium in Auschwitz, when old man Ludwig burst through the door. He was flushed with excitement and all smiles as he walked right up to Kurt and said loudly, "What did you do?"

Kurt looked innocently at him and spread his hands wide as he said, "About what?"

"The army just told me I have a *permanent* deferment!" Ludwig shook his finger at Kurt with a broad smile on his face. "Somehow, I think you were behind this. I respectfully ask you again, sir, what did you *do*?"

Kurt's face transformed from innocence into a beaming smile. His eyes twinkled, and he looked like a cat that had just dropped a mouse in front of his owner. "Well, I had a chat with my friend Mr. Bischoff. He suggested that his superiors would not allow a man critical to the design of their new crematoriums to be taken from us. I agreed that that could set back our whole program by months, and he made a few calls." Kurt Prüfer shrugged and then said, "How were we to know that they would misconstrue that *you* were the critical designer?"

After a pause, Ludwig smiled conspiratorially and bowed formally. "An honest mistake. One which I shall never forget. Thank you."

And with that small stroke of politics, Ludwig Topf would forever back Kurt Prüfer on anything he wanted to do. And Kurt Prüfer would do all he could to make Karl Bischoff's career advance. It was the seed for an unholy alliance.

#

Karl Bischoff's discussions with his bosses at the SS building office got people thinking that Kurt Prüfer was some kind of a genius at cremation. The head of technical operations for the SS building department in Berlin invited Kurt to talk about some plans for a new camp's furnaces. Kurt dragged me along to the meetings so I could take notes and provide him some technical backup.

Berlin was lovely but cold. I could see many of the construction projects my father had worked on, some half completed because of the war. The SS had nice offices, as you might expect. They wanted to discuss with Kurt some new requirements for crematoria in a camp in the small town of Mogilev, far away in Russia. While a tiny town now, in the 1600's it had been a big trading stop between Turkey and the Ukraine.

General Kammler, of the SS building office, was the chair of the meeting. He was in charge of most of the construction projects run by the SS and was Karl Bischoff's boss. A large man, he was used to being obeyed, and used to being in charge. "First of all, we want to do this on the cheap."

Kurt Prüfer laughed. "We've come to assume that as a requirement on *all* your projects."

Melting Point

I was surprised that Kurt would say such a thing to this man, but Kammler just laughed and grabbed a cigar from a holder on his desk. I was always amazed at the way Kurt Prüfer could read people.

Kammler lit his cigar. As he exhaled the first cloud of smoke, he said, "Well, maybe this one more than most. We don't expect this camp to be around all that long. It's not a destination; we just have a lot of *special guests* up there." Kammler took another puff.

A colonel named Bruker chimed in. "Another difference there is that there is no coal nearby, and we don't want to import it. But there is a large forest nearby, so there's plenty of wood. We were thinking of a wood-fired oven."

Without thinking, I blurted out, "Wood-fired ovens are suitable for bread, not people." Only after saying it did I realize it wasn't my place to say such things. I should have let Kurt Prüfer do all the talking.

Kurt Prüfer dramatically leaned over to me and patted my arm, as if comforting a child. "Yes, Albert, it will be a challenge." He then turned to General Kammler. "Wood-fired will be harder because it's difficult to reach the temperatures required. However, with adequate blowers to pump air in, and a large fire box men can feed continuously, I suppose we could do it. Though it will take longer to cremate each body." He turned back to me. "Take some notes, Albert." He stood and paced the floor. "Hmmm. We'll need a very large fire to get enough heat, so we better arrange as many muffles as we can around that fire."

Bruker chimed in, "If the fire was in the middle of a bunch of muffles, maybe the amount of fire-brick could be minimized and you could use regular bricks farther away from the fire. That would lower the cost."

I looked at Kurt and asked, "But if the muffle is hot enough to incinerate a body, doesn't it need fire-brick throughout?"

143

Melting Point

Kurt nodded, "Yes, yes, it does. But perhaps only a thin layer of fire brick right on the wall of the muffle, and regular bricks for the bulk of the structure." Kurt pulled a large sheet of sketch paper from his valise and started drawing. He asked me for some specific sizes and dimensions, and pretty soon had a rough sketch.

General Kammler grunted and set down his cigar. "OK, so I see the fire box in the middle. You've got two sets of four muffles, a total of eight muffles. How does this make it cheap?"

Kurt had drawn the crematoria as a square, with four muffles facing out to the left and four out to the right. The fire box was in the middle, at the back of all eight muffles. Kurt gestured towards the fire box, "The wood can be loaded from both sides of the furnace, away from the muffle openings. This way the piles of wood can be on both sides and the fire men won't interfere with the loading of bodies."

Kammler grunted and picked up his cigar, took a big puff and listened intently.

Kurt circled the ends of the fire box. "When running, wood will be loaded continuously, so there's no need for metal doors or other fittings on the fire box." Tracing over the lines between the pairs of muffles, he said, "Since the wood fire is cooler than coal, we won't need as much thermal insulation, nor as many fire-bricks." He turned to Kammler. "With only one fire, we need only one set of fans, one air duct, and one chimney. All in all, much cheaper."

General Kammler was puffing his cigar again, the smoke filling the room. He nodded. "All right, I get that it's cheaper. How much cheaper, do you think?"

Kurt Prüfer turned to me. "Albert, you're good at the math. Work up an estimate." He turned to General Kammler. "We should assume that local labor does most of the unskilled work?"

"Of course; they have nothing better to do," agreed Kammler.

Prüfer, probably hedging his bets, said, "And, again, I think the bodies will cremate more slowly with a wood fire than they would with coal."

"Excuse noted," grinned General Kammler good naturedly. "It's not like we are in any rush at this camp. Like I said, it's not a destination for trains like the others."

After a few moments, I had a rough calculation done. "Well, this is rough, but it looks like it will come out at about 1,700 Reichmarks per muffle."

Kurt Prüfer quickly chimed in, "If you recall, the original Auschwitz furnaces were about 5,000 Reichmarks each, and the new ones are about 2,100 each."

After some more talk, the meeting wrapped up. "Well, Kurt, I'm impressed with you and the Topf team." Kammler shook hands with Kurt. "You've done a great job over at Auschwitz and Birkenau, and I like the way you think. Keep up the good work."

Kurt acted shy and said, "Well, sir, I have to say I've enjoyed working with Karl Bischoff over at Birkenau. He's really first-rate. I can't think of a finer man I've worked with in your organization."

Kammler stubbed out his cigar. "Thank you, I appreciate that. What about the Auschwitz construction folks?"

Kurt's expression was pained, as if he didn't want to say anything bad. "Well, sir, as I say, Bischoff is really the best man out there. It is difficult supervising large projects like ours, and it takes a special man."

Kammler grunted. "Thank you; again I appreciate your honesty. Well, can you firm up these plans and send us a formal proposal?"

"Certainly," Kurt said. "About 13,600 Reichmarks, then." To me he said brightly, "A good day's work, Albert."

Melting Point

I was just starting to smile in agreement when Colonel Bruker chimed in, "Oh, no, you don't understand. We'll need four of these."

Four eight-muffle crematoria? Thirty-two muffles to cremate bodies? What in God's name was going on there?

After we left the SS offices, Kurt whistled. "Astonishing. Truly astonishing."

"Yes, unbelievable, Kurt," I agreed.

He smiled at me and clapped me on the back. "I couldn't have done it without you, Albert. Outstanding; a good day's work, indeed!"

#

A few days after we got home, Kurt got a phone call from Karl Bischoff. The building offices at Auschwitz and Birkenau had merged. Karl, who had been in charge of just Birkenau, had been made the head of all of the building in the entire Auschwitz/Birkenau complex.

"General Kammler said I worked well with contractors," Bischoff said. "He mentioned Topf by name, and said that was one reason for my promotion."

"You're welcome," was Kurt's reply.

#

Early in December, 1941, the Japanese attacked Pearl Harbor. Now, every major country was involved in what had truly become a World War. I was a little surprised when, a few days later, Hitler declared war on America, because I was hoping that America and Japan could fight each other and leave us out of it.

#

Kurt asked the Mogilev SS building office for half of the money for their furnaces up front, but the SS wanted in return to get something, anything, shipped up to the site before the end of the year. The factory at Erfurt quickly scrounged together enough hardware to build half of an oven, four muffles, and shipped it to Mogilev on December 30th, with just one day to spare. Of course, half of an oven wouldn't do them much good, but at least we had shipped *something*. We set about to manufacture more parts for the ovens up there. Though, as it would later turn out, we were not going to deliver any more parts to Mogilev.

Melting Point

The Holocaust – 1942, 1943

The rain in Bodega had slowed to a drizzle, but there were drips from the roof still hitting the porch, and raindrops were still collecting and running down the windows. We took another quick break to refill cups and glasses and to empty our bladders. I was avoiding looking at my family, especially at Magda.

Tom came over and said quietly to me, "I've never heard this viewpoint of the Holocaust. It's fascinating and, well, disturbing at the same time."

I nodded at him and sighed heavily, and could only imagine what Magda was thinking. I saw Magda out of the corner of my eye, dabbing at her eyes with a tissue. *What does she think of me now?*

We all moved back to our seats and sat down, so I continued the story.

#

1942 was another year of tremendous effort and success for us at Topf. By spring, parts were being shipped by train from the home office in Erfurt up to Auschwitz to complete the third oven and to start building the new crematoria at nearby Birkenau. Meanwhile, Kurt Prüfer went to Buchenwald to supervise the installation of our prototype triple muffle oven, the first of two

The Holocaust – 1942, 1943

planned for there. This would give us a chance to see how they performed before installing five such ovens at Birkenau.

Kurt also discussed plans with Karl Bischoff for a backup cremation facility in Birkenau, since we had been having so many problems with the old crematoria. Kurt proposed some cheap and flimsy, stripped-down furnaces. We worked on the plans for a while, but the plans were eventually canceled by Bischoff's boss, General Kammler, after he visited the camp. Both Kurt Prüfer and Karl Bischoff were upset about losing the sale and about having their work second-guessed, but Bischoff convinced the central office to pay Topf for the work we had already put into the plans.

There was still a lot of work going on at Auschwitz involving Topf, though, and Kurt decided to send me there as a kind of 'resident Topf representative.' I would be the eyes and ears of Topf as all of the construction progressed. I'd still come back to Erfurt, of course, when there wasn't much happening, but I packed my bags in anticipation of staying a long time.

In late May, I was up at Auschwitz helping with the construction of the third and last furnace in the original crematorium. I also looked over the foundation of the new crematorium building being built in Birkenau. The digging had started after the beginning of the rainy season, and the prisoners in the pits of what were to become the cellars of the furnace building were ankle-deep in a clay-like mud.

The Birkenau camp was immense, and now that the buildings were taking shape I could see how big it really was. It took up the space formerly occupied by several farms! A couple of the small farmhouses were still there.

Everywhere there were prisoners in their striped gowns. Construction was going on all over the camp, with tens of thousands of prisoners working on foundations and roads, a sewage treatment plant, warehouses, dormitories, guard towers, and all kinds of other projects. The cavalry's horse stables were

Melting Point

still in use, but many more wooden dorms were being built with small brick stoves and chimneys in them. We had again been cautioned to stay away from the prisoners because of lice, so I didn't stay at Birkenau long before returning to Auschwitz.

The evening of May 27 I was in the Auschwitz officers' dining room. Dinner was rabbit, potato pancakes, and bottled mineral water. As a manager from a contract firm, I was able to dine with the officers.

"Bottled water?" I said offhandedly to Otto, a construction supervisor sitting next to me. "I know the water wasn't very tasty, but ... bottled?"

In a hushed voice, he said, "You can't drink the tap water anymore, it's polluted. Typhoid fever has broken out among the inmates. We're working on a water treatment plant, but it's slow going. Meanwhile, we all drink mineral water."

"That must be expensive, giving mineral water to all the inmates," I said naively.

The supervisor stared at me with raised eyebrows and didn't say anything. It dawned on me, and my face showed that I understood. *The prisoners don't get bottled water.* "So, how are they going to stop the disease, then?" I asked.

"Boiling kills the germs, so the inmates are eating a lot of soup these days; or drinking water that has been boiled. But that's not the only problem," he said, again lowering his voice conspiratorially. He glanced around dramatically and said, "The lice problem has gotten out of hand too, and now there's a typhus epidemic. We thought that shaving the prisoners' heads, having them take showers when they get here, and delousing their clothes would be enough, but it hasn't helped. We're not sure *where* the typhus is coming from. The prisoners are starting to drop like flies from the two diseases."

"Typhoid fever and typhus are different?" I asked quizzically. "I thought they were the same thing."

"Completely different," Otto said through a mouthful of rabbit leg. "The fever is from bad sanitation and typhus is from fleas, ticks, and, in our case, lice." He took a swig of water, swallowed, and continued. "If untreated, they are both disastrous. And, it's too expensive to treat properly in this place."

I was struck with an odd feeling, a kind of incongruous notion that we were doing our best to incinerate prisoners at a phenomenal rate, so what was the big deal about disease? "You know, in any other place in the world, a disease that kills people is bad." I chuckled, trying to make light of it, "But, here, it almost seems like we're in *competition* with them."

"Well, it's true that lots of people aren't surviving their arrival here, and those that can't work, or won't work, don't survive, but those that *can* work are useful. The epidemics are depleting our work force, right?"

A ray of light shone through the fog of my understanding, and like a diamond cutting through glass I suddenly understood with complete clarity. All along I had thought that only the brutalities, privations, hard work, and diseases were causing a high death rate. I had never considered that people were being *weeded out*; that there were valuable people and superfluous people. Those who could work were valuable, the rest weren't, and so should die. How insanely obvious.

Just as I was valuable to the German work force even though I was just a college student, these prisoners were valuable to the German work force as well. The prisoners worked sand and gravel pits and made bricks. And Birkenau had been created to supply workers to the German industries up here in Poland. One of the biggest construction projects was the chemical giant I.G. Farbin making a synthetic rubber plant near here. I didn't know much about synthetic rubber plants, but I knew that they were huge, like a small city, with

Melting Point

large numbers of buildings. They were going to build it where now there was farmland. If I.G. Farbin was going to build a plant, they needed thousands of workers to build it. Thousands more would be needed to supply the sand, gravel, bricks, cement, and other materials. You can't find thousands of German men to do this kind of work; they are in the army or doing other necessary jobs. *Like building furnaces.*

"Anyway," he said, "your ovens will be working hard this month."

That stung: *my* ovens. *Well, they were, weren't they? Just as the construction sites were his. The camp was the SS'. The ovens were Topf's. And therefore, mine.*

"Yeah," I said stupidly. What else could I say? People were being weeded out. That meant that there must have been lots of people sent here who were never meant to be housed in the prison, or at least not for long. Did that mean that someone or some group sent people here specifically to die? That would be murder, wouldn't it? I wasn't ready to accept that yet. Maybe 'callous indifference,' but not murder; not Germans.

#

When the third two-muffle oven in the old ammo bunker in Auschwitz was finally completed, all three were started up, and almost immediately the chimney had problems again. The metal bands put around it to stabilize it broke off and cracks formed in the brickwork. We men from Topf were glad that it wasn't *our* workmanship failing. The chimney needed overhauling *again*. It needed more draft so the hot smoke didn't linger in the chimney. This time, the proposal was to raise the chimney to 90 feet tall! This was absurd, and the SS men who worked in the nearby buildings were rightly concerned that the chimney could topple on them. They wanted the chimney to be no more than 30 feet tall. So, the SS' central building office proposed putting up a 30-foot tall chimney, with 60 feet of flue underground, making it a 'virtual' 90 feet tall.

The Holocaust – 1942, 1943

There wasn't enough room between the crematorium building and its neighbors for a huge flue like that underground, so Kurt Prüfer suggested to Karl Bischoff that he should ask Topf for a bid on the new chimney. We bid a 45-foot tall chimney with 36 feet of underground flue. It was a compromise, but it was accepted. Work started on that in June and finished in August.

As part of the expansion of the ventilation systems, the crematoria needed additional electric power brought over to it. Additional power was to come from the building behind the crematoria. While the ground was all torn up for the new chimney, we had a trench dug for a couple of new power lines between the two buildings. We should have run one large cable for power, but electrical supplies were scarce, so we ran a few smaller, cheaper lines. We used some cheap low-power fuses on those new lines, as high-power fuses were in short supply as well. I helped to install the fuses and lines in the basement of the other building.

With the exception of a brief run at the end of May, there were no cremations in Auschwitz for most of May, all of June and July, and some of August. It felt sort-of good that 'my' ovens weren't working, though I knew that people were still dying. We did send another railcar of materials for the new ovens to Birkenau, however, and so our cremation capacity was only going to increase, despite the short break.

At the beginning of July, a letter from my father reached me in Auschwitz. It had been mailed some time before to our offices in Erfurt. I had been spending so much time in Auschwitz that Gitta had forwarded the letter to me there. In my youth, my father had been reserved with me, but lately he had been writing to me in a tone I had never heard him use in person. He must have been a little lonely, but also fairly happy, from the tone of his letters. It helped me see him in an entirely new light.

#

Melting Point

Dear Son,

I haven't talked with you for a little while, and I wanted to let you know what's been going on with your father. I hear from Carl and Mary that you come by to visit once in a while, because you are sometimes working at a facility nearby. I'm proud of you for being involved in the war effort, as much as I'm proud of Herman.

Speaking of Herman, he has been galloping through southern Russia this spring, and seems to be having a great time. He has been promoted and is in charge of a battery of guns. He said he would try to send you a letter soon.

Last January, I was in the southern Ukraine in Dnipropetrovs'k (it's harder to pronounce than spell!) working on figuring out how to repair the Russian railroads. We need them to supply our troops, but the sheds were destroyed, the roundhouses burned, and it was generally in bad shape. The Russians did a good job of destroying everything useful as they retreated, and our troops have just added to the devastation. We have now repaired the tracks, but all the support facilities are in disarray. The distances back to fully working rail lines are enormous, and there are serious problems getting supplies to our freezing troops. I am part of the 'Speer Construction Staff' and was housed for a time with my co-workers in a sidelined train, in a spare railway sleeping car. It was freezing there, and once in a while we got the locomotive fired up enough to run some steam through the cars. We worked in an adjoining dining car, with the tables turned into desks and drafting surfaces.

Our boss, Albert Speer, came out to visit and organize the reconstruction at the end of January. He flew in on a plane just before snow closed the runways. The roads and rail lines had been nearly impassible for most of the month. We were pretty isolated there, without a lot of supplies, even food. What supplies got through for the troops were ferried along the river Dnieper. Getting any useful work done was very difficult. Mostly we were waiting for spring.

Just before Speer arrived, a small Russian tank group had broken through our troop's lines nearby and headed towards the town where we were. We didn't have much besides some rifles here, and were getting concerned for our safety. What we didn't say out loud was that while our army was bogged down in the snow, the Russians seemed to be moving around freely. Fortunately, the Russians didn't know what they could have done, because they got close to the town and then seemed to just mill around. Perhaps they thought we were well defended. Had they pressed on just a bit farther, they could have cut off our supply lines across the river Dnieper and put the entire army in really bad straits. And they could have captured your father and Albert Speer! They didn't, thank God.

After being stranded for a week, his plane grounded from the cold, Speer decided to try to get home on a train that was going to attempt to go west, and had a snow plow on the front of it. The train pulled out very slowly, with prisoners shoveling the deep snowdrifts off the tracks in front of it.

After he left we had a small party to celebrate his safe trip home, and, I'm afraid, we got rather drunk. We passed out in our freezing train and woke up the next morning with hangovers. And Speer was back! Apparently his train had to turn back. We were depressed. That very day, the weather was way below zero degrees with gusty winds, but we were determined to help his plane get unstuck and get him out of there. Prisoners shoveled snow from the runways and we trampled the ground

Melting Point

and preheated the plane's engine. At last he took off. We were glad to see him go. His nervous energy made us nervous too.

He flew to Rastenburg, Hitler's eastern command center, and had an oddly wonderful thing happen to him. He was going to fly back to Berlin the next morning with the Minister of Armaments and Munitions, Dr. Todt. As you likely know, Todt built the autobahn, and was in charge of roads, construction, and a whole lot of other things that keep the wartime economy moving. Todt had been at Rastenburg having arguments with Hitler. Hitler seemed to think that Todt wasn't doing all he could to keep supplies flowing to the army in Russia. Also, Todt had recently been having heated disagreements with Goering, who was responsible for the four-year plans and the war economy, over responsibilities.

Todt and Speer were going to leave together very early the next morning, but Speer was called in to chat with Hitler at one in the morning. I understand Hitler keeps late hours often. Anyway, Hitler and Speer talked until three in the morning, so Speer decided not to fly with Todt. Speer was woken the next morning by a phone call telling him that Dr. Todt's plane had crashed, and that Todt had been killed! Hitler again called for Speer, and unexpectedly told him that he, Speer, was to take over all of Todt's duties!

Then, Goering swept in and demanded that Todt's duties be turned over to him! Goering had come by train at least 60 miles to see Hitler, and so must have jumped on the train the moment he heard of the crash. Hitler told Goering that Speer was taking charge of all of Todt's duties. Speer later told us that Goering was furious with him for this, as if Speer had been maneuvering to get the job.

Now I work for the new minister of armaments, director of road building, builder of the West Wall and U-boat pens and on and on and on. And, best of all, I kept the same boss! As you can imagine, our workload has increased and gotten more hectic. However, I think I'll be able to get out to Herman's unit on business later this year, and that will be nice. Perhaps I can come by and see you too at that place near Carl and Mary's.

Well, keep up the good work, and may we all be victorious. I hope to see you and Herman later this year. Until then, Heil Hitler!

Regards, Papa.

P.S. Do you remember the summer before you went off to the University, when we were at the park? It looks to me like the same thing may have happened here, but tell no one.

#

That final comment was odd. The summer before I went to the University, Mother, Father, Herman and I had gone to a park near our home for a picnic. We came upon a couple of boys who were playing with toy airplanes made of balsa wood and paper. One of them had placed a large firecracker inside the toy cockpit, and lit the fuse just before throwing the plane. The plane blew apart mid-flight in a spectacular shower of burning paper and balsa wood splinters. Was my father implying that there had been a bomb on board Todt's plane?

So my father, by virtue of providence and perhaps a little sabotage became part of a powerful ministry, working for the most powerful civilian man in the government. I wondered what my father was saying by the plane being blown up by a bomb. He had been careful to tell me that both Hitler and Goering had reason to kill Todt. Of course, he couldn't come out and say that outright in the letter, it would be too dangerous. But he did make it plain that there were at least two people who could have wanted him dead. Goering came a long distance quickly upon hearing of the crash, so maybe he was waiting for the explosion? I don't know. "Oddly wonderful," my father had said. Very odd; if the top men in government were capable of this kind of plotting of important people's deaths, perhaps they could also plot the deaths of the prisoners of Auschwitz? That was something for me to think about, anyway.

#

In mid-July, Heinrich Himmler visited both Auschwitz and the nearby Birkenau, which was still undergoing a lot of construction. As the Topf representative, I was invited along as a part of Karl Bischoff's engineering group. We were to stay in the background but be ready to answer any questions Himmler may have.

Heinrich Himmler was the head of the SS, and reported only to Hitler himself. As head of the SS, he was head of the Gestapo, the camps, and the reign of terror that gripped Europe. He was the reason that people toed the line. After the army moved through an area, Himmler's men moved in. Everyone was terrified of Heinrich Himmler, not the least the SS who worked for him. He was cold and seemingly arbitrary, merciless to those under him who failed to do whatever he thought they should do.

There were a number of preparations underway before his visit. The camp was cleaned up, even *beautified* with flowers and shrubs. Specific inmates were chosen to be visible, their placement and actions carefully choreographed. The evidence of typhus and typhoid fever were hidden away, they being evidence of sloppiness. Himmler was going to inspect a number of aspects of the camp, but I was to be present only when he saw the crematoriums.

He arrived on July 17. General Kammler from the central building office came with him, as well as a number of other men. Himmler was introduced to Karl Bischoff and some of the other higher-ups in the camp. He already knew the director of the camp, Rudolph Höss. They were apparently friends from way back. After introductions, we all went over to Birkenau. I

The Holocaust – 1942, 1943

went over to wait by the foundations of the new crematorium as Himmler and his entourage viewed an arriving trainload of prisoners. Having walked from the train station, the prisoners walked through the gate of Birkenau. Himmler's group followed the progress of the prisoner's processing as they were selected into two groups, and one large group was marched off past a row of trees beyond where the crematorium foundation was being built. I didn't see what happened to them after that. The other group entered the quarantine area, where prisoners were kept separate from the main population until they could be determined to be in good health.

About two hours later, the group came over to inspect the new crematorium facility. Himmler asked questions of Höss and Bischoff, and I stayed in the background, available if Bischoff needed me, but otherwise out of the way. After that, the group went off a mile or two northeast to Monowitz, the town where I.G. Farbin's new synthetic rubber plant was being built. I stayed behind.

There was a big reception for Himmler that night. I wasn't invited, so I rejoined the group the next morning in the Auschwitz crematoria furnace room, where Himmler inspected the three double-muffle ovens and observed progress on the construction of the new chimney. Again I kept to the background in case Karl Bischoff needed me, but he didn't. Himmler left later that day, and the camp command seemed pleased and relieved.

Late that evening, Karl Bischoff summoned me. This was unusual, especially so late at night. I went to the camp building office, which was deserted except for Karl. He sat with his feet up on his desk. A bottle of good French brandy stood next to a half full glass. Karl's eyes stared somewhat unfocused at the bottle, as if trying to imagine it being something else, a woman perhaps. He rubbed his bushy black eyebrows and ran his hand through his thinning hair as he offered me a drink. I politely declined.

Melting Point

"You'll need it," he said, taking his feet off the desk and sitting up. "Please."

I took the glass he offered, and he poured me a generous amount. He poured himself more, too. Then he took a large swig from his glass. I had worked with him for a few months now, but this was the first time we had been together socially. I took a sip and it burned my throat.

"Are you a religious man, Stohl?"

"My mother used to take my brother and me to church, but I, well, haven't gone to church in years."

"You may need to start going again," he said, taking another gulp of brandy. "What did you think of Himmler?"

I wasn't sure what to say. Himmler was Bischoff's boss', boss', boss', boss or something. The most feared man in Germany. At least Hitler had his charismatic, mythic side.

"Uh, very nice."

"Right," Bischoff said with a cynical smile and raised eyebrow that indicated that he understood precisely what I meant.

Bischoff stared down into his glass for a moment, gathering his thoughts. Then he said very softly, without looking up, "He's insane, you know." He looked up at me sharply and demanded, "Can I trust you to be discreet?"

Here he had just called the most feared man in Germany insane, and *then* asked if I could be trusted. He must have been drinking for a while now. From the tone of this conversation, I decided I had better start catching up. I took a large gulp from my glass and winced as it burned all the way down my throat.

"Of course, sir. Nothing you say will leave this room."

The Holocaust – 1942, 1943

Bischoff nodded and a smile flickered across his face. "I like you, Albert. I like Kurt, too. So many of these people I work with here are all caught up in the system. Kurt is a self-made man; bright, industrious, a Great-War vet; like me. And you remind me a little of myself when I was younger. Kurt told me of your concerns about what we are doing here, and I respect you for that. You are right to be concerned."

He took a final sip from his glass before setting it down and refilling it. He held the bottle out to me, and I quickly drained my glass and held it for him to refill. I could feel that there was something inside him he wanted to let out, and I knew I should be properly anesthetized before hearing it. I thanked him for refilling my glass.

"Do you know what I saw yesterday?" He waved his glass vaguely in the air. "That trainload of people walking into the camp? Dutch Jews. The train pulls up to a stop just before the civilian train station. We wouldn't want civilians seeing them, of course. The people get off the train and are walked over to Birkenau. They walk into the camp in a long line, and are seen by a doctor. He glances at the people and decides their fate in a second or two. Those who could work were sent to the quarantine area. Those who couldn't work were marched off into the woods. I saw you there at the crematorium. Be glad you didn't come with us."

"I knew where we were going, of course." He took another gulp and licked his lips. "I oversaw the reconstruction of the farmhouses. There are two back there, near each other. One is made of red brick and so is called *the little red house*. We headed past that one to the other one, made with bricks too but covered in white plaster, called the *little white house*. We've replaced the thatched roof with thin concrete, and divided it up into four rooms, with one door for each room on the south side and one on the north side. When the entrance doors are swung out, the signs visible on the doors say *to the baths*. The people

Melting Point

undress in a wooden shed next to the farmhouse, and then they all go in to the four rooms. All of them, all at once." Karl Bischoff closed his eyes as if remembering the scene. He took a deep breath, and gulped more brandy. He topped my glass off from the bottle without asking as he continued, "The doors are closed and sealed, revealing the signs on the outside of the doors: *High Voltage - Lethal Danger*."

My eyes narrowed. This didn't sound good. I gripped my glass tightly and took a big swallow of brandy. It felt good as it burned down the back of my throat, and my mind was beginning to feel pleasantly fuzzy.

"Ever heard of Fritz Haber?" Bischoff asked lightly, refilling our glasses.

"Of course!" I said brightly, though a little puzzled what this had to do with the prisoners. "Nobel prize in 1931 for inventing a process to make nitrate fertilizers – the foundations of modern farming!"

"Yes, well, less known was his invention of the insecticide we use to kill lice here. A hydrogen cyanide product called Zyklon A. It has this foul odor added to it so you will know if you smell it. Sort of like they add to natural gas they pipe into homes." Bischoff swirled around the brandy in his glass and then took a sip. "Turns out they have another version now called Zyklon B. It doesn't have the odor added to it. That would make it pretty dangerous to kill lice with, of course."

Karl Bischoff set down his glass and leaned closer to me. He lowered his voice to almost a whisper. "The High Voltage sign was just to keep people out, you understand. After they closed the doors, some cans of Zyklon B were poured into the rooms from a hatch in the roof. There was muffled screaming from inside, but only for a few minutes. By the time half an hour went by, it was all over. Both sets of doors were opened to ventilate the gas. After some time to clear the air of poison, the bodies are dragged out the rear doors and taken a hundred feet or so to mass graves and buried."

We both took a drink.

"But, as bad as that was for me, Himmler was *delighted* with the operation. He talked the whole time to the men around him about the possibilities. About how this was only the beginning. About how this was *good for a start*. In fact, the only thing he didn't like was the burying of the dead. He likes the idea of cremation. I think it's because it makes people just vanish, without even a grave left behind. That's why he was so interested in the crematoriums."

We sat silent for a moment then. I wasn't sure what to say. This was murder, plain and simple. Murder of those *unfit to work*.

Karl Bischoff looked at me and nodded slowly as he said, "Do you know why I'm here in my office tonight, Albert?"

My heart seemed to be beating irregularly. I shook my head slowly and could barely breathe. "No," I whispered.

Karl ticked the items off on his fingers one by one. "Himmler ordered us to double the size of Birkenau to house 200,000 inmates. He ordered the creation of satellite camps to house inmates for work at I.G. Farbin and other factories. He ordered us to speed up the repairing of the chimney in Auschwitz to get the furnaces back on line. He ordered us to hurry up the new crematorium in Birkenau. He ordered us to more than double our cremation capacity. He ordered us to put a rail line from the train station right into the heart of the camp to speed up the unloading process," He paused to drink. He sounded disgusted and angry as he said, "And he told Höss that we should be prepared to receive an average of one trainload of Jews a day, every day, from now until there are no Jews left in Europe."

Melting Point

He threw his glass across the room and it smashed against a metal filing cabinet. "That's why I'm working late. I have to plan how to kill thousands of people a day, every day, from now until God himself pulls me down into the fires of hell." Bischoff buried his face in his hands.

I was silent for a while, and then quietly said, as much an option for myself as for him, "You could refuse. Leave. Transfer into the army."

Bischoff sighed heavily and shook his head, still buried in his hands. "A week ago a civilian worker illegally gave a bottle of mineral water to a Jewess who was thirsty. Höss had the worker shot. Himmler personally assigned me the responsibility for carrying out the construction. He gave me unprecedented authority to get materials, and unprecedented responsibility to see that it all happens. Can you imagine what would happen to me if I refused? Especially on the grounds that the Jews didn't deserve this fate? Can you imagine what they would do to my family?"

I didn't have Bischoff's authority or responsibility, but I could well imagine what would happen if I asked to leave on moral grounds. I hadn't considered that there might be repercussions to my family as well. This was horrible, a disaster.

In a defeated tone, I said quietly, "But this is murder."

Bischoff just pursed his lips and nodded. "It may help to imagine them as enemies of the state, a threat to the nation. Your brother is off killing Russians; we're at war. Imagine the Jews as the enemy. Or imagine them as being a threat to our security. Imagine anything but the truth, Albert. Bury yourself in your work, keep your head down, and wait for this to blow over. It can't last forever. Hitler won't let it. He can't."

We both drank in silence then, Karl drinking directly from the bottle. After a while, I went back to my room and collapsed in bed. I felt trapped. I think he did too. This was a new low. I was very depressed.

The Holocaust – 1942, 1943

We both buried ourselves in work. On August 8, the smokestack in Auschwitz was finished and we fired up the three ovens. There was, as you can imagine, a large *backlog*. The ovens ran at full capacity for five days, and then the chimney had a minor breakdown again. For a brief moment, I wondered if there was a message in that. But it was clear that this crematorium was nearing the end of its useful life. There just wasn't the room to make a chimney large enough to handle the load here. The new crematoriums would have an immense smokestack, with fans pushing the smoke out. They'd be more suitable for the job.

Kurt Prüfer came out in late August to discuss plans with Bischoff for new crematoriums, a direct result of Himmler's visit. One was to be a mirror image of the one under construction, though without the trash incinerator. Another two were planned for extra capacity to handle the influx of Jews being shipped in. These would be smaller, and located by the little red house and little white house, respectively. They wouldn't need five triple-muffle furnaces like the 'main' crematoriums. Instead, Prüfer decided we could use the cheaper furnaces of the type that we were building for Mogilev. At this point, we had shipped one half of an eight-muffle oven to Mogilev, but there were lots of parts becoming ready in Erfurt. Bischoff was in a rush, actually a panic, and didn't want to wait until after we built all the ovens planned for Mogilev. Himmler wanted results from Bischoff, not excuses. Kurt figured he could hijack the shipments to Mogilev and use them in Birkenau, provided that Karl Bischoff could pull the right strings in the SS to give priority to Birkenau.

For the first time, the crematoria were given numbers, so we wouldn't have to identify them as 'the new one by the little red house,' and so on. The original crematoria in Auschwitz was designated *Crema I*, and the new crematoria already under construction in Birkenau was designated *Crema II*. The proposed one that was its mirror image was designated *Crema III*, and the two smaller crematoria by the farmhouses were named *Crema IV* and *Crema V*. They

Melting Point

used Roman Numerals as an ironic touch – the Romans had expelled the Jews from Jerusalem. Now apparently it was our turn to expel them from Earth.

#

Meanwhile the typhus outbreak had become an epidemic. Camp Commandant Höss ordered huge quantities of the insecticide Zyklon B, the one without the added odor, to combat the problem of lice. The epidemic was to be kept secret, lest Himmler think the camp wasn't working well and his labor force in jeopardy. Ironically, Höss was able to hide the epidemic in part because his superiors thought that the massive amounts of insecticide being ordered were to be used to gas the Jews. But in fact, it takes a lot more of the insecticide to kill lice than people. The SS leadership would have been very upset to supply tons of Zyklon A to exterminate lice, but they were happy to supply Zyklon B to exterminate people.

It turned out that the epidemic was originating among the thousand or so civilian workers and not the prisoners. The civilian workers didn't have their heads shaved and didn't take the other precautions, so they were spreading the disease to the inmates. The camp was put under quarantine. Trainloads of people could come in, but no one could leave. The workers were divided into those who had contact with inmates and those who didn't, like me. I got an inoculation against typhus, and had a high fever for a day as a reaction.

Summer and fall were spent in construction and getting the parts together for the various crematoriums. There were thousands of prisoners working on foundations and brickwork and carpentry and plumbing and all the other trades to get the buildings up. Asphalt needed for water-sealing the basement morgues was hard to come by and delayed construction for a time. Vedag, the construction firm overseeing the building of the cellars, got the asphalt delivered and installed just in time to keep out the rising water tables in October, thanks only to Karl Bischoff's intercession.

The Holocaust – 1942, 1943

There had been relatively minor changes to the design of the new Crema from Kurt's initial designs. The two cellars had been changed to aerate the same way, with both intake and exhaust vents. However, where before they had been planned as morgues, now one cellar had been designated as a dressing room and the other a gas chamber. Another small but crucial change was that the chute that was to be used to slide the dead bodies down into the first morgue had been changed into a stairway. The dead would be able to walk in now.

By the end of the year, we had finished installing the two prototype triple-muffle ovens in Buchenwald. The ovens did not have the capacity we expected. The heat from the coal came in to the outer two muffles, and then flowed into the center muffle. The center muffle was therefore cooler, and didn't perform as well. Because of the bigger muffles, the ovens ran cooler, too, causing bodies to take longer to cremate. Overall, the oven performed at only about half of the estimated capacity of five-bodies-per-muffle-per-hour.

This was a potential disaster for Topf, and so we kept it quiet. It wouldn't do to tell everyone that all the capacity we were building was only half as effective as we had promised. Kurt Prüfer told Karl Bischoff, of course, because they were friends, and Karl deserved to know what was going on. Quietly they agreed that it was important to complete all four new crematoriums so that the combined power would come close to the demand.

I suppose, looking back now, I should have been happy that the furnaces were not working as well as planned. However, the fact was that prisoners were going to die whether there were furnaces or not. And, yes, I suppose there was some pride at stake; we said these furnaces would work at a certain capacity, and we wanted them to work at that capacity. I imagine medieval blacksmiths took great pride in the swords they made, even if they didn't respect the way they were being wielded. I took pride in the work I did.

Melting Point

The quarantine was getting to be a real problem for the camp. The SS wouldn't let any of the thousand civilian workers leave for Christmas holiday until they had gone twenty-one days without an outbreak of typhus. But on December 10, someone came down with the disease, so it would be at least the 31st before the workers would be allowed to leave. The workers were outraged, because they would miss Christmas. On the 17th they stopped working in protest. The SS relented and let them all go home for Christmas on the 23rd, and they could stay away until the 4th of January.

I took advantage of the work stoppage to go home and visit my mother for the holidays. Father and Herman were both off in Russia, and so couldn't celebrate with us. It was kind of a somber Christmas with both of them gone. Mother and I knew things had gone poorly for our army the year before in the bitter cold Russian winter. We worried that the coming winter would be tough again. In addition, the war hadn't been going as well this year as it had in past years. The British and Americans had begun 1,000-bomber air raids against German cities by midyear. After roaming with impunity most of the year in Africa, Irwin Rommel's army had been thrown back at El Alamain, and the Americans had landed in North Africa. We were still convinced of our eventual victories, but it just seemed that winters went poorly for Germany.

Christmas day we went to a church, the first time I had been in one for some time. It felt terrible. Here I was in the house of the Lord, celebrating the birth of His Son, when I had just completed a year in which I was inexorably tied to the deaths of hundreds of thousands of people. Halfway through the service, the minister talked about all the good people of Germany working in the Lord's service, and I excused myself and went outside into the cold air and snowy grounds of the church. I was sweating and breathing hard and my chest burned and ached. There were good people in Germany, of course, but I couldn't have been counted as one of them.

The Holocaust – 1942, 1943

After the service, my mother came out and chastised me for leaving early. As we walked home, with me limping slightly, I tried to tell her what was bothering me.

"Where I'm working, up in Poland, terrible things are happening," I began. I couldn't tell her the whole truth, but I wanted her to understand why I felt so bad.

"Your father was almost caught by Russians earlier this year. Are you close to the front?"

"No."

"Herman has people shooting at him. Do you have people shooting at you?"

"No."

"Well, then," she admonished, "I'd say you probably have it easier than they do. Try to keep things in perspective, Albert."

What could I say? How do you explain it without telling the truth? Mother, I'm part of a system that is killing hundreds of thousands of people. Well, so is Herman. So are the Russians.

"I'm not being shot at or near the front, mother, but I'm building crematoriums for prison camps, and lots and lots of people are being treated horribly and are dying there," I said tentatively. I would be in big trouble for telling even this much, but I felt I had to tell her *something*.

My mother sighed and then remained silent. As we walked down our block towards home, she nodded at a house across the street. "Mrs. Schmidt over there lost her two sons and husband. One son to the British and one to the Russians. Her husband was on a train that was bombed. They never found his body. I have a son in the army and a husband running around the front."

Melting Point

She stopped and turned to look at me. "You, Albert, are not in the army or at the front. I think that is wonderful. I know you are doing important work for the Fatherland and I pray every night that you are safe, just as I pray for your brother and father. I want you to come home safely after this war is over, and I don't really care what you have to do to make sure you come home to me. Do you understand?"

I slowly nodded, and she hugged me. End of discussion. *Do anything you have to do; I don't care, as long as you come home afterwards.* As she was hugging me, she started to cry.

"I'm so worried about Herman up there in Russia. The rumors are that this winter is worse than last," she said, trying to wipe her eyes.

I started us walking back down the street towards our house. I said, "Herman is a big lug, and he'll be coming home soon. I know it. You know it too."

She smiled through her tears, and we walked into our home.

My mother was lonely and worried. Christmas was somber. New Years was as well. I tried to cheer Mother up, but soon it was time for me to go back to work. At least she had a pet bird to keep her company. Right after New Year, I headed back to Erfurt for a brief stop before going back to Poland. I arrived on January 2.

"Gitta, where is everybody, the place looks deserted!" I said after looking around the office. "Is everyone still on vacation?"

"All the younger men have been called up to the army, silly." Gitta looked at me with a bemused expression. "You wouldn't know, of course, being *exempt*."

I couldn't tell for sure if that was a hint of disgust in her voice. It wasn't my fault I was born different.

The Holocaust – 1942, 1943

"We're spread pretty thin here. I've been working days here, and evenings over at the women's club, mending clothes and writing letters and other jobs that need doing. The older engineers and those with special exemptions like Ludwig or with deferments, like you, are still here."

I stood awkwardly for a moment, noticing that she had lost some weight, and then she asked, her tone softer, "How are things going in Poland?"

I thought of my mother. "I'm not being shot at, but it's grim just the same. Lots and lots of death. We do seem to have plenty of workers, though, even if it is forced labor."

"It'll do 'em good," Gitta snorted. "We're suffering; they may as well, too. No point in making it a country club, eh?"

It was hard to remain somber around someone as pretty as Gitta, and it was pointless to try to tell her the magnitude of what's wrong in Poland. A smile flickered across my face and I said, "It is no country club, I can assure you. Not even for me."

"Well, good. Weren't you just visiting your mother?" she asked, and with that we moved onto happier topics.

Heinrich Messing was getting ready to go to Auschwitz, too, in order to install the forced draft systems for Crema II, the new triple-muffle furnaces. Our deadline was rapidly approaching, and we had a lot of work to do. Gitta told us that she had heard that Karl Bischoff was in a state of near panic up there as the days ticked by. Heinrich was leaving on the late night train, so I told him I'd go with him.

Late that afternoon, Gitta caught me on her way out. She said, "I don't have a lot to do this evening, and since you are the only available young man for a hundred miles, perhaps you would like to take me to the beer hall for a drink?"

171

Melting Point

I didn't need a second invitation, so I told Heinrich I'd meet him at the train station that night just before the train left for Poland. Gitta and I went to the local beer hall and ordered some thick dark beer. I had been drinking mostly brandy since that night with Karl Bischoff, but the beer felt wonderful going down my throat. I quickly gulped down the beer and ordered another.

"Slow down, you're not heading to the front," Gitta said, shaking her head and raising an eyebrow at me. She had a trace of a smile.

"It sure feels like it. It helps to get drunk. My mother doesn't approve of drinking, and so I've been depriving myself while on holiday."

"Well, we're all having a tough time. Look around, you don't see any young men who aren't in uniform here, do you?" She asked, gesturing around the beer hall. Indeed, the only young men were some boys in the corner who looked younger than me, all dressed in crisp new army uniforms.

One of the army boys looked up and saw us. He stood up and came over unsteadily with a friend, beer steins in hand, to flirt with Gitta.

With a big smile, he said, "Well there, young Frau, what are you doing with this civilian? Why don't you come over and sit with some *real* men? Men who aren't afraid to fight." He looked at me with an expression of disgust, as if to say, "Why aren't YOU in uniform?"

Gitta batted her eyes at him and then looked at me with a bemused smile to see what I would do.

I was never very strong, and had often relied on Herman for protection. There was no way I could take on one of these boys, let alone all of them. As always, I had to rely on my brains.

"I work for the SS in the East. I'm heading back tonight on the train. We're always looking for new men like yourselves. Why don't you give me your names and unit?" I said politely, pulling a pen and a pad of paper out of my

The Holocaust – 1942, 1943

pocket, smiling what I hoped was a dangerous smile. What I said wasn't exactly true, but it wasn't exactly a lie either. I hoped that the young soldiers would think the worst.

Apparently they did; the two boys stiffened. They nodded curtly at Gitta, and then said quietly, "No thanks," and quickly returned to their seats. Shortly afterwards, the group left.

Gitta looked appreciatively at me, "Well, I didn't think you had that in you. I'm impressed."

The barmaid came over. "Thanks a lot. There went a nice tip."

"Sorry, I'll make it up to you," I said, breathing a sigh of relief.

And for the next two hours we had a great time drinking and talking. When it was time for me to go, I left a fat tip and Gitta and I unsteadily walked arm in arm to the train station. Messing was there with his bags. He got on the train first, and I stayed behind to say goodbye to Gitta.

"Thanks, I had a good time," she said, leaning in to kiss me.

"Me too," I said clumsily, kissing her lightly on the lips.

I got on the train and found Messing's compartment. I watched Gitta through the windows as she headed out of the station. Heinrich Messing had pulled out a paper wrapper with some cooked sausages and bread in it. He offered me some.

"Nice girl?" asked Messing, with a hint of something I took to be envy.

"Very nice. She seemed so cold before, but we had fun tonight," I said. I passed over the sausages in favor of the bread. I needed something to help absorb the alcohol.

"I hear she likes dangerous men," he asked with a smile, taking a bite of sausage. "Are you dangerous, Albert?"

Melting Point

"Tonight, for once, I think I was. A bit," I said, smiling towards the window as Gitta turned a corner and was lost from view.

#

The work stoppages and holidays set us back a couple of weeks, but there was still incredible pressure to get Crema II up and running by the end of January. On the first day back for the workers, January 4, Heinrich Messing and I arrived from Erfurt to install the forced draft air systems. We worked for 22 days straight, 11 hours a day, installing the fans and ducting. After that we went on to install compressed-air systems to feed the ovens.

We did allow ourselves some extra time on Sundays. I took to praying in my room. I was out of practice, but I was honest and sincere. I hoped that would matter. I couldn't get out of my mind the image of Karl Bischoff and me being pulled down into the fires of hell for what we were doing.

In spite of my worries and shame, I pressed on. I mostly felt trapped and alone. Karl Bischoff kept me supplied with fine brandy, which I enjoyed in my room in the evenings.

My father came to visit. He looked older and more tired than I had ever seen him. He didn't stay long, but I showed him around the new crematoria building. Karl Bischoff met my father, and Karl told him what a wonderful job I was doing, for which I was grateful. My father told Karl that he was very proud of both his boys. That made my heart feel lighter than it had been in weeks. That evening, after dinner, Father told me that he was leaving on a late train. I walked with him to the station and stood with him on the platform. He was quiet. When we could hear the train coming, he cleared his throat.

"Ah, Albert, I visited your brother in Russia. He wrote you a letter. He gave it to me, which was wise, because it wouldn't have made it past the censors, and would have landed him in considerable trouble. I'm entrusting the

The Holocaust – 1942, 1943

letter to you on the condition that you destroy it completely after you read it. Maybe put it in one of your incinerators. Promise me," he said, holding out an envelope.

His tone was one of sadness, desperation, fear, and embarrassment; a combination of dark emotions bound together. He didn't look at me directly as he handed me the letter. "Of course, Father, I'll burn it when I'm done. But what's the matter? What's going on?"

"You'll understand when you read the letter, Albert," he said, still not looking at me.

I couldn't imagine what might be in the letter. Some secret revealed? "Yes, sir." I said.

He again was silent as the train pulled into the station. Some soldiers and a few civilians got off the train, and then others got on. As the train was getting ready to leave, and my father was ready to get onboard, I noticed his eyes brimming with tears. He held his hand out to shake mine. When I took his hand, he unexpectedly hugged me tightly. When he let go, he sniffed once and wiped his eye as if a speck of sand had gotten into it. A flicker of a smile appeared on his face.

"Goodbye, Son. Take care of yourself, and stay safe."

"Goodbye, Father. I will."

And he was gone. I stood on the platform watching the train pull away from the station heading west. I was baffled and concerned at the same time. What was going on? If the letter was this important, and maybe even dangerous, I was going to read it in the privacy of my room. I headed back to the camp.

#

Greetings from Russia,

Melting Point

I will give this letter to our father to give to you, because I can't mail it in the usual way. I'm sure you will understand as you read. Please see that this letter doesn't survive long after you read it. I would be most grateful.

We had a pretty good summer up here. We rule the summers, we really do. If only they were longer. The distances are so vast, though, that we live at the end of a very tenuous supply line, and that is a big problem. Thin supply lines are easy targets for partisans, and in the winter, the lines get bogged down something awful. This winter particularly.

I've come to begrudgingly admire the Russian soldier. We kill ten of them for every one of us they kill. Yet, they keep coming at us. Against hopeless odds, they continuously attack us and push on us. During the summer, this is suicide for them – they suffer terribly. During the winter, though, we are at a disadvantage. They come and come and come, by the millions.

I spent the summer as part of a huge army group in a quest for Russia's oil fields. We were doing pretty well, but then were diverted to join Paulus' sixth army taking Stalingrad. Stalingrad is a large city that had become well defended, and we spent much of the fall using our guns to shell the city. Because of our long supply lines, we didn't get the replacement parts we needed, and so our guns began to break down for the lack of those parts.

Supplies dwindled further when the rains started. Everything here turns to muck. The trucks can't get around and we can't move well. Even the horses get bogged down. They get exhausted and cold and frequently get sick and die. Still, we made continuous but very slow progress. Until November 19. That's when the Russians, led by

'General Winter' (their best general - ha ha), attacked. They encircled us in five days, cutting us off from the rest of our front.

There are 300,000 of us against a million Russians. We are bogged down and under-supplied and worn out and hungry. These Russians are troops we haven't fought before, so they are fresh and seem to have incredible amounts of new equipment. We're fighting for our lives here.

Hitler won't let us retreat. If only we could fight our way back to the German front, we'd be all right. But we can't. Supplies have been reaching us by air, though not enough to sustain such a huge battle. Father flew in with one of the supply planes as Speer's representative. I'm giving him this letter now before he returns. He says there is an effort to get an attack from the south to reach us with supplies. I desperately hope that it succeeds.

Albert, I wanted to take this opportunity to tell you my feelings, should I not survive this battle. I know Germany will win in the end, but my contribution to this war may be drawing to a close. I'm hungry. I'm freezing. We have no horses left, almost no ammunition, and as many of my men are dying of dysentery and cold as from shells and bullets. It looks pretty bleak here.

Albert, I love you. I've always looked up to you as my big brother. I so appreciate the help you gave me in school, getting past some of our monstrous exams. You were always there for me, and I tried to be there for you. I had always hoped to raise a family and pass on the Stohl name. If I don't return, it will be up to you. Maybe you can have several boys so you can name one after me!

If I don't return, Albert, know that I will be waiting patiently outside the gates of heaven for you to arrive. I'm sure I'll need help with the entrance exam. But take your time big brother; take your time. Live a full long life and do good things. If given the opportunity, avenge my death. Father says you are helping build prison camps. If you come across any Russian prisoners, please make life as miserable as possible for them. Respect them for their bravery, but remember what they are doing to me and to what is left of Paulus' third army here in Stalingrad.

With love, Herman.

#

What a startling letter. Herman in trouble? Freezing, starving, men dying all around him? My stomach felt like it had been kicked. I re-read the letter. It was unbelievable that Herman could die – he just *had* to make it. Even though he was on the front lines of the war, it had never even occurred to me that Herman would actually die in this war. Really, I had never even considered that possibility. Herman was brave and bold and had one of those lives where everything seemed to go his way.

But it wasn't Herman alone. An army of 300,000 men in trouble? A million Russians are attacking them? We had been hearing that the Russians were as good as beaten, that we were essentially *mopping up*. And, while we know that the winters go poorly for us, the magnitude of such a battle in freezing weather is unimaginable. It made me dizzy to think of these things.

That's why my father had been so sad. He had seen what was going on. He must think the army up there is doomed, or he wouldn't have been so emotional.

Herman, come back to us. Come back to me.

#

I didn't sleep well that night. Though it was very cold outside, and near freezing in my room, I was sweating and had bad dreams all night. *Herman sitting in a snowfield with men starving, freezing, dying. Herman waiting impatiently at the gates of heaven for me. My father crying over his favorite son.*

The next morning my attitude towards our prisoners had subtly changed. While my brain knew that we were still using innocent prisoners as forced labor and killing those we couldn't use, my gut somehow felt that these people were now the enemy, somehow responsible for my brother being in peril. They looked different to me. It was a subtle shift, and I didn't realize at the time that I had changed. It wasn't a big shift, either. I didn't suddenly hate the inmates or anything that overt, but somehow, what we were doing to them didn't seem quite so wrong. Almost like what Gitta had said, "We're suffering; they may as well too." That sounds terrible now, but it seemed that if my brother had to suffer, why not them?

#

At the end of the month, the ovens of Crema II were supposed to be up and running. Topf was behind, though, with many aspects of the work. Karl Bischoff was very nervous, and concerned that Himmler might think it was his fault. Karl's boss, General Kammler, was also nervous, and so he called constantly to check on progress. If Karl failed, then Kammler failed, too, so he would yell at Karl with all kinds of threats, though it was becoming obvious there was no way to get back onto schedule. Even as work progressed at a frenetic pace, Karl Bischoff walked around with a cloud of doom over him.

Kurt Prüfer 'fell on his sword' for the good of the project. He told General Kammler that the construction was done as scheduled, but it was going to take another fifteen days for finishing the ventilation systems. It was our fault, though, in part because of the work stoppage over Christmas. It was definitely *not* Karl Bischoff's fault. In fact, it would have been a month later if not for Karl's tireless dedication and supreme management skills.

Melting Point

Kurt Prüfer was a man who could pull that kind of thing off. He would flash his baby blue eyes at you and get an expression on his face like a schoolboy caught stealing a cookie. He looked so innocent and honest. After his confession, he would smile and talk about how he had to learn from the SS how to run projects more efficiently. If only he was as good at his job as Karl Bischoff was at *his*. The first time you heard the routine it sounded so sincere. But I'd heard Kurt do both his great sales jobs and his sincere apologies for our setbacks so many times by now that I just had to admire his form. At times it was hard not to applaud after hearing one of his *we're innocently guilty* speeches. When you were in trouble, Kurt was the man to have arguing your case.

General Kammler accepted that the crematorium would be late almost gratefully, since he could now blame a private contractor. He even promoted Karl Bischoff to a Sturmbannfürher, which is about like a Major. In gratitude, Karl Bischoff asked Kurt to bid on a contract for heating the delousing rooms. They needed to be heated in the winter so the Zyklon B would vaporize. The Kori Company had already bid 5,000 Reichmarks to do the work. We bid 39,000 Reichmarks to do the same work. Bischoff awarded us the contract. He also ordered some elevators for the crematoriums from us and ordered a sixth crematorium, yet to be designed. The total of all the work contracted or promised was 90,000 Reichmarks! Not bad money for a little face-saving. Kurt and Karl definitely had a good arrangement going.

#

On February 3, 1943, I was installing a three horsepower motor with Heinrich near the chimney of Crema II. I was just connecting a power wire to the motor's fuse, when a worker came running in. He was flushed and talked rapidly.

"Have you heard? It was just on the radio! Paulus' sixth army has surrendered! Stalingrad is lost!"

The Holocaust – 1942, 1943

Herman. No.

My stomach contracted and I dry-heaved. I got cold and clammy and felt faint. I got on my knees and held my head in my hands and started to cry.

Heinrich quietly told the worker, who was staring stupidly at me, "His brother is at Stalingrad."

The worker nodded, bowed his head, turned, and left quietly.

Three hundred thousand men lost; my brother lost. This was the worst defeat of the war so far. Three days of mourning were proclaimed, and the radio mostly broadcast funeral marches and slow, somber music. Men all over the camp were somber – they all knew someone who had been there.

My father must have known what was to happen when he had seen me. He knew his son was doomed. That is why he was emotional and why he hugged me. I wonder what he's feeling today? I wonder what Mother is thinking? Our only hope was that Herman was a prisoner and would come home after the war.

That night, after a bottle of brandy, it occurred to me that by this time we had probably killed at least 300,000 Jews in our gas chambers at Auschwitz. Yet there had been no national mourning for them. It didn't make me feel any better about Herman, but it did help put the loss in perspective. This war stunk, in all aspects. The Russians murdered us and we murdered Russians and Jews. Everyone killed everyone and it all stank.

Now I felt even less ashamed of what I was doing. True, we started the war with the Russians, and the actions against the Jews. But I started to think of what I was doing as a kind of revenge for what the Russians did to Herman. Logically, this made no sense. However, my brain was grasping for anything, any reason at all, to believe that I was doing some good. Some weak rationalization and a lot of alcohol, and I was fine.

Melting Point

Well, not fine. But, I could function at work, not look at what was going on, drink a lot at night, and that kept me going.

A few days later we finished the ventilation work. Other work was still going on, so the first real test of the crematorium wasn't until late in the month, and then the first full-blown firing and tests were set for March 4. In the meantime, there was a problem with the furnace up in Mogilev. It was the same kind of cheap eight-muffle oven we were going to use in Crema's III and IV. Since the heat all came from the center, with four muffles on either side, the farthest muffles were a lot cooler than the closest ones. The heat stress caused the brickwork to crack wide open. Actually, up in Mogilev, we had only gotten around to installing a half of an oven, or four muffles with a furnace on one side. But we were going to have the same problem here with Crema III and IV. The oven for Crema III had already been delivered, so it was too late to fix it. Kurt immediately ordered that the oven for Crema IV, now being built in Erfurt, be reinforced with more brick and steel, so that it would have more of a chance of lasting a while.

On March 4, 1943, several men were on hand for the initial cremations in Crema II. Besides me, there was Kurt Prüfer, Heinrich Messing, and Karl Schultze from our office. The SS was represented by Commandant Höss, Karl Bischoff, General Kammler, others from the SS building offices both locally and in Berlin, and a few men I couldn't place, who probably were involved in the supply of prisoners.

Karl Bischoff and the men from Topf knew about the disaster at Buchenwald. The two triple-muffle furnaces had been working at about half the rated capacity of five bodies per muffle per hour. At Buchenwald this wasn't a real problem yet because the six muffles were keeping up with the workload. But here, we were already at a disadvantage with less planned capacity than we needed. There were also a lot of higher-ups, including Himmler, who were keeping their eye on us.

The Holocaust – 1942, 1943

We had fired up all 15 muffles early in the morning so they would be ready for the demonstration. At the appointed time, each muffle was filled with two bodies. Overweight men had been chosen, because fat bodies burn better than lean ones. According to the design, it should take about 25 minutes to cremate two bodies half way in the upper chamber, before moving the bones and ash to the lower chamber for another 25 minutes.

With some ceremony, the bodies were inserted into the muffles on command, and stopwatches were started. After 25 minutes, the doors were opened, and we peeked in. And then we closed the doors again, immediately. The bodies were no where near half done. We men from Topf looked at each other nervously. Karl Bischoff shuffled his feet. He kept looking nervously at Kurt Prüfer. Would Kurt have to offer up another excuse?

After 30 minutes, a few doors were opened for a peek. Another door was opened after 35 minutes. Still another after 40 minutes. At 45 minutes, with a signal from Höss, the bones were moved from the top chamber to the lower chamber with the scraping tool. Nothing was said, but even I could tell that the bodies could have used several more minutes.

"What is this, Prüfer?" demanded General Kammler. "We were assured that you could manage five bodies an hour per muffle!" As long as he could pin this on someone, his job was secure.

Kurt knew that this was not the time to be accepting blame – this was too big. He walked over to one of the furnaces and touched and poked at the bricks and mortar. With all eyes in the room on him, he called me over. He drew me in close and pointed at the mortar.

"Put your finger on this," he said quietly to me, pointing at the mortar, his head near mine.

I put my finger on the mortar. Kurt nodded his head vigorously.

Melting Point

"Yes, you are right, Albert," Kurt said loudly. Kurt turned to his audience, "Just as we thought. The mortar had been mixed too wet by the prisoners and is now still too wet. The ovens need time to dry, and then they will work to specification."

And with this explanation, the observers had to agree that they had seen a good demonstration. They would expect improvements, but were satisfied that today's demonstration was a *worst case*. We dodged a bullet that day. But we had a real problem on our hands. If we couldn't get the cremation rate up, almost double what was going on at Buchenwald and what happened here, we were in trouble.

After the other SS men had left with Höss for a reception, Karl Bischoff and those of us from Topf stayed behind briefly to figure out what to do about the ovens.

"We're in real trouble," Karl Bischoff said.

Kurt Prüfer nodded slowly, lost in thought.

I opened my big fat mouth. "It is ironic that we designed these ovens to routinely handle what the Crema I ovens handled when totally overloaded, yet these ovens remain cool. Maybe we should overload these ovens . . ."

And as soon as I said it I realized that I had said too much. I shut my mouth abruptly. Kurt Prüfer looked quickly up at me and then over at Karl Bischoff. They exchanged glances.

"Start with more coal," said Kurt quietly to Karl.

"Maybe three bodies would fit at a time," Karl replied, nodding.

"We'd have to keep the temperature under 1,100 degrees or we'd have major problems," said Kurt, rising to the idea.

The Holocaust – 1942, 1943

"We could use the door color as a guide – when it gets white hot we've gone a little too far," said Karl, "Maybe we'd have to play with the total body fat in each muffle. Some mix of fat and thin bodies."

"Run ovens hotter with more coal for thinner loads, or less coal for fatter loads."

"Mix adults and children."

"And run the ovens with careful timing for fast turnaround."

"Grind the remaining bones with mortar and pestles to finish what we don't have time for, like they did at Crema I."

"We may have to increase the draft fan power."

And on and on at a dizzying pace. After a few moments I didn't hear what was being said, I could only think about how I had once again caused another small outrage, one more in a series of worse and worse things we were doing for *our part* in the war effort. I wondered briefly if Herman has days like this, and then I remembered that Herman may not even be alive any more, and I winced.

Kurt Prüfer noticed my wince and said, "You may have just saved us, Albert. Don't be upset."

Over the next several days Karl Schultze, Heinrich Messing, and I upgraded the ventilation systems to draft out more smoke for the intended higher furnace heat, and we put in fans to blow hot air into the second morgue, now a gas chamber, intended for vaporizing the Zyklon B. In winter the cellars would likely be freezing cold, so we assumed we would need to heat the room.

On Saturday, March 13, 1943, we declared the venting system for the furnaces and gas chambers done. By this time, the Sonderkommandos had been briefed on how to run the ovens hotter. Specialists were assigned the task of managing the body ratios in the muffles and monitoring the oven door color.

Melting Point

Everything was ready, though they would need practical experience to make the system run as efficiently as it needed to.

We went for a light dinner, and were asked to come back to supervise the inaugural full run. A trainload of 2,000 Polish Jews had come in earlier that evening from the ghetto of Krakow, just a short distance away. They had come right into the camp on our new rail spur. Some 1,492 women, children, and old folks were deemed *unfit for work* by the doctors. They were then marched, not to one of the little farmhouses, but to our new facility.

Topf was still finishing the ventilation system for the dressing room, and there were construction materials strewn about, so the people undressed in a temporary wooden building next to the new crematoria. Then they walked down the stairs, and through the nearly-completed dressing room, and on into the heated and aerated gas chamber. The dressing room had been set up to look like a typical dressing room for a shower facility, and the signs said innocent things like "To the Showers."

Above in the furnace room, the prisoners who ran the ovens, the Sonderkommandos, and their prisoner bosses, the Kapos, had rehearsed for this evening and were standing ready to receive the Krakow Jews. I was with them watching over the ovens, which were roaring hot, and so I didn't see the people come in.

I was later told that all 1,492 people went from the dressing room into the gas chamber at once. The doors were sealed, and six kilos of blue Zyklon B pellets were poured through special openings in the roofs of the gas chamber. The heat of the people and the heat from the ovens being forced down into the room made it extremely hot, and the Zyklon B vaporized instantly. Within five minutes, they were all dead. Karl Schultze's 8,000 cubic-meter-per-hour aeration and the matching 8,000 cubic-meter-per-hour de-aeration systems were started up. They changed the air completely inside the room every three to four minutes. In 20 minutes the air was judged clean enough for Sonderkommandos to go in and remove the bodies. The chamber was stifling hot from the heat still being pumped in from the ovens upstairs.

The Sonderkommandos untangled the bodies and moved them out of the room. Hair was cut, because the SS was using it to make blankets, socks, bomb fuses, and other products. Jewels, valuables, and gold fillings were removed; these were intended to help fund the SS efforts with less drain on the national treasury. However, I believed the guards and other SS men would eventually pilfer much of it.

When ready, the bodies were taken up from the underground cellars to the ground floor on the new Topf elevator. It was more like a forklift than what we would think of as an elevator, because it just raised a platform with the bodies up to the furnace room. The bodies were then slid down a trough along one side of the oven room, opposite from the oven openings. The trough had a small amount of water in it to make the bodies slide easier along the smoothed concrete. From there they would be lifted onto the carts that rode on tracks to the oven doors.

The furnace room was noisy. The furnaces had a roaring noise to them, partly from the flames, partly from the forced air being blown into them. Kind of like the sound of a fireplace when you blow on it, that low pitched roar. Only with fifteen muffles, the roar was very loud. Add to this the noise of the oven doors clanking shut, the Sonderkommandos shouting to be heard, the Kapos and guards yelling commands, and the room was filled with noise.

The furnace room also had a strange light to it. There were windows in the room, but no light came through because it was nighttime. There were electric lights, of course, but there were also the lights of the fires. As the doors were opened, the interiors of the oven chambers were alive with small tornados of blue, white, and yellow flames. When closed, the doors and their iron frames

Melting Point

glowed various shades of red. The glowing and flickering bounced off the walls, ceiling, and floor. Shadows danced on the walls.

The furnace room was hot and smoky and crowded. The room, for all the equipment and people, wasn't that large. Anyone standing anywhere but against a wall was in the way. The small space and the superheated ovens made for a very hot environment. The Sonderkommandos had their shirts off and were glistening from sweat. They wore just their striped pants and caps. There were eight men per oven, or 40 in all. Another several men took the bodies from the elevator and slid them down the trough. Add to that the Kapos, guards, runners, and me, and the room was packed. The windows were open as wide as possible and the wintry air was coming in, but it stood no chance against the hellish heat we were generating. Ventilators were on, helping to pump in fresh cold air. It was Karl Schultze's fans, installed by Messing and me, which were stopping *us* from being cooked. I could easily believe that Dante had seen this room when he described Hell in *The Inferno*.

The first time I saw the bodies was when they started to slide down the wet trough. Naked, shaved, bluish in color from the gas, they did not look human. Some were big; some were small; a few were fat; most were thin. They weren't easily recognizable as *people*, and that was a relief. Really. I tried not to look at them much, and when I did, I tried not to recognize human parts. Occasionally, though, I would see a pair of lifeless eyes staring at me, and I would look quickly away.

This was our first time doing an extended, hour-after-hour cremation in this new facility, and there were some kinks to work out. The Sonderkommandos were still learning their jobs. There was a hierarchy, a pecking order, of Sonderkommandos. Those few at the top, the Kapos, supervised those at lower levels. To be at the top meant better living conditions – more food, better bedding, and better treatment. There were specialists, too. Just as in the old Crema I, one man would work the door while another pushed

The Holocaust – 1942, 1943

the cart. Others fed coal and hoisted bodies. One man was assigned to each triple muffle oven to just manage the amount of coal versus the fat content of the bodies being loaded into that oven.

The furnaces ran all night, all the next day, all that night, and into the next morning. One thousand, four hundred and ninety-two bodies. The ovens weren't yet running at their designed capacity, but we were getting closer.

I stayed with the operation for many hours, until dawn broke and the room started to fill with natural light. I left then, totally exhausted, as the cremations went on and on. I went back to my bed and lay down on top of the covers, not bothering to take my smoky clothes off. I stared at the concrete ceiling of my room. I tried to sleep, but I was too wound up. Though the room was very quiet, there was still a roaring in my ears from all the noise in the furnace room. The cold air of my room felt good after the prolonged exposure to the heat. The air smelled so fresh and clean, too, after having spent so many hours in the haze of smoke.

My eyes were very tired and they had a hard time focusing on anything. The concrete ceiling swirled into patterns, like staring at clouds in the sky. My mother's bird was looking to the left, its neck very long. A thick horse, perhaps one of Herman's, was leaning forward, its front legs buried in snow. A pair of hands with long bony fingers was reaching out from a cloud of smoke. Two eyes stared at me. The face they were on seemed to have horns.

I did not sleep well that day.

Melting Point

The Girl with the Curly Hair

Distant thunder could be heard outside the house at Bodega Bay. Inside, the house was deathly quiet. I cleared my throat and said, "I need some water." I was parched.

Slowly the others stood up and stretched and moved around, all except Magda. She was staring at me with her mouth open slightly, a look of shock on her face.

"Papa," she whispered hoarsely. She said nothing else.

I sat down next to her. "I know, Honey. I know." I patted her hand sadly.

"How awful it must have been for you," she said. She put her arms around me. "Where was Mama then?"

"I don't know, exactly, but we're getting to that part soon," I reassured her.

Magda wiped her eyes with her hands and said, "Did you say you needed some water? I'll go get it."

I watched her walk out of the room. The others seemed to be avoiding looking at me. I turned and walked out to the porch, leaving the door open behind me. It was cold outside, but the air smelled wonderful and I took some deep breaths. In the distance I could hear the surf crashing on the shore, and the occasional rumble of distant thunder.

"Appropriate," I mumbled, after another boom of thunder.

Magda came out on the porch behind me. "Here's your water, Papa. Now let's get back to the story; I can't wait to hear about Mom."

"Well, okay, but there's still a ways to go," I said as I entered the house after Magda, closing the door behind me. I sat down on the couch, took a large drink of water, cleared my throat, and continued the story.

#

Late on the Saturday evening following that first large-scale cremation in the brand-new Crema II, I had been writing a letter to my mother and enjoying some of the fine brandy that Karl Bischoff had been providing me, when I received a frantic call to come to the furnace room. That was on the eve of March 20, 1943, a cold and windy night. A small fire had broken out in the electrical room. It had been extinguished by the time I got there, but without power the furnaces had no forced air draft, and so could not operate. This was a real problem for the camp administration, because about 2,000 Greek Jews were awaiting cremation. More trains were on their way, and the administration was impatient.

The electrical room was more like a closet. It was located in the small rear wing of the building, behind the furnaces, which housed the refuse incinerator and the base of the chimney. By the time I got there, the main power switch had been thrown and some prisoners were busy cleaning up the mess from the fire-fighting efforts. Flashlights and lanterns had to be used for light. The pungent aroma of wet burnt wood and plaster hung in the air. Water from the fire-fighting was still in large pools on the floor.

Melting Point

The camp administration was still looking for their resident electrician. He was probably at a beer hall in town. With all the civilian workers employed here, there were quite a number of new drinking establishments, so it might take a while to locate him, and even then he might be useless. Though I had been drinking some, I wasn't completely drunk. Still, around electricity, I wanted to be extra careful in the state I was in.

"Take it slow," I muttered.

The wiring close to the fuses was a mess. All the insulation had burned off, and the white porcelain insulators were black with soot. The fuses themselves, about the size of a roll of quarters, were completely destroyed. This was where the fire started.

"Ah ha," I mumbled.

The fuses had become so hot that they caught fire before they did their job of breaking the connection. They aren't supposed to catch fire, of course, but these were a poor-quality fuse we didn't usually work with. My only prior experience with this kind of fuse was when we laid the wire between the old crematoria in Auschwitz and the building next to it, back when the chimney was being rebuilt. When there are shortages of parts, you take what you can get.

The real problem came from the large power draw of the various ventilation and blower systems. The parts for this electrical panel had been delivered months before, even though the plans had changed in the meantime to call for more blowers, and more powerful blowers. Getting new electrical parts was near to impossible these days, so we had made do with what we had, turning a blind eye to the possibility of disaster that had just now happened.

"Well, what do you think?" asked the camp supervisor, a short ugly man, for the crematorium. His eyes darted back and forth and he kept taking deep breaths and puffing his cheeks as he blew the air out. He was responsible for keeping the ovens working, and there were thousands of bodies awaiting cremation. He chewed a fingernail. His eyes darted around the room at the damage.

"The panel was overloaded. Power consumption has to be reduced. Eventually we need to get more power in here," I said. "For tonight, though," I started, then looked at him and slowly ticked off a list. "Shut off the aeration and de-aeration systems in the cellars. Shut down the cellar heating system as well, because that fan takes power. Find whatever lights are optional and turn them off. I'll go over to Crema III's worksite and take some replacement parts for the things that are burned-out here."

He was relieved to have a plan of action in place. He went off barking orders at people, mostly prisoner workers, to implement his part of the plan. I scrambled over to the site where Crema III, a mirror-image of Crema II I just left, was being built 100 yards away, and went into its electrical closet. There, awaiting their first use, were wires and fuses identical to those that had burned.

"Sorry about this," I said to no one in particular, as I reached up with a screwdriver to remove them from their panels. It seemed a shame to be pillaging a brand new building like this, but we had time to get replacements for this building, and I needed the parts *now*. On my way back to Crema II, I the cold night breeze blew my hair around.

After a couple of hours of work, I reapplied the power to the system, and the fans and blowers all came back on. I breathed a big sigh of relief. I put tape over the switches that would start up the blowers in the cellars so they wouldn't accidentally be turned on again. Then I called Kurt Prüfer at home to tell him what had happened. He sounded tired and annoyed, but thanked me for handling the problem. Then I went back to my room to go to bed, and I slept late on Sunday.

#

Melting Point

Upon arising Sunday, I finished my letter to my mother, and decided to send another letter to Aunt Mary and Uncle Carl as well, to see how they were getting along. Living as close as I was, I still never seemed to find the time to get over to their farm. Things should be getting busy on the farm, since spring was on the way. Outside my room, the blossoms had appeared on the trees, and the last of the snow was on the ground. I was tired of the wet and cold and mud of winter.

I imagined the farm with the new life of spring. I thought of Uncle Carl cleaning and repairing his plow, getting ready to till the fields. I thought of the rooster looking a little pluckier, eyeing the chickens. The tomcats were snuggling next to their chosen tabbies. New life is born after surviving the winter.

"It's always winter in here," I sighed.

There was no new life here, only death. Spring might come to the trees and grass, and the sun may warm the air, but in Auschwitz it was always winter.

#

Monday, Crema IV, over by 'the little red house,' was officially handed over to the camp. Crema IV was smaller than the either of the huge twin Crema's - II and III. This one was the first of the two Cremas with the simplified eight-muffle ovens like the one installed at Mogilev. Coal was put in a firebox in the center, with four muffles on each side pointing away from the fire; eight muffles in all. We had told people they would handle about four bodies per muffle per hour, but that was optimistic. The official capacity was 768 bodies per day, which assumed four bodies an hour over a 24 hour period, but Kurt Prüfer knew it would never reach that capacity.

Karl Bischoff and I knew about the problems with the identical oven at Mogilev. Well, to be fair, Mogilev only had *half* an oven, with a furnace and four muffles on just one side. We had yet to deliver any more of the four full

The Girl with the Curly Hair

ovens they had ordered. Two of their ovens had ended up here in Cremas IV and V. But the heat in the muffles nearest the center of the furnace was much higher than that in the muffles farther away, and the stress on the brickwork had caused the furnace at Mogilev to crack wide open.

Crema IV, then, was poised for the same disaster. Its ovens had been assembled before the Mogilev furnace failed, so it was too late to fix it without starting over. It had been quickly designed and intended to be extremely cheap. As it turned out, it was *too* cheap. Since the senior SS staff had wanted quick results, with dire consequences for Karl Bischoff for failure, it was decided to go ahead and complete the flawed furnace rather than delay construction. At least there had been time to change the design for Crema V, which was originally going to be a twin of IV.

Now, it was time to pay the piper. We hoped the furnace would last long enough to delay the inevitable blame, to delay one of Kurt Prüfer's now all-too-common command performances. This furnace was fired by coal, whereas the one in Mogilev was fired with wood, so it was likely this furnace would break sooner than the Mogilev one. When that happened, we'd have some explaining to do.

Wednesday, Kurt Prüfer arrived by train with Karl Schultze. Kurt was there to inspect Crema IV and maybe lay some groundwork for the excuses later on. He hadn't originally planned on bringing Schultze along, but Prüfer wanted Schultze to figure out what to do about the electrical problems in Cremas II and III.

Karl Schultze, Karl Bischoff, and I talked a while about the electrical problems. Since the gas room was warm enough with all the people in it, the extra heat from the furnaces was not really needed to vaporize the Zyklon-B into a lethal gas, so we decided to permanently shut off the gas-chamber heating system. The gas-chamber exhaust fan blade had been made of wood to prevent

Melting Point

corrosion from the Zyklon-B gas. Because wood was very heavy, requiring a larger motor to drive it, we replaced the wooden blade with a metal one. If it did corrode, we could replace it again later. That allowed us to replace the fan's motor with a smaller one. We also doubled-up some of the overloaded wires and fuses. It was easier to double the number of wires and fuses than to acquire thicker copper wires. Again, we *borrowed* from the stockpile of parts going into Crema III. We would have to replace all these parts eventually, of course, but we had some time for that.

Kurt Prüfer only spent a few days at the camp before heading home to Erfurt. I walked with him to the train platform to see him off. He seemed somber.

"Albert, you are doing a great job here. I don't know how you put up with it, and I admire that."

"Thank you sir, this has been a huge project," I said.

"Albert, I . . ." He looked down, and then away, at a loss for words.

I wasn't sure what he was trying to say, and kept quiet. The train approached slowly and came to a halt. Kurt Prüfer picked up his bag and took a step towards the train. Then he turned to me and said, "You were right, Albert. You were right to be concerned. This is not. . . This wasn't what I. . ."

The train blew its whistle and the conductor shouted "All aboard!"

"I'm sorry, Albert. I'm sure this will all end one day soon." Kurt boarded the train and it pulled out of the station.

#

A week later, at the very end of March 1943, Crema II was officially finished and fully in business. Because of this, and because of all the chimney problems in Crema I, the old Auschwitz furnace room, Crema I was taken off line. Its use as a gas chamber and crematorium was nearing an end.

The Girl with the Curly Hair

On April 4, Crema V was delivered, minus its gas chamber, which was due to be delivered two weeks later. Originally, IV and V had morgues in the basement just like the other buildings, with the thought that the 'little red house' and 'little white house' would continue to serve as gas chambers. At some point, the administration had decided to convert the morgues into gas chambers, so as to reduce the distance that bodies would have to be moved. The 'little houses' could then be closed.

We had high hopes for Crema V, because it was reinforced more than the flawed Crema IV. The very next day, our worst fears were confirmed when Crema IV split wide open. It looked like an eggshell cracked down the middle. We patched the crack temporarily.

Two weeks later, Kurt Prüfer arrived again to talk about the problems of Crema IV. The temporary patch wasn't holding, and had to be constantly repaired, making the oven almost useless. This was another occasion when Kurt and Karl Bischoff being friends helped. Kurt boldly stated that the warranty on Crema IV had expired, so we wouldn't repair it. He also said that the morgue cellar in Crema IV would work better as a gas chamber if it were aerated, and came away with an order of 2,500 Reichmarks to build an exhaust system!

Karl Bischoff also discussed some problems he had been seeing in the internal linings to Crema II's dampers and underground flues. Topf didn't build the flues and dampers, but Karl Bischoff asked Kurt Prüfer to draw up some new blueprints for them so they could be repaired or replaced. Crema III was still under construction, and Kurt and Karl Bischoff also discussed how to replace the borrowed parts for the ventilation and electrical systems.

In May, the 'little red house' and its undressing barracks were dismantled. The incinerator pits behind it were filled in and leveled. Trees were planted on the spot where thousands were buried. Himmler was finally getting

Melting Point

his wish; bodies were disappearing without even a grave left behind. Perhaps Himmler was just forward thinking, because in mid-May, things again were bleak for Germany. Our troops surrendered in North Africa, and we lost almost as many men there as we did at Stalingrad. Thousands of allied planes dropped bombs on our biggest cities, leaving hundreds of thousands of people homeless. Admiral Dönitz was forced to suspend U-boat operations in the Atlantic because the allies were getting too good at sinking our U-boats. The world was beginning to close in on Germany.

In the Warsaw Ghetto, Jews had risen up and revolted. By mid-May, the uprising had been quelled, but Himmler decreed soon afterwards that all Polish ghettos must be eliminated. The trains into the camp picked up their pace.

Meanwhile, we had looming disasters of our own. Crema IV was shut down permanently in mid-May because of the large cracks. Late in May, Crema II was shut down for extended cleaning and repairs of the underground flues and ducts. Unfortunately, this was held up because the camp was waiting on Kurt Prüfer for those blueprints for duct improvements Bischoff had asked for. Kurt Prüfer hadn't realized they were that important, so had done nothing about it. Now the furnace was offline and stalled waiting for the blueprints that we hadn't delivered. Though we eventually did deliver them, Crema II would remain down for all of June, July, and August waiting on those repairs.

Crema I, the original furnace room at Auschwitz, was pressed back into use for the last time while Crema II was down for repairs and Crema III wasn't finished. By July, Crema III was working and so Crema I was shut down for good. The old furnace room and morgue were turned into a bomb shelter for the SS. The large-scale bombings and setbacks were beginning to make them nervous.

The Girl with the Curly Hair

I had a small personal disaster as well. I got a letter from Gitta, saying that she had gotten engaged to a soldier. He had given her a nice engagement ring and everything. I should have felt happy for her, but I felt a little jealousy. No, I wouldn't ever have had the courage to ask her to marry me, but somehow it stung that now I *couldn't*.

#

In June, since the ovens of Crema II were down for flue repairs anyway, Kurt Prüfer thought it would be a good chance for me to check the interior of the muffles for cracks and other problems. It was critical that these ovens keep working once they were back online. We couldn't afford another disaster like the cracking of Crema IV's oven. Since Crema III was a mirror of this Crema, any problems here could be expected there as well.

On a warm July morning I went into the furnace room of the inoperative Crema II. The furnace room was quiet and deserted, so I could work undisturbed. The room smelled faintly of smoke and sweat, and though it was well lit from the windows and lights, it still seemed gloomy and dark.

I shined a work light into the first muffle of the far-left oven and saw that the interior looked like it was in pretty good shape. Naturally the curved walls and ceiling of the muffle were various shades of black and gray, but the floor looked like gray bricks with brand new white mortar. Closer inspection revealed that the floor of the muffle was covered with a fine coating of ash and soot, and the mortar between the bricks had caught enough ash so that what looked like clean mortar was actually just ash. I blew on a spot between two bricks and a small cloud of ash blew up into the air. I sneezed.

I suppose it is telling that the ash didn't affect me except as an irritant. I had been working with death for so long, that the ash was as much a byproduct of my work as scraps are to a butcher. The ash had become an annoyance to me, no longer the respected remains of humans.

Melting Point

I got a pail and filled it with water from a faucet near the fire hose, and poured the water into the muffle. The water sloshed and slurped around the inside, then some splashed out the front and some washed down the rear grate, simultaneously exiting both the top and bottom doors of the muffle. The muddy water sloshed over the floor, working its way towards the room's drain. There was a sizzling sound, not from heat, but from the water seeping into the porous brick and from the air bubbles escaping. It was still pretty wet inside, and I didn't want to lean into the muffle and get soaked. Instead, I went down the line, pouring a pail of water into each of the fifteen muffles in turn. By the time I was done, the first muffle had dried enough that I would get damp, but not soaked. Someone else could hose down the muddy floor later.

I took the work light and leaned into the muffle, closely examining the bricks in the front. The mortar had blackened from the heat and flames, but it had no cracks. I looked a little farther inside the oven, and the mortar looked fine. With a nervous prickle on the back of my neck, I leaned in as far as I could and shined the light towards the rear. I noticed that some of the mortar at the back of the muffle was shiny.

"Well, of course, it's wet," I muttered.

But wait, there are patches shining brighter than the rest. Perhaps these were pools of water that had collected. That would indicate that some chips of mortar had come out, and water had collected in the holes left behind. I thought I should investigate further.

This, however, presented a problem. To get back to the rear of the muffle meant climbing all the way inside it. As if leaning over a cliff, I wanted someone to hold my feet. At the very least, I wanted someone I could trust outside, making sure that the door didn't slam shut on me when I was inside. I looked around the furnace room. There was no one there. I looked inside the muffle. It looked awfully deep. I shuddered.

I knew my fears were silly, but my stomach was starting to churn at the thought of going inside the muffle. But a job is a job, and I knew there was no real danger.

"Make a list," I said under my breath.

Lately, I'd found that mentally making a list would help calm me down a little. Whenever stressful things happened, or I was starting to doubt my own humanity, I'd make a list of what I had to do, or what I saw, or even what I ate. Just making the list seemed to calm my mind enough that I didn't get sick. Without the list, my stomach would sometimes start to feel like it had been kicked.

Lately I had been making a lot of mental lists.

"Get some rope," I began. "Tie the door to the muffle open. Make sure no one's around. Put the light in as far as it will go. Take it slow. Make sure my shoes hang out the front."

I busied myself satisfying the list. I got some rope and tied the door open firmly so that it wouldn't swing shut on me. I carefully looked around again to see if anyone was about. I looked behind the ovens where coal was loaded, in the coal storage area, by the elevator, out the back door, anywhere I could think of where someone might lurk, waiting for a chance to shut me in the oven.

"Like Hansel and Gretel, shutting the witch in the oven," I said to myself with dread.

Then I slowly approached the opening of the muffle. I tested the strength of the rope holding the door open. I rubbed my hands together and put the lamp in as far as I could by leaning in. I looked around one last time and then put my knee up just inside the opening, and with a small heave I pushed myself into the muffle. There was a slight echo in the muffle, and it

Melting Point

smelled like a hot asphalt road after a summer rain. The shadows cast by the work light were sharp and long.

My breathing picked up, and my hands and forehead became clammy. Half of my mind was thinking about being put in the oven to be cremated, while the other half was telling me that the bricks were cool, no one was around, the door was tied open, and all was safe.

"Relax," I said aloud, slightly angry with myself for being irrational. My voice echoed on the walls.

Just then I reached the first splotch of shiny stuff. It wasn't water; that much was obvious now. I dragged the work light over to it and inspected it closely.

Gold.

What an odd sight – gold-coated mortar. Of course, if someone had been wearing a gold ring or earrings, the gold would have melted and puddled on the floor of the muffle. When the bones and ashes were scraped towards the rear of the muffle, some of the gold would be pushed out with the bones and ashes, and the rest might have oozed over to the gaps between the bricks. That would explain why it was back here in the rear of the muffle, too.

But jewelry wasn't supposed to get this far. The victims were instructed to leave it behind when they undressed. If they didn't, the Sonderkommandos removed it from the bodies long before they got here. Even gold fillings were removed before the bodies got here. So how did the gold get here? My mouth was dry, and I swallowed hard.

Swallowed. People who didn't want to leave the jewelry behind had swallowed it. They must have assumed it would be stolen.

In a way, they succeeded. The SS confiscated all the jewelry, effectively stealing it from the victims. At least here, no one had it. The gold had bonded

The Girl with the Curly Hair

itself with the rough mortar, and would be difficult to extract. Not much of a victory for the victims, I suppose, but a tiny victory nevertheless.

I inspected other shiny areas and found that they were all splotches of gold, some mixed with a little silver. It was hard to tell exactly, because the ash had mixed with the gold enough to discolor it. In another splotch, a tiny pebble or bone fragment had been caught in the gold when it was liquid, and now was stuck in the cooled metal. Wait, if it were bone, it would have eventually turned to ash, so it must be a small pebble. I poked at it a bit. It wasn't a pebble at all.

It was a diamond.

That made me ill. Gold was a curiosity. It was unexpected, but a curiosity, almost abstract. Even as jewelry, gold was found in all kinds of things – watches, pendants, rings, whatever. But a diamond would belong to an engagement or wedding ring. It signified the love between a man and a woman, and their marriage together. Perhaps a wife had been in this very spot that I am in now. In a final act of defiance, she had swallowed her wedding ring, her symbol of attachment to her husband and their family. Now she's gone, and maybe her husband and children too. Probably all that remains of the entire family is this diamond stuck in a puddle of gold in this oven.

If it hadn't gotten stuck, it would be gone too. The bones never got the time in the lower chamber to completely disintegrate, and so they were taken outside and ground with a mortar and pestle into dust. Stray diamonds must be found in the ashes – they won't crush. So, many of the diamonds people try to hide from the SS get into their hands anyway. This one didn't.

My mouth twitched briefly into a smile. "Well done."

Here was one diamond that had stayed out of the hands of the SS - for now, anyway. If it stays in this oven for long, someone like me will discover it and confiscate it. It would be nice if it never fell into the hands of the SS. That was her final wish, after all.

Melting Point

I reached back into my pocket and took out the tiny folding knife I keep with me. I unfolded the blade and pried at the diamond gently until it popped out of the gold. I picked up the diamond and folded the knife, then put both into my pocket. I had broad smile on my face.

I wasn't stealing it. I wasn't exactly sure what I would do with it, but I didn't want the SS to get it. I didn't plan to spend it, just protect it. So, I took it.

I looked around carefully at the rest of the splotches, but didn't see any more diamonds. I then inspected the other 14 muffles, each one in turn. I would carefully tie the door open and crawl inside. There, I found in each muffle more splotches of gold and silver, and, occasionally, a diamond. I pried each one loose and put it in my pocket.

In the two hours I spent examining the muffles I found seven diamonds. I vowed that I would periodically inspect all the ovens' muffles, and do something noble with the diamonds, perhaps bury them, perhaps throw them into the river, something. At least keep them away from the SS.

#

In July, the Allied armies landed in Sicily. In Hamburg, an allied air raid caused a firestorm, dooming hundreds of thousands of civilians. The Allies were animals, bent on revenge for our bombing of London. I hoped the Eastern summer campaign went well enough to give us some fighting room this winter. With Herman gone, I no longer had much interest in what was happening in the war, but I didn't like the idea that we might be losing.

#

August 7 was Commandant Rudolf Höss' wedding anniversary. I was invited to sip champagne and join in the celebration at his villa on the grounds of the camp that evening. The prisoner orchestra played Straus waltzes and Beethoven sonatas and old patriotic ballads, and we danced and sang and drank the evening away. I think the pressures we were feeling from Germany's failures caused us to celebrate with a little more abandon than we might have done otherwise.

At the party, I met an inspector from Berlin, SS Major Konrad Morgen. He was plying Höss' wife, Hedwig Hansel Höss, with champagne, trying to get dances with her. Mrs. Höss was pretty tipsy, and she did dance a fair amount with him. I saw them chatting away as they danced. I don't think the commandant would have approved, but he was tending to other guests at the party, particularly the women.

Rudolf Höss danced with a beautiful woman named Irma Griese, a woman about my age who was the chief of the women's camp at Birkenau, and the camp's highest ranking woman SS officer. After that dance, Höss moved on to another woman, and Irma came over to where Karl Bischoff and I were standing.

"Care to dance?" She asked me, taking my hand and pulling me onto the dance floor.

"It would be an honor," I said, hurrying to keep up with her.

She smelled of a lovely perfume. Her eyes were sky blue. She was in uniform, but such a uniform never looked so good. Her jacket matched her eyes. She had a dark tie and skirt. Her shoes were decidedly non-regulation, being elegant high heels. The one odd note was a whip, coiled at her waist.

The music was a slow, sad song. She held me close. "I'm Irma. Irma Griese."

"Albert Stohl."

We danced slowly, with many eyes on us. She smelled good, looked good, and danced good. I had heard rumors about her having affairs with several men at once, but that only added to her mystery.

Melting Point

"Enjoying yourself here?" she asked.

"Very much, now that I'm dancing with you," I said.

She laughed, "No, I mean here at the camp."

"Oh, well, no. Not really. It's very difficult on me. Not physically, but mentally."

She got a gleam in her eye and a far-off look as she said, "Well, I *love* it! I absolutely love having the power of life and death over people. The kind of people who used to look down their nose at me and sneer. Well, they're not sneering now!"

That sent a chill down my spine. As we moved about the floor, I passed by Dr. Joseph Mengele, later to be known as 'The Angel of Death.' He looked at me with an evil eye. Irma noticed this.

"He is so jealous," she whispered to me. "But I'm honest with him – I tell him that I have several lovers, not just him. He just doesn't know who they are, and that makes him insane with jealousy."

"Wonderful. Now Dr. Mengele thinks I'm the competition."

"Don't worry, I'll tell him you aren't. I don't go for young men, anyway. You're cute, but I prefer older men. Unless you are a general?" She asked a smile with one eyebrow raised.

"Engineer."

"Ah, a nobody. I used to be a nobody. Not anymore."

The music stopped and we broke apart. I thanked her for the dance, and she nodded to me, and then went off to find Mengele. I went back to stand with Bischoff. When I got there, he handed me a large glass of brandy.

"Enjoy yourself?" He asked.

"Yes and no. She's very beautiful, but she scares me," I said, and took a large gulp of the brandy. It felt good going down.

"She should scare you. She personally selects thousands of women to go to the gas chambers. That whip? It's not just for decoration. She uses it frequently, and for the slightest infraction."

My brow furrowed. "Such beauty and ugliness in one package."

Karl took a gulp of his brandy, "And, so young. Twenty-two. What will she be like ten years from now?"

I shuddered as Mrs. Höss came over.

"Karl, how are you this evening?" she said, extending her hand.

"Very good, Hedwig, and you?" Karl said, taking her hand and kissing it.

"A little drunk, but well enough other than that. Who's your handsome young friend?"

"Albert Stohl, meet Hedwig Höss. Hedwig, Albert."

I took her offered hand and kissed it, bowing formally.

"Ah, a charmer. I see why Irma was interested in you. Alas, if only you could keep her busy full time," she said, with a bit of a sigh.

I said, "She makes me nervous."

Hedwig said, "Me too, but probably for a different reason. I wish Rudy would stay away from her."

"Dr. Mengele seems to keep her busy," I volunteered.

"Ha," she said in disgust. "The good doctor can barely tear himself away from his precious experiments to meet the trains. I doubt she does more than provide him with intriguing victims."

Melting Point

She leaned towards me and I could smell the alcohol on her breath as she said, conspiratorially, "Twins."

I wasn't sure I understood. I raised my eyebrows in a quizzical expression. I was about to ask her what she meant when Karl Bischoff grabbed my arm hard and said pleasantly, "Albert, why don't you dance this next dance with Hedwig, and you can tell her about your Uncle's farm near here."

He then gave me a stern 'don't-ask' look as he took my glass from me.

"Marvelous," Hedwig said, leading me away.

We went onto the dance floor and she clung on to me. Well, maybe hung on me is a better term. She was a little clumsy from the alcohol.

"Do you really want to hear about my uncle's farm?"

"No. I just want to dance."

We danced in silence for a moment, and then she sobbed once. I looked at her, and a tear was coming down her face.

"I hate this place," she said glumly.

"Me too," I said, surprised.

"I much preferred Dachau. Even Sachsenhausen was better than this hellhole. Rudy drags me along to each of his assignments. But, here there are no opera houses or decent shopping districts, and nothing for me to *do*."

Apparently we disliked this camp for different reasons. I changed the subject. "How long have you been married?"

"Fourteen years. We got married in 1929, right after Rudy got out of prison."

"Prison?" I asked.

"Didn't you know? He killed a man. He did it to protect the Nazi Party, but he went to prison. That was before the Party was in power, of course. He spent six years in prison before Hitler was elected. Then the Party let him out and rewarded him with good jobs in the SS."

With a look of disgust, she added, "Until now." She nodded towards Major Morgen and added, "With weasels like that poking their noses into everything. There used to be some trust. Not anymore."

The music came to an end and I bowed to her. She smiled and curtseyed, thanked me, and wandered off to another man, a sergeant this time. I returned to where Karl Bischoff was. He handed me back my glass of brandy.

"Twins?" I asked Karl.

"No. You don't ever want to know, Albert. Don't *ever* ask."

Twenty years went by before I found out that Dr. Mengele had done inhumane experiments on 3,000 twins. Most of the experiments ended in death. Karl Bischoff wanted to protect me from that. He was good to me like that.

#

In September, we finally got Crema II back online, after months of work. With the twin Crema's II and III running smoothly now, we were able to shut down the eight-muffle Crema V and keep it in reserve. This was partly because Crema II and III were capable of handling the workload, and partly because we didn't want to test out Crema V's increased stamina over its weaker sister, Crema IV, which stood broken and useless as a monument to our hurried work.

Major Morgen was poking around the camp a lot. I noticed him several times wandering through the Crema buildings, making notes in a small book he kept. I wasn't sure what he was after, and he kept to himself, so I would just smile and nod at him. He would scowl back.

Melting Point

The celebration over Crema II's return was short lived. General Kammler, Bischoff's boss, convened a meeting to discuss who was going to pay for the repairs to Crema II. He was pretty upset that the chimney systems had ended up needing so much time and money to fix.

General Kammler met with Kurt Prüfer, Karl Bischoff, me, and a representative from the Köhler Company. Köhler had done the original construction work on most of the chimney systems, and also much of the repair work. Kammler started off the discussion on a sour note.

"This whole camp has been a screw-up right from the start," he said bitterly, to no one in particular. To Kurt Prüfer he added, "And the crematoriums are the biggest screw-up of all."

Kurt Prüfer drew himself upright. I could almost see his mind trying to decide whether to be contrite or honest. He chose honesty.

"The SS is the cheapest customer I've ever worked with, and I've worked with a lot. Everything has to be done as fast and as cheap as possible." Kurt's bald head was tinged with pink, giving away his anger.

"We may be cheap, Prüfer, but we expect that we should get what we contract for," Kammler said menacingly.

Kurt wouldn't back down. He said defensively, "We delivered everything we said we would."

General Kammler snorted. "Ovens that crack wide open, chimneys that won't vent smoke, electrical systems that catch fire, and my favorite, ovens that burn at half their promised capacity! I let you fool my superiors because I need this stuff to work as much as anyone, but you're not fooling *me* with your wide-eyed innocent acts!"

Kurt sighed heavily and tried to calm down. He appealed to reason. "When you asked for Crema IV, you wanted and approved an extremely cheap, stripped-down design. This design had only been tested using wood fires, but we had to convert it to run on coal for use here. I had no way of knowing it would fail."

General Kammler scowled, but listened.

Kurt shifted in his seat and went on. "The chimney in Crema I was designed for one furnace running at its rated capacity. You ran the furnace at a much higher capacity, and tripled the number of furnaces feeding it. I can't be held accountable for the vastly higher temperatures being fed into the chimney."

Try as he might to keep calm, Kurt's voice raised a little and he started gesturing with his hands as he went on, "The electrical system of Crema II was overloaded because we specified it back when you weren't gassing *half of Europe* in the basements, demanding vastly increased ventilation. By the time the specifications changed, we could no longer get the high-current parts needed to modify the electrical service panels."

Kammler sat up straighter, and narrowed his eyes at Kurt. He wasn't used to people arguing with him. In his world, people obeyed his orders. Kammler didn't like this.

Kurt continued, "As for the oven capacity of Crema II, we have increased the capacity considerably since it first went into operation. Had we stuck with tried and proven ovens like those in Crema I, there would have been many more furnaces, at much greater cost, than we ended up with." Kurt became a little sarcastic as he said, "Yes, I overestimated the furnace capacity, but this is a new technique, incinerating several people at once. It has never been done before in commercial crematoriums. You know, usually people *respect* the dead."

Kammler lost his temper. He threw up his hands. "Enough! Let's talk about this latest fiasco with the chimneys, or is that my fault too?"

Melting Point

"No, it's Köhler's fault," said Kurt abruptly.

The Köhler representative was startled. "What, our fault?"

"They used inferior materials," said Kurt, addressing himself to General Kammler. "Yes, we supplied blueprints, but we didn't do the actual work."

The Köhler representative became indignant. "That's a lie! It's because the ovens are being run much hotter than originally planned! The SS is burning too many bodies! If the blueprints had taken that into account, there would be no problem!"

They traded barbs and accusations for a short while, and then Kammler called a halt to the argument. We sat in silence for a long moment while he thought. Then he sighed and spoke quietly and slowly.

"I think we're all a little at fault here. I'll admit that even I have made a mistake or two, mostly in not foreseeing the vast increase in capacity we would be asked to provide to the special operations. I'd like to ask the Köhler Company to keep their eyes out for potential problems in future construction, and notify us of them immediately. Topf should also do its best to keep us informed of the ramifications of our decisions, especially if we seem to be asking for inferior or unreliable systems."

He looked around at us for approval. We all nodded, and he added, "I'm asking that each of the three parties here pay a third of the reconstruction costs. That would be about 1,600 Reichmarks each, I think."

Kurt, looking relieved, said with a smile, "You still owe us 90,000 Reichmarks for work we've completed. The SS is not only cheap, but they don't pay their bills on time. We'll deduct our payment from what you owe us."

Karl Bischoff winced at this smiling jab directed at his boss, but Kammler chuckled and said, "All right, Kurt, that would be fine." He looked at us all again and wagged a warning finger at us. "And remember, boys, this stays in the family. No one outside finds out about our problems, okay? To the outside, and especially to my boss, everything is rosy here."

All in all, it was a little like a family fight. We had yelled and let off some steam, but in the end, we all smiled pleasantly and pretended everything was fine. The 1,600 Reichmark fine was a trifle next to what we had made at Auschwitz.

#

Things were changing at Auschwitz in the fall of 1943. There were escapes and openly rebellious acts. A Jewish woman refused to go from the dressing room into the gas chamber, and was threatened by an SS guard named Shillinger. She grabbed his pistol away from him and shot him. He died on the way to the hospital. She wounded another SS guard, Wilhelm Emmerich, shooting him in the leg.

Then there was *The Scandal*. The guards had a thriving black-market going where they would loot the property stolen from the prisoners. I know it sounds silly when I say it that way, but the Nazis took everything away from the prisoners to help fund SS operations. Some of the guards figured that they could personally help themselves to the loot. This was a serious crime; not stealing from the victims, but stealing from the SS's stocks of confiscated items. Crazy, I know; like stealing from thieves.

"Hey, Albert, have you heard the news?" asked Karl Bischoff one day, as I was inspecting a fan motor that had stopped working.

"News?"

"Höss has been fired."

"Why?" I asked, surprised.

Melting Point

"Major Morgen, the guy who's been poking around for the last few months? Apparently he's been uncovering the black market pilfering going on here, and he blames Höss," Karl replied.

The black market had been widespread enough that everyone knew about it, and everyone looked the other way. For one thing, there were dozens of warehouses in Birkenau with loot piled high in them; a few baubles here and there weren't going to make any difference.

I asked, "Did Höss really have much to do with it? What about all the other men?"

"Apparently Morgen and his boys have been collecting evidence against a large number of guards, and they intend to prosecute. It's pretty serious. I don't think Höss is implicated in the stealing, just in losing control of the men. If you're convicted of stealing from the SS, the penalty could be a trip into one of our cellars."

I thought of my diamond collection. It had grown since my initial seven diamonds, and I just kept them in a little cloth pouch in my room. I realized all of a sudden that I could be accused of pilfering SS property. I felt flushed and hot.

"They've collected evidence?" I asked, becoming nervous and wanting to go back to my room.

"Quite a bit, apparently. They've taken over the building next to the bomb shelter, our original furnace room, to store the evidence," Karl said. He raised his eyebrow at me, smiled, and said, "You look nervous, Albert. Is there something I should know about?"

"No," I said abruptly. I must have looked guilty.

Karl said quietly, "Well, if I were you, I'd find a good hiding place for it, whatever it is. I have."

The Girl with the Curly Hair

My eyes opened wide and I stared at him, and then slowly nodded. I took a deep breath. *He has.*

"Well, I guess I'm done here for the time being," I said, a little too obviously. "I'll come back later and finish fixing it. I, uh, need some parts."

Karl said quietly, "You know, now that Crema IV is shut down, no one ever goes in there."

I nodded, thanked him, and left. Crema IV was indeed a good place to hide my small collection. The furnace was cracked in several places, and had several loose bricks. I picked the least obvious place I could find, and hid the diamonds in their pouch behind a loose brick. If they were found, there was nothing to tie them to me.

#

All during the autumn, the Russians were pressing forward. They recaptured Mogilev, ending forever the question of how we were going to install all those eight-muffle ovens. The Russians had proceeded as far as Kiev in the Ukraine, only about 500 miles to the east of us.

In the extermination camp of Sobibor, on the eastern Polish border, there was a large prisoner escape in mid-October of 300 prisoners. The largest death-camp escape of the war. The camp was closed and plowed under. Around 250,000 Jews had been killed there. Two other extermination camps set up specifically for disposing of Jews, Treblinka and Belzec, were also closed and hidden. Belzec had killed well over 500,000 Jews; Treblinka something like 900,000.

By the end of 1943, the only major extermination camp still open was Auschwitz. Of course, we were also a work camp, with tens of thousands of workers building the synthetic rubber factory, and tens of thousands more involved in all kinds of industrial labor at the dozens of sub-camps. But for

Melting Point

every worker that came into the camp to live a few months toiling for the SS, at least two people came into the camp and went straight to the cellars.

An interesting arrangement was going on with our prisoner workers. They were *hired out* to the industries that employed them. Those German firms would pay the SS for the workers. By the end of 1943, the SS was making over 2,000,000 Reichmarks a month off the labor of Auschwitz's inmates. Likely, some of that money was used to pay the SS's bills with Topf.

In early December, the trial was getting close for all the SS men accused of being a part of the black market. The guards were still working at the camp, but weren't allowed to leave until the trial was over. Men were coming from Berlin to hold the trial. Everyone was depressed. Many of the guards took their feelings out on the inmates.

On the evening of December 7, Karl Bischoff came up to my room, something he had never done before. He knocked on the door and I let him in. He was as white as a ghost.

"What's wrong? What happened?" I asked with concern.

Karl sat down heavily on my bed. "Morgen has accused me of stealing."

"What? You? That's preposterous!"

"He caught me," Karl said with resignation.

"Doing what?"

"You know that good French brandy we've been drinking?"

Karl had always been generous with his brandy, and it was much better than the swill available to us in town.

"You didn't," I said with alarm.

Karl just nodded, a glum expression on his face. "I would get it from a sergeant, who got it from a private that worked in one of the storage houses.

Morgen caught the private, who squealed about the sergeant, who squealed about me."

"What are you going to do?" I asked.

"Just await my fate along with the other men caught, I suppose," he said, flopping back on my bed, defeated.

"Are they still storing all the evidence in the old building next to Crema I?" I asked.

Karl just nodded silently and stared at the ceiling. I thought for a moment. *Karl Bischoff, despite preventing me from joining the army, had tried to make my stay here bearable. He was my friend. Drinking good brandy was a refuge from this place. And, if he hadn't taken it, someone else in the SS hierarchy would have. I should try to help him.*

But what could I do? All the boxes of evidence on the men and all the records and notes were stored in the building next to the old Crema I, the building that the SS had been worried about the chimney collapsing on. I had been in that building only once before, when installing the supplemental wiring from that building to the fans in Crema I. I had used the same crummy fuses in the electrical panel in the basement of that building as the one that caught fire in Crema II when it was overloaded.

The fuses caught fire when overloaded.

I felt a chill run down from the top of my head through my neck and down my back. As if some huge weight came off my shoulder, I felt lightheaded and a bit giddy.

I thought out loud, "It's an old building. Brick on the outside, but all wood on the inside. Old, dry wood. The electric panel is in the basement. Poor construction from the turn of the century. The wires aren't even insulated in most places. And, in spite of there being an ancient electrical panel there, we

Melting Point

brought power from that panel into Crema I to supply the additional needs for the fans for the second and third oven. I used those crummy fuses that catch fire, too."

Karl Bischoff sat back up and stared at me. "What are you thinking? You're not going to *do* anything," he said. "They've got special guards posted around the building to prevent any of the accused from getting in. You couldn't get near the place. And if they catch you, Albert Stohl, you'll be shot!"

I should have been scared. But here was an opportunity to do something against the system. *An opportunity to do something to help my friend.* True, it would help the guards who didn't deserve any sympathy, but all I saw was that Karl Bischoff needed my help, and by helping him I could lash out in a way that wouldn't hurt Germany, but would still be a thrust at the system. What was happening here was inhuman, and to accuse the SS men involved in the system of *stealing from the SS* seemed insane.

With calm I hadn't felt in a year, I said to Karl, "Stay here. I'll be back in an hour."

Karl looked alarmed, but was speechless. I left my room and walked to Crema I. There was some frost on the ground but a clear sky. The frost crunched under my shoes as I walked to the old camp. The moon was out and I could see my breath. Crema I had long since been shut down, and was now reserved as a bomb shelter, but the furnaces were still in place in the deserted building.

Unused, there was no one around the building. The door was unlocked, in case of an air raid. Once inside, I peered out the windows of the furnace room towards the building with the evidence stored somewhere within. There had been additional power needed in the furnace room to run fans and lights. By a stroke of fate, I had been involved with the changing of the panel in the other building back in 1942. It had been easy, because the ground between

The Girl with the Curly Hair

the chimney and the building had been all torn up to install the underground flues for the chimney. Since most of the ground was torn up anyway, it wasn't expensive to run power lines underground from the panel in the basement of the building across the way.

I walked over to the main power panel in a small room next to the furnace room. It was unchanged from when I had last seen it. I took out a screwdriver and removed the cover to the panel. The panel in the basement of the neighboring building had no fancy cover. It was just wires stuck to fuse holders bolted onto the bare wood beams holding the rooms above. The service coming to Crema I went through one of those dangerously bad fuses on the old panel.

The key was the fuse. It was the exact same kind of fuse as had caught fire in Crema II back in March. If I could get the fuse in the basement to catch fire, that could cause some damage. Maybe enough damage, maybe not. The building was deserted at night, so I was hoping that a fire would go unchecked until it was too late.

The power came to the crematorium building from the neighboring building through the fuse in its basement. If I added power drains onto this wire, it could overload the fuse in the other building.

I had to work carefully, because I couldn't turn off the power. That might have alerted the guards. Instead, I moved wires around carefully so that all of the electric motors in Crema I were now attached to the line from the other building. Where before there were two fans and a couple of lights, now there would be all eight fans for this building on this one wire, and on the one fuse. Next, I started to power up the blowers and fans. The three ovens came to life, albeit cold, with air rushing through them and up the chimney for the first time in months. I powered on the fans in the morgue room, later turned into a gas chamber, and now abandoned. Fresh air was being sucked into the

Melting Point

room by the high-powered fans. I powered on the extra draft fans in the chimney. I looked through the windows at the other building.

Nothing. At least the guards didn't seem alarmed by anything going on in the crematorium. There must have been a rushing noise from the chimney, but they paid no attention. Probably lights in the other building had dimmed a bit. I hoped that with no one inside, no one would notice.

I stared out the window for about twenty minutes, fans and blowers going all around me. I was getting a sinking feeling as I realized that this wasn't going to work.

"Well, I tried," I sighed.

I heard some whistles blowing in the distance. Something was wrong. But it was in the distance, so it wasn't about the building, and it wasn't a fire. I heard some shouting and saw a couple of men rush away in the distance, but none of the guards left the building they were guarding.

"Maybe another escape," I mumbled. Escapes were becoming more frequent. There was even rumored to be an organized resistance movement. *Asylum Strike*, it was rumored to be called. It made me shudder to think about it.

Just then the blowers all shut off, startling me. It was now dark and silent in the old furnace room. I'd been discovered! My heart pounded. I looked around, but it was still silent. Where were the guards? Surely they were coming for me?

Oh, the blowers have shut off.

The fuse had finally blown. I hadn't been discovered; I had overloaded the fuse, and now it had blown. It was time to restore the wires to their original position so my sabotage couldn't be detected. I was nervous and began to sweat. It wouldn't do for someone to find me here. I quickly shut off the

The Girl with the Curly Hair

switches for the fans and blowers, rewired the panel as it had been, and screwed the cover back on. I needed to return to my room, but I took one last peek towards the old building across the way.

It was dark, but all was quiet. Damn. *I Failed.*

Dejected, I headed back to my room, taking a circuitous route so no one would think I was coming from the furnace room. On the way, a man was running by with a toolkit and I asked, "What's going on? What's happening?"

"The trap door on the water tower broke, releasing the water. Now there's no water in this part of the camp."

He kept running towards the old water tower. It, too, was from the turn of the century, and prone to breakage.

I got back to my room and stamped the frost off my boots. Karl Bischoff was no longer there, which was just as well. I was cold and damp, my sweat having soaked my clothes. I took off my clothes and fell onto the bed.

I'd failed. The one time I tried to rebel against the awful goings-on here, I failed. *I'm a miserable failure. Like Irma Griese said, a nobody.*

Just then the fire alarm wailed.

Suddenly I didn't feel cold anymore. I just felt tired. With the sounds of men running and shouting outside, I fell into a deep sleep; contented and smiling.

The next day I slept late. Karl Bischoff came to my room and pounded on the door. I opened it up to see a broad smile on his face. He sat down.

"Electrical fire," he said by way of greetings. "Too bad the water tower failed, or they could have saved more of the building."

He was all smiles.

Melting Point

"The bolt holding the trap door looked so secure, too," he said wistfully. "Took a lot of effort to break it," he said with a wide grin. "The electrical fire was genius, Albert, sheer genius."

I nodded. "Thanks. How did you know?"

"You talked about the panel. I knew you couldn't get into the building, but I remembered the work you'd done pulling cables to Crema I, and I thought I'd give you a hand," he said with satisfaction.

"And the evidence?"

Karl shook his head, a mischievous smile on his face, "Sadly, it was all lost, I'm afraid."

All the evidence had been destroyed and the SS decided to call off further investigation. They may have suspected foul play, but they knew the problem was an electrical fire, and they knew no one was in the building. Karl Bischoff was charged with fixing things, and he asked *me* to fix the damage to the electrical panel. I did so gladly and with pride.

#

I went to Carl and Mary's farm for Christmas. Travel was being restricted because of shortages and the war, so I couldn't go home to visit my mother. Instead, I used a bicycle to get to the farm, using the same route Herman and I had taken all those years ago. The farm was pretty with snow on the fields and roofs. Yet when I got there, Carl was fuming because their housekeeper and a farmhand had run off a few days before. Most of the rest of the farmhands lived in a nearby building, huddling together in the cold. There wasn't a lot of work to do in the winter except care for the animals, so the farmhand wasn't missed. The housekeeper was a different story.

"Now Mary has to do the cooking and cleaning. It's not right. That's servant's work," complained Carl.

I laughed at this, "A few years ago you had less land and no servants or farmhands. Now you can't live without them."

"Bah. Times are different. This is the new Poland, the German Poland. I like the new Poland a lot more than the old Poland," he said gruffly, but with a smile.

Mary spoke up, "Polish girls are being useful by being servants. Most of them have been sent south to Germany, so it's harder to find one now. Ours wasn't great, but I miss her help. I wish I could find another."

"There are Polish women at the camp I work at, maybe they could loan you one," I said. *Maybe that would save a life.*

"That would be great, Albert," said Mary.

Christmas was kind of somber. The Russians weren't all that far away, and they had just launched their massive winter campaign all along the Ukrainian front. They were heading for the Polish border, just a couple of hundred miles away. Each year they get closer. It seemed like only a matter of time before they got here.

"They won't be happy when they get here," I said.

"They hate the Poles as much as we ethnic Germans do. I wouldn't worry about them being angry over us using Poles as farmhands and servants. They'll like that idea and do the same," said Carl.

"No, it's not that. It's Auschwitz."

"The town or the prison camp? The Russians have prison camps too, you know," said Mary.

"Not like this one. You should know about it, so if they should get this far you'll be prepared," I began.

And I told them everything I knew. About the 100,000 Russian POW's used to build Birkenau. About the Poles, the Gypsies, the homosexuals, the criminals, the children. And about the many hundreds of thousands of Jews, maybe a million so far.

They didn't believe it. They couldn't believe it. They accused me of lying, or at least exaggerating. It was incomprehensible. We yelled; we stomped around; at last we came to a truce. They wouldn't believe. I couldn't convince them.

"Well, just believe this: the Russians will be extremely enraged at what they find there, if they get this far. If that happens, you don't want to tell them you are German," I said.

I was glad to leave there the next morning. They resented me for what I said, half believing that I was lying, and half knowing that there must be truth to it. Carl had delivered food from his farm to Birkenau, so he knew the scale of what was happening, just not the specifics. And they couldn't deny the huge number of trains that lumbered within a few miles of their farm on their way to the Oswiecim station. Full going in; empty coming back.

When I got back to camp, I asked Karl Bischoff to help me find a replacement housekeeper for Carl and Mary, and he said that he would take care of it.

#

By early January, the Soviets had reached the Polish border, just a few hundred miles away. We were all nervous. The tensions in the camp were raised when the BBC broadcast the names of many of the guards in the camp, and said that they would be held accountable for their actions after the war. Men started to get nervous, and several joined the army or SS combat battalions to try and salvage their honor. The army was getting desperate for men, and they were even willing to take me, too. I was willing to give up my hell at Auschwitz for the army, even if it meant the eastern front. Alas, that was not to be. Events were conspiring to keep me at Auschwitz, and when I asked Kurt

The Girl with the Curly Hair

Prüfer or Karl Bischoff for permission to leave, they both said no. I wouldn't have made a good soldier, but I would have been away from here.

Though the end looked near at the time, there would be another year before we were through at Auschwitz. And things were happening on the world stage that would affect both me and this camp. The three other big Jewish extermination camps had been closed. Even though there were many concentration camps and other prisons, the main *Factories of Death* besides Auschwitz had been closed for business, largely due to the lack of Jews to kill from the occupied areas.

All occupied areas but one: Hungary. For years, Hungary's government had been fairly autonomous, and had become a relative haven for Jews. Some 500,000 Jews were in Hungary, comprising most of the remaining Jews in Europe. As the Soviets were getting closer to Hungary, Hitler decided it was time to take more complete control of the country, and Himmler ordered the Hungarian Jews rounded up and shipped to Auschwitz.

Auschwitz, for its part, was told to prepare for one last influx of Jews. Topf was asked to install de-aeration systems for the gas chambers in Crema IV and V, to shorten the turn-around time of the gas chambers. We were also asked to repair Crema IV's broken ovens so they could at least contribute some help. Crema V was to be put into shape to be used again, having been shut down soon after Crema III came online. The 'Little White House' was pressed back into service. The 'Little Red House' had been destroyed, and so was no help.

In return, all our bills were finally paid up. Well, all except for the cost of the Mogilev furnaces. Even though Mogilev had been overrun and we never delivered the ovens we said we would, we had already been paid most of the money for them.

Melting Point

Since the SS was desperate for us to get things in shape for the arriving Hungarians, it was a good time to bargain with them. It was also a confusing situation, and with the Mogilev camp overrun, the confusion worked in Kurt Prüfer's favor.

We had priced the eight-muffle furnaces at 13,800 Reichmarks each. We had planned to deliver four furnaces to Mogilev for a total of 55,200 Reichmarks. We installed only a half of one furnace, but had been paid 41,400 Reichmarks (the price for three *complete* furnaces). Meanwhile, Auschwitz ordered two furnaces and paid us 10,000 of the 27,600 Reichmarks they owed us. We had asked to be paid for all six furnaces (which was outrageous), but the SS remembered that the two Auschwitz furnaces were *borrowed* from the Mogilev order. So, the SS concluded that they should pay for the balance due on the four furnaces actually purchased. In the end, we were paid for four furnaces when we only delivered two and a half. A neat profit.

We had until mid-May to get things ready for the Hungarians. It would take the Germans that long to take control and organize transport. We fixed up Crema IV, and I had to find a new hiding place for my diamonds. We added ventilation systems and cleaned all the ovens. In the meantime, the Soviets started offensives on the Byelorussian front, and in the Crimea. They recaptured Sevastopol. Berlin was bombed in daylight by the Allies. Prisoner escapes had escalated. Amidst this, Commandant Höss returned, having been forgiven for his earlier crimes; he was needed to efficiently run the Hungarian operation.

#

And when it started, it was a flood.

#

On May 15, 1944, the first trains loaded with Hungarian Jews left northeast Hungary. The closest ones arrived the very next day. Six thousand, three hundred Jews were on the first day's trains. About one in ten was selected to work, to replace the fallen workers in one of the industrial areas. The rest went to the various gas chambers. After that, there were three or four trains each day, each train with 45 cars or so, and each car with 80 or so people on board. About 10,000 people a day, 9,000 destined to be gassed immediately, the rest allowed to work to death.

There was such a crush of people that there were large groups waiting to go into the various gas chambers at all hours of the day. Kapos, the prisoners who served as guards, kept people in line and moving. Like the Kapos that supervised the Sonderkommandos running the ovens, they were given extra food and privileges to be supervisors of other inmates. In this way, just a few SS guards could manage thousands of prisoners.

We had five gas chambers in all; one in each of the Crematoriums and the 'Little White House.' Our furnace capacity wasn't nearly as great as our gassing capacity. We were able to manage as many as six bodies per muffle per hour in the 30 muffles of Crema's II and III, and optimistically four an hour in IV and V. Total daily capacity was under 5,000 bodies per day. With 9,000 people a day being sent to gas chambers, there was no way we could keep up with the demand. We fell behind by almost 4,000 bodies a day! At the peak, there were some 950 Kapos and Sonderkommandos working the various gassing and cremation facilities.

In the heat of the sun, the extra bodies quickly became a health hazard. They stank and bloated and gathered flies. Soon the stench of tens of thousands of rotting bodies moved like a fog over the entire camp.

Pits were used to burn and bury the overflow of bodies. Fuel was poured on the bodies so they would burn. Smoke poured out of chimneys and pits all day and all night for about eight weeks. The smoke and rotting smells

Melting Point

combined together to make an unimaginable pall over the entire valley, visible for miles. Folks in the nearby town stayed indoors. This went on for weeks.

Eight weeks of concentrated mass murder. Four hundred forty thousand people murdered and incinerated. About one person every nine or ten seconds - all day, every day, for eight weeks. The piles of bodies took another few weeks to incinerate and bury.

#

Right in the middle of all of this, the Americans and British invaded France on June 6, 1944. The Soviets attacked Finland. The Soviet summer offensive, called *Bagration*, began. The first German V-1 rockets attacked Britain. The soviets captured Minsk. The Allies bombed Blechhammer, northwest of the camp. The world was very busy and wasn't paying attention to Auschwitz.

And what about me? What was Albert Stohl doing during the deadliest eight weeks of the war? I was running constantly from one disaster to another. Ludwig Topf had decided that Kurt Prüfer, Karl Schultze, and the other lead members of Topf were no longer to go to Auschwitz. Somehow, I think he felt that he could bury his head in the sand and escape some blame. I was the sacrificial lamb. I was the least important person at Topf, and so was the one chosen to stay and help out during the eight weeks of hell.

And for me, it *was* a kind of hell. Not like what was awaiting the victims, but a hell just the same. I would literally run from building to building, visiting each of the four crematoria in turn, and fixing problems constantly. Ventilation motors would stop working. Wires running next to the furnaces would melt from the heat. The fragile oven in Crema IV was constantly in need of repair.

The cremation of victims ran around the clock. Normally, each furnace would have some downtime during the day for cleaning and inspection, but that

The Girl with the Curly Hair

was eliminated. Now, the furnaces ran 24 hours a day. This meant I tried to inspect the furnaces as they were running to see if there were any impending problems. There were many.

The Sonderkommandos had become good at the job of regulating the ovens so they stayed almost white-hot without melting and cracking, but that took a lot of finesse and care. Sometimes an oven would get too hot and would need some iron parts pounded back into shape, or pipes would crack and need re-welding. It was hot, backbreaking work. Fortunately for me, prisoners did most of the heavy work, but I still had to be there, to supervise and inspect and direct.

#

One day, I was at Crema III working on some melted wires that ran too close to an oven. We had to repair the wires while the oven was still running. Since the oven was hot enough to melt the wires, you can well imagine that it was too hot for us to be close to it. It took some time and careful work, and we were all sweating from the exertion.

I had to leave the heat and noise and smell of that furnace room for a few minutes of fresh air. I hated to see what went on in there, and I felt a little faint. I walked out the side door and slowly shuffled along the gravel path around the side of the building, breathing in lungfulls of air. A light wind was blowing the stench away from me that day. I inhaled the summer air and enjoyed looking at the trees and shrubs. I felt a little better. The bushes rustled in the breeze.

The small path I was walking along was between the building housing Crema III and a shrub-covered fence. I came to a larger path perpendicular to mine that went from a shrub-covered gate to the main entrance of the dressing room for the victims. The bigger path was empty. Indeed, I didn't see anyone

Melting Point

around me, and so I stopped at the intersection, leaning against a tree on the smaller path.

Where was all of this going? What can I do about it? Make a list. On the one hand, we're at war, and by the looks of things, losing. So, we're desperate. The army was screaming for new people. At this point, they would take almost anyone. Maybe I should once again try to convince Kurt and Karl that I should join, and get away from all this.

But that was too simple. There must be horrendous killing and death on the battlefields, and even if I didn't end up like Herman, I would still be in the midst of gruesome things. At least here, no one was shooting at me. On the other hand, being a warrior was noble, wasn't it? Certainly it was nobler than being here. Many of the veteran SS guards had opted to join the army rather than stay here.

Herman died a noble death. Trapped in Stalingrad, told by Hitler they can't retreat, they were unprepared for the massive assault by the Russians. The rescuing army was not able to reach them. Maybe he was in a Russian gulag, a place like this.

No, not like this. There had never been a place like this. We were unique in all of history to have created such an efficient death machine. Others had brutal camps where lots of people were killed, but here we applied modern manufacturing techniques to the problem. Here we could tell you exact yields in hair, gold, shoes, combs, everything.

So where did that leave me? Let's, see, what else could be on the list? I could join the army and be a combat engineer. Build bridges, that sort of thing. Maybe that would be noble. At least it would be away from here. I imagine they need engineers. I should look into that.

I suddenly heard some music start up; a string quintet. A beautiful Straus waltz. I looked towards the dressing room entrance and there were five prisoners playing instruments. Small groups of Kapos were nearby. I hadn't

The Girl with the Curly Hair

heard them come into the yard in front of the building, but there they were. It seemed odd and certainly paradoxical to be hearing a waltz out here.

At that moment, the gate near me swung inward, and a crowd of people moved along the path towards the building. Kapos were with them, shouting at them to keep moving. The crowd was mostly quiet, but there were occasional coughs, sobs, and moans. The music was louder now, the prisoner musicians playing for all they were worth. Old men, old women, mothers with babies, small children. They all moved forward to the dressing room. They weren't in prison garb; they were dressed in civilian clothes. Yet they had no luggage. They must have left that by the train.

My stomach began to churn and ache. I had always stayed away from this part of the operation. But here I was, frozen to my spot against the tree, no more than six feet from the moving crowd. People mostly stared at the ground in front of them. The musicians didn't look at the people; one looked at the ground, the others seemed to have their eyes closed. After several hundred had passed by, the group was mostly past me. A Kapo bringing up the rear went to close the gate after the last two people in the group came through it.

An old woman, stooped and taking small steps, was holding the hand of a little girl with long curly hair. The woman had a shawl around her head so you couldn't see much of her face. She wore a long coat that was stained and frayed. The girl's hair was long and unkempt. It had a striking deep mahogany red color, and must have been beautiful in other circumstances. The girl wore a thin dirty coat over a dress that had a faded pattern. Her bare feet were filthy. She clutched a doll's hand in hers, the doll swinging slowly back and forth as she walked. The doll looked homemade, like a rag doll with a bright yellow tuft of yarn for hair. While the girl's clothes were dirty and stained, the doll looked clean; its yellow hair bright in contrast to the girl's dress. The girl must have taken great care to make sure the doll stayed safe.

Melting Point

The girl looked up at the old woman and spoke in Yiddish. I couldn't understand it completely, but from the few words I knew I think she said, "Will I see my mommy again?"

The old woman said to her, also in Yiddish, something like, "I'm sure you will soon, dear. And the rest of your family."

The girl said impassively, "No, she's all that's left."

Apparently this woman wasn't related to the girl. They probably just met at the train platform when the girl had been separated from her mother. My heart beat faster, and my stomach was tight. This girl had been taken from her mother, and, rather than walk her last mile alone, a stranger was holding her hand and comforting her.

By this time the pair had come to be right in front of me, not six feet away. The girl turned and looked at me, her face filled with sadness and defeat. She looked apprehensive and afraid. Her brow was crinkled and her nose was running. She got a pleading look on her face, and she asked me a question in German.

#

"Will it hurt?"

#

She knew. So help me, she knew what was going to happen.

"Nonsense, it will be fine," the old woman said. She looked at me with a stern look that said, *don't tell.*

So she knew, too. They probably all knew. How could they not know? They were separated from the strong and marched to a building with a chimney spewing ashes and smoke. But, just as I have been in denial about this place, so were they. They saw the sign *To the Showers* and accepted it. One side of their brain was probably screaming at them to run, while the other was telling them

The Girl with the Curly Hair

that it is impossible that civilized people would do such things. I had been feeling that a bit myself, lately. I can see why they would think that too.

And so, the little girl looked up at the old woman and they continued down the path, the doll swinging slowly in the girl's iron grip. That instant I realized that the old lady had more courage than I'd ever had. She knew what was going to happen; she knew she was about to die. Yet she spent her last few minutes comforting a stranger's child. That was strength. That was courage.

I felt weak. Humiliated, I suppose, by the courage that those two had shown. And fear, for what they faced. No longer could I rationalize that these were prisoners of war, or *enemies of the state*. How could those two be a threat to Germany? I felt anger, for what my part was in all this. And I felt helpless; helpless to stop this machine. I had to get out of this place, while there was still some humanity left in me.

By now the gate had been closed, and the Kapo bringing up the rear had ushered all but the old woman and curly-haired girl down the stairs into the changing room. As she started down the steps, the little girl turned and stared at me. I couldn't take my eyes off her. She continued to stare at me until she disappeared through the door to the dressing room. My eyes hurt with the pressure on them, and tears began to run down my face. I had to leave.

With her last look haunting me, I went back into the furnace room. The outside air was no longer a relief. The noise and heat and smoke were enough to drown out my thoughts. Near the door to the furnace room was a wooden chair, and I sank into it, my head in my hands. The Sonderkommandos were working the ovens as efficiently as ever, dragging the bodies down the watered-down trough up to the next available muffle. Watching the men do their jobs helped to empty my mind.

By the time a body is in the watered trough, it no longer resembles a person. Head shaved, skin bluish gray from the gas, no clothes or jewelry. It

Melting Point

was easy to not recognize human features, and therefore to not think about what was really happening. I suppose it's a little like a surgeon who only sees a tiny exposed part of the body, and doesn't have to see the whole human being. You can get on with your work, and not focus on who the person is.

I was able to start my list of options over again. *Soldier? Combat engineer? Run away? Stay here?* No, I can't stay here. Running away is out, too, after all Herman has sacrificed. I would ruin the family name by deserting. *Find some non-war engineering work?* That's not likely. I'll have to think more about this later. For now, I just need to stop thinking. I closed my eyes and tried to ignore the throbbing in my temples.

I'm not sure how long I sat there with my eyes closed, but it was quite a while. I opened them again because I became aware of a disturbance. Something was wrong. I opened my eyes and looked around. Men were staring at the wet trough with bodies. I felt it before I saw it, and I saw it before I registered what it was.

A bright yellow tuft of yarn.

The Sonderkommandos, who were used to seeing the very worst of the world, all stopped and stared. The killing machine paused for a moment to see what had happened. One of the bodies had held on to something with a yellow tuft of yarn.

There was a young girl's body, clutching tightly, even in death, her doll. She hadn't left it in the changing room. She hadn't let go of it in the gas chamber. The Sonderkommandos downstairs who were supposed to take it from her didn't. They had let a little humanity slip through. She had thrown a wrench into the machine.

One by one, the Sonderkommandos would look, recognize what it was, and then look away or down at the floor. Disgust? Shame? I don't know.

Feelings weren't supposed to get into this room, and they had. For me, I felt as if my heart had been ripped from my chest. I wept.

Did it hurt?

Two Sonderkommandos came over and carefully lifted her body up and put it on top of two other bodies on a trolley near me. I was apparently the closest man in charge and one of the men took hold of the doll and looked at me with a questioning look and a gesture that said, "Shall I take it away?"

I shook my head. *No.* We've taken everything else from her. Her family, her mother, her old lady friend, her life, her clothes. The great German war machine doesn't need her doll, too. The man let go of the doll and nodded at me. He swallowed hard. He had tears in his eye.

I was having a hard time seeing through my watery eyes. I blinked a lot. The cart men continued their routine, slowly wheeling the cart up to the oven. Other men stopped what they were doing and faced the muffle she was in front of, looking at the bright clean doll. I heard a man sob. I heard another wail. The men who wore caps took them off and held them in their hands. All work stopped for a brief moment. Three dozen men stood silently in tribute to the doll and its owner. That doll represented all the children lost. Not hundreds, not thousands, but millions. Many of them incinerated in Topf ovens all over Europe. Maybe hundreds of thousands of them incinerated in the ovens right in front of me.

The moment passed and the three bodies were pushed into the oven. I couldn't take my eyes off the tuft of yellow yarn as it slid into the red-hot oven. It burst into a puff of orange flame. Even after the oven door was slammed shut I stared at the door, glowing bright orange-red. Our company name on the iron door in raised letters, **TOPF**, was a little darker than the surrounding iron. It could just as easily have read **STOHL**.

Birth and Rebirth

It was raining again in Bodega Bay. The thunder was closer, and now and then flickers of lightening could be seen. Lightning storms aren't common on the North Coast, and it seemed like a commentary on my story.

I got up, not bothering to announce another break, and went to the bathroom. When I came out, the family was up and about. Magda and Amanda were putting out some desserts. Amanda served a piece of cherry pie and handed it to me with a fork.

Tom came over and shook his head, "I never understood why people went willingly to their deaths. I still don't completely understand, but what you said makes sense. They couldn't bring themselves to believe it was really happening."

"Excuse me?" Amanda asked with incredulity, "You are walking into a building with a huge smokestack spewing ashes? They had to know."

"But what else could they do?" Tony piped up. "They had dogs and guys with guns herding them along. Getting out of line would just get you shot."

"Enough!" shouted Magda. She was visibly upset. "Papa, if you don't mind, let's just get this over with."

We all silently returned to our seats, everyone having some dessert except Magda, who nervously chewed on her fingernails. I took a bite of pie and then continued telling the story.

#

It became clear to me that Auschwitz's days were coming to a close. The Russians were moving nearer to it, and the end of the trains from Hungary signaled the end of the majority of Jews in Europe. There were still trains coming in now and again, but the vast majority of Jews had already been shipped to Auschwitz and other camps. Most of the camps in Poland, primarily designated as *death camps*, had been closed for lack of Jews. For our part, we still had workers; 11,000 building the synthetic-rubber factory nearby at Monowitz, now called Auschwitz III; another 7,000 working at chemical plants in the area; 8,000 worked in mines; 4,000 turned human hair into bomb fuses and socks; 4,500 worked to make cement and bricks. Thousands more were still employed trying to turn the marshy land nearby into productive farmland. We were a work camp too, not just a death camp. Though, as I've come to realize, the distinction has always been a minor one.

For my part, I had resigned myself to my fate, whatever it may be. I had begged Kurt Prüfer to let me join the army, but he had said I was too valuable here. Karl Bischoff had been forced to let most of his staff join the army, and he relied on me to keep things going in the various crematoria. There was no new construction going on, but there was still a fair amount of maintenance needed to keep the various furnaces and venting systems in working order. I was stuck at Auschwitz until the very end.

I began to look for ways I might atone for my behavior. Open rebellion was out, I was too afraid to do that. Besides, I didn't want to disgrace

Melting Point

my family by becoming a traitor. Sabotage might work, but it was a little late for that, what with the camp's use nearing an end. After a while, my quest for atonement seemed nearly as futile as the rest of my endeavors. But just knowing that I *might* do something seemed to help my mood. Meanwhile, life and death at the camp went on.

#

Then there were the bombers. On Sunday, August 20, I had been walking from my quarters to a store room when the air-raid siren started up. This was the cue for prisoners to return to their wooden huts, in which there would be no protection from the bombs, and for the rest of us to dive into one of the makeshift bomb shelters. The old crematorium in the original camp, no longer used for cremations, had been turned into a bomb shelter. I was nowhere near that shelter, though.

I looked around hurriedly for the nearest shelter. They had been hastily built and marked with painted yellow signs. I ran for the nearest one. It was just part of a drainage ditch that had a small concrete roof over it and some sand bags. Fortunately, it hadn't rained recently, so the ditch was not filled with water. Still there was mud in the bottom and nowhere to sit. The ceiling was only about five feet from the deepest part of the ditch and so I crouched and waited.

Nothing happened for a long time. Then, though the sky was nearly cloudless, I heard some thunder. Then more and more thunder, with some distant rumbling and rolling, and some much sharper. I thought back to what Herman had said about battles and the rolling thunder sounds. After another twenty minutes or so things quieted down and I heard the all-clear signal.

That night at dinner, I found out that over 1,200 bombs had been dropped by 120 American bombers on the synthetic rubber factory that was still under construction just a few miles from here.

"Do you think they will bomb us? Right here in camp?" I asked.

"Nah, they won't want to hurt prisoners," one man said.

"They would if they knew what we were doing to them," another said. After that we were all pretty quiet.

Tuesday that week, another raid was made by 260 American bombers on the nearby oil refineries at Blechhammer and Odertal. On Friday, August 25, 1944, Paris was liberated. The following Sunday 350 bombers attacked Blechhammer again. The following Tuesday some 210 bombers attacked other targets within 45 miles of us. Also in August and early September was the dissolution of the Lodz Ghetto. Some 68,500 people were transported to our camp. However, that only amounted to a train a day or so, something that had become fairly easy to deal with by now. All but one of the crematoria had been shut down, their use at an end.

On September 13, I was again forced into a bomb shelter when the air raid sirens sounded. This time I sought out a little better shelter than the ditch. I ran into a slightly better constructed shelter about 20 yards behind and to the west of the big crematoria. Once again I found myself waiting for a long time for something to happen, and wondering if they would attack the camp.

The thunder started again, and it was loud but far enough away that I knew that at least those bombs weren't falling on the camp. There seemed to be fewer bombs.

A nervous looking man with a bushy mustache and a sunburned face was sitting across from me in the little shelter, looking at the ceiling. I was nervous as well, of course, but felt better now that the bombs seemed to be getting further away. I could tell the man was nervous both because of the way his eyes darted around, and because he was sweating profusely, even though it was fairly cool in the shelter.

"Maybe fewer planes this time, eh?" the nervous man said.

Melting Point

"I hope so," I said. I was regretting not bringing some brandy with me into the shelter to pass the time.

The nervous man asked, grimacing as more thunder rolled through, "Maybe the Americans are running out of planes, eh?"

I said, "It's not the Americans I worry about, but the Russians."

The nervous man's eyes widened. "Russians?" he asked quietly.

I was about to say more, but just then there was a loud THUD, followed by another and then another and then seven more quickly in a row, each getting louder and louder, like a big bass drum being hit as it came towards us.

"Ah! Help!" yelled the man, his eyes wild, as he jumped up and ran to the door.

I should have told him to sit down, but I was too terrified to move or speak. Fortunately, the nervous man didn't open the door, or he could have endangered both of us. He stood listening.

Silence.

I realized that I hadn't been breathing and now took a big breath and sighed. The bombs had all stopped. After a few more minutes there was the all clear siren and we both climbed out of the shelter. From the direction of Auschwitz III, the synthetic rubber plant, there were clouds of smoke. A few smaller plumes of smoke made a line from Auschwitz III over to our camp, the last one being directly south of the camp. This last bomb hit the rail line that goes between the nearby civilian train station and the camp. For a while, the arriving prisoners would be walking the mile or so from the train station to get to their last destination.

#

Birth and Rebirth

By now, it was time to think about evacuation. Our use as a 'death camp' was just about at an end, though we still had a lot of factory work going on. Kurt Prüfer came to the camp for one last time to discuss moving the ovens to a safer location. The SS believed they would continue to use their ovens, just in another camp. The trouble was that we just didn't have the workers or transportation we would need to move them. The camp administration was also making plans to get rid of the Sonderkommandos, their work being near an end.

'Get rid of' meant just that – the Sonderkommandos who ran the gas chambers and ovens for us would meet the same fate as the other victims of the camp. For a long time they had had better rations and sleeping quarters, helping to ensure a longer life, but now that was nearing an end. The issue for the camp administration was how to do this in a way that wouldn't cause a revolt. After all, the usual pretenses of going to showers wouldn't work on these men and women. And, getting *other* Sonderkommandos to deal with their own kind was bound to cause troubles.

There had been purges of Sonderkommandos in the past, of course, but then they would be mixed in with a trainload of 'regular' prisoners, and were not as noticeable. With fewer transports, it would be harder to hide them. And, since everyone knew that the camp was nearing its end, the working Sonderkommandos would know that their time was coming soon as well. I heard there were discussions about moving the Sonderkommandos elsewhere to be killed, but it was finally decided to kill them here.

Trains from Lodz came into camp until about mid-month. Occasional trains came in from Theresienstadt, in France, late in the month and throughout October. Only 18,404 people over a thirty-day period; most of the crematoria were no longer needed. And most of their workers were no longer needed.

Melting Point

Did I just say 'only' 18,404 people? How numb I had become to the proceedings here. These poor unfortunate people were the last to be gassed and cremated at Auschwitz, with the last train arriving at the end of October.

I was still trying to think of some kind of good deed, some kind of atonement I could perform before the end. I had been careful to *inspect* the ovens occasionally, and had collected many more diamonds. I was sure I could find some way to return them to the families of the dead, or a synagogue, or something. I was determined to keep them from the camp administration. Not that this was my good deed, but I felt that it had to be done. It felt like, well, 'honest work'.

#

On the morning of Friday, September 22, Karl Bischoff pulled me aside. "This would be a good weekend to take a holiday," he said.

"Holiday? I couldn't go very far with all the restrictions now."

"What about your Aunt and Uncle's farm? Can't you go there for the weekend?"

"I suppose. But, why?" I asked.

Karl looked at me seriously and said, "This is the weekend of the first Special Action against the Sonderkommandos. But don't tell anyone."

Special Action was a phrase used a lot around the camp, and generally meant that people were to be gassed and incinerated. This weekend, then, the first of the Sonderkommandos would be killed. Most likely, they would take the Sonderkommandos from one of the four crematoria in camp, leaving the other teams intact. Karl was right; I didn't want to be around for that.

"Yes, maybe I can stay with my Aunt and Uncle this weekend," I said, nodding.

Birth and Rebirth

I thanked Karl Bischoff, who had become a good friend over the few years we had spent together. Time and time again, he had looked out for me, helping me through this horror of a job. In return I was loyal to him and did whatever I could to make his job easier. I was lucky to have him here, in this awful place.

That afternoon I borrowed a bicycle from camp and rode to Aunt Mary and Uncle Carl's house. I took with me a loaf of bread and some margarine, so that I wouldn't be too much of a burden on them. As it turned out, I needn't have worried. Mary and Carl had a good harvest that summer and had plenty of vegetables to eat. The bread was welcome, though.

Mary and Carl had a few farmhands living on their extended property. They were Poles who were slave laborers as much as any of the Poles in Auschwitz, but here their chances of surviving were much better. And their rations were much better too. Knowing that their fate could be much worse, they were unlikely to flee. Until the Russians came, of course. I could see the laborers in the distance working in the fields as I stood in the front yard of the farmhouse.

Inside the house was another servant; the one I asked Karl Bischoff to arrange for after the previous servant had ran off. She acted as cook and maid, and slept in the straw in the barn. She had a cold hard determination in her eyes, but nevertheless smiled briefly at me as I walked into the kitchen to set down my bread and margarine.

"Etta, set a place for my nephew, Albert," Mary said as I sat down at the table.

The servant girl, Etta, brought over a fork, bread knife, and cloth napkin.

\#

Melting Point

Back in Bodega Bay, Magda perked up. "Mom!" she shouted. I nodded and continued.

#

"Thank you," I said to the young girl. I noticed her square face and thin lips and thought how they sort of resembled the curve of a violin. She was short and stout, but about my age.

She nodded at me curtly. She wasn't really pretty, but she was young, and carried herself with a determination that I found attractive. She smelled faintly of onions, which I also found appealing.

Dinner was my bread with some boiled onions, potatoes, and cabbage in a nice broth.

"I don't know how long it will be, but the Russians are only a hundred and fifty miles away or so. There's not much time left," I said to my Aunt and Uncle, while sopping up the juices with my bread.

"For you there's not much time. For us, this is our home," Uncle Carl said grumpily. He took a large bite of boiled potato.

"I don't think they'll let you keep your servants, Uncle," I said earnestly. "They may want you to give back the land that was taken from your neighbors, too."

"Hah. My old neighbors are all dead; and good riddance to them. This is all *my* land now," Uncle said with defiance, stabbing another potato with his fork.

"Uncle, you are *German*. The Russians won't like that."

Uncle Carl pounded his fist on the table, "I'm a *Polish* citizen, this is *my* land, and that's that!"

I wasn't going to fight with him, so I changed the subject a little. "Things are starting to shut down at the camp where I work, now. We're thinking about moving equipment to the West," I said.

"Most of my vegetables go to your camp. I know what goes on there; it's disgusting."

Well, at least we agreed on that subject.

"What a waste of perfectly good food; feeding Jews. Bah."

I felt flushed. I didn't understand my Uncle at all.

Mary spoke up, "Carl, please, they *are* people."

"We've been killing hundreds of thousands of them there, Uncle," I said, a little angry. "And, it's not just the Jews, but Poles and lots of others." I nodded towards Etta, "She was there, and would probably have died if she hadn't come here."

Etta's eyes widened for a moment, and then she turned quickly away.

"Well, I'm sure most of them deserved what they got," Uncle Carl said grumpily. He looked at me with narrowed eyes, and asked "Are *you* killing them?"

I was shocked. "No! Not me. I work on maintaining the, uh, crematoria that incinerate the bodies after they are dead." It didn't sound like much of a distinction, but for me it was.

Aunt Mary blanched and said, "Is *that* what all that smoke is about? For several weeks this summer there was so much smoke from over there it looked like a volcano had gone off."

I said slowly and quietly, "That smoke was the entire Jewish population of Hungary." I looked hard over at my Uncle, inviting no more insensitive utterances.

Melting Point

Mary put her hand over her mouth. Carl blinked twice and looked away. Etta hurried back to the sink to busy herself with dishes.

I said quietly, "Early in the war with Russia, Germans killed one hundred thousand Russian prisoners of war in the camp. Off and on through the years, lots and lots of Russians have died there. That's why they won't appreciate Germans on Polish soil."

"But we *are* Polish and we are lowly farmers, not *executioners* and *murderers*," Uncle Carl said curtly. With that he stood up and left.

"Well, I've got some work to do too, dear," said Mary quietly, and she left as well.

I sighed and twiddled with my fork, unsure of what to do or say. Etta busied herself in the kitchen. After a few moments, I turned to her and opened my mouth to say something. I couldn't think of anything to say, though. I'm sorry? That doesn't amount to much, does it. I closed my mouth and studied my fork again.

While continuing to wash a dish, she suddenly shuddered and said to me, "That is a horrible place. I heard about the prison camp at Majdanek, that doesn't sound any better." She hesitated a moment, then nodded in the direction of the camp and asked me, "How many Poles have been killed there?"

I looked up at her, then down at the floor. "I, I don't know, a lot. Hundreds of thousands," I said. We were quiet after that; I didn't know what else to say. The sheer enormity of it; hundreds of thousands of people killed, and that was from only one of the many countries represented by victims there. I wanted to brighten her mood. "Have you heard about the resistance movement there?" I asked. "Asylum Strike, I think it's called."

Etta looked at me a moment, "I have heard of it," she said quietly, narrowing her eyes. "But never was part of it or knew anyone in it."

"I have heard of it too, but never saw any evidence of it in Birkenau," I shrugged.

"Maybe," Etta continued quietly, "That's because it started in the old camp. A long time ago; back when the camp was first put into use."

"Really? How did it get started?"

"No one knows," she said very quietly, almost conspiratorially. "Each group of prisoners passes down the story. It gives hope." Then she stiffened up and said, "I've already said too much. I will say no more about it."

#

I spent the rest of the weekend trying to help out around the farm. Being the end of autumn, there was still some harvesting to be done. I also spent some time helping Etta with cooking and doing her other chores; not so much because she needed the help as, well, I enjoyed being near her. We didn't talk any more about our pasts or what I did, only about food and the weather and other simple things. I liked that. I couldn't tell if she liked me, or even appreciated the help. But I liked being around her. She made me feel happy.

#

Early Monday morning I rode the bike back to the camp. When I got there, I could sense that there was something different. The guards were a little on edge, and the prisoners seemed more nervous than usual. The guards inspected my papers carefully. When I got to Karl Bischoff's offices, the few remaining workers were sitting around and talking. They stopped and looked up when I came in.

"Stohl, you picked a good weekend to be gone," said Erik, an architect, grumpily.

Karl Bischoff came out of his office and smiled weakly at me. "Have a nice weekend?"

Melting Point

"Yes, thanks," I said. I helped myself to some coffee. It was cold and bitter.

Erik filled me in. "Two hundred Sonderkommandos were killed this weekend. It was bad. They knew right away what was coming, of course, so they fought tooth and nail. It took many of the camp guards to deal with it. We were assigned guns and told to watch the rest of the prisoners to make sure they didn't escape." He guffawed, "Imagine me, with a gun."

"Be glad you weren't here, Albert," Karl Bischoff said. "We came close to having some breakouts. A couple of guards were badly hurt. Next time, it will be harder."

"Next time?" I asked, raising my eyebrows.

Karl said quietly, "There are six hundred and thirty left. A couple of weeks from now, another three hundred or so will be killed, probably starting with the ones living over Crema IV."

I winced and said, "That sounds really bad." Even though Crema IV was no longer running, the loft above the furnace room was used for Sonderkommando living quarters.

Erik shrugged and said, "Can't be helped, though. We're shutting this place down. We can't let the Sonderkommandos tell their stories to the world; they'll think we're monsters."

I raised my eyebrow at him. *We are monsters.* "We're witnesses, too."

Laughing dismissively, Erik said, "The thief doesn't tell the police who stole the jewels, eh?"

Karl coughed and changed the subject, "Albert, we're not going to be able to move the ovens, but we need to start salvaging parts where we can; why don't you start with tearing down the electrical systems in Crema V? See how much of the ventilation and wiring you can save."

"Crema V sounds like as good a place to start as any," I said. Crema IV had been shut down longer, but neither Crema IV nor Crema V were needed anymore.

"While you're at it," Karl said, smiling encouragingly, "See what you can do to salvage the hard-to-make metal parts; doors, hinges, pipes, whatever." He added gently, "The faster we tear this place down, Albert, the faster we can all go home."

If I was going to rip out wiring and metal parts to the ovens, I could use some help. At a minimum, I needed someone who could crawl around in the rafters. That meant someone small and agile. The thought came to me that if I employed one of the Sonderkommandos, I might be able to keep them away from the purge when it came. That seemed like just the kind of atonement I'd been looking for.

Crema IV, though no longer functioning as a crematorium, was home to many of the Sonderkommandos. The attic of the building was crammed with men and women. Still, living in the attic was preferable to living in the regular barracks. They ate better, and had more clean water. In Auschwitz, clean water either came from a bottle or had been boiled. Prisoners didn't get bottled water. Here at Crema IV, there was plenty of boiled water; a luxury that regular prisoners weren't given enough of.

It was easy finding the office of the SS man in charge of the Sonderkommandos living in Crema IV. He took up the largest office in the building, right next to the furnace room. The sign on the door read "August Brück."

"What can I do for you son?" August Brück stood and shook my hand. A large man with short black hair and piercing blue eyes, he gestured to a chair and I sat down.

Melting Point

"I need a helper, and I was hoping you could supply one," I said. "I need someone who is small and agile enough to do light work crawling around the rafters over at Crema V. I'll need him for several days."

August stroked his chin in thought. "We have lots of surplus people right now, what with the workload down and all."

I thought to myself, *we're running short on people to kill, you mean.*

August continued, "So you can have as many as you want. They don't have to come back, either."

I winced at that. "No, I just need the one, thanks."

August stood up and called out of the office in a commanding voice, "Foreman!"

A brutish looking man ran into the room, and August said, "This man needs a worker; someone who can crawl around the rafters." The man nodded and ran out again.

"He'll fetch someone for you," August said, standing. "Let me know if I can do anything else for you."

I waited outside August's office for just a minute or two before the foreman returned with a small, frail woman in tow. When they got to me he pushed her towards me. She was staring at the floor in front of her. Her hair was just beginning to grow back out, having been shaved when she entered the camp. She was wearing a long, dirty, faded, baggy dress, many sizes too large for her. It draped over her almost comically, and she had tied the bottom up so it wouldn't drag on the floor.

"Come with me," I said, and walked out of Crema IV and over to Crema V. She followed silently. When we got inside Crema V, I looked around to make sure no one was there. Crema V had been completely abandoned. I walked over to the fuse box and pulled the master power switch. The lights went out, leaving just sunlight filtering into the room.

"We're going to be taking down the wires, fans, lights, and switches," I said to her. She looked so pale and small that I couldn't imagine her doing much work at all. "We're going to dismantle the salvageable metal parts of the ovens." I put my hand under her chin and lifted it up gently. "Look at me." She did. "You and I are going to *destroy* this place."

Her eyes flickered around the room, taking in the ovens and gurneys. "Good," she said, and then looked at me, slightly frightened. "Sorry, sir," she said and looked down at the floor again.

"No, it *is* good." I pulled a screwdriver from my pocket and handed it to her. I led her over to the nearest light switch. "Start here. Remove the switch from the wall, and then unscrew the wires from the switch. Follow the wires up the wall, removing the fasteners as you go. Coil the wire up. When you are done with that one, move on to the next one you see. There should be a ladder somewhere around here you can use."

She nodded and set about unhooking wires and rolling them up, while I took inventory of the various metal parts of the ovens, and tried to figure out which ones were salvageable without tearing down a lot of brickwork. I definitely wanted to remove the oven doors with 'TOPF' emblazoned on them. The rest was much less important.

The young woman worked quietly and steadily, though not very quickly. That was alright by me, though, because I needed her to keep busy working until after the next purge, if I was to help her survive. I had to think. *What is my plan? Get her past the next purge, and then the next and the next and the next? That sounds awfully difficult. Maybe I can get her a job at my Uncle's farm. That will get her out of here for good. Then if she can hang on until the Russians arrive, she'll be safe.*

Melting Point

Sometimes, when she thought I wasn't looking, she stopped working, clutched her stomach and seemed to be gasping for air. She looked pale and weak. I thought that she might be hungry, or sick. It wouldn't do for my atonement to die of disease before being rescued by the Russians!

If she was to be my salvation for all I'd done here, I needed to make sure that she survived. On the other hand, helping prisoners by giving them food or medicine was a crime punishable by death. I couldn't be too overt in my help.

My first decision was to find out if she was sick. Sick prisoners are often put to death, but not always, so I needed to get her to trust me. Since we were alone, I decided the direct approach.

"You look pale, are you hungry or sick? Can I help you?"

Her eyes widened in fear and she shook her head violently. *So much for the direct approach.*

I put my hands out to calm her and shook my head, "My name is Albert Stohl. I'm an engineer here, and I'm not going to hurt you. In fact, I want to help you. I'm tired of all the killing in this camp and it is clear the Russians will be here soon. I really want to help you if I can. Do you need food, or a doctor?"

She looked into my eyes for a long time, the fear gradually subsiding, and then she narrowed her eyes and peered at me suspiciously. She asked, "You want to help me so I'll put in a good word for you with the Russians?"

"No, no," I shook my head; she didn't understand. "I just want to help you; I don't want to hurt anyone. I want to atone . . . " It sounded ridiculous now. Maybe she was right, this was silly. I can't redeem a million deaths by helping one woman. I sighed. "It sounds stupid now. I don't expect any help with the Russians. I just wanted to do something other than helping to kill people."

Birth and Rebirth

I slumped into a chair and put my head in my hands. *So, this too was doomed.* How foolish I'd been to think that some simple atonement would make any difference at all. How foolish to think I could save even *one* life. She continued to look at me, her eyes seeming to pierce through to my soul. After only a moment, I was ready to admit defeat and just go back to work. I sighed and stood up.

As I turned to leave, she quietly said "Hungry, mostly."

I looked back at her, brightened, and said, "That, I can fix."

I left her working there and went to the camp commissary and got some rolls and a bottle of water. I stuffed them into my pockets, telling the workers there I was starved. I went back to Crema V and gave the rolls and water to the woman. I shook my finger at her, "Now, not a word about this to anyone, right?"

She nodded as she greedily ate the rolls. We both knew we'd be in a lot of trouble if anyone found out. That made us bonded to each other in a small and strange way. While she ate, I asked her name. She just pointed to her tattoo and said, her mouth full of a roll, "No name, now, just the number."

It was illegal for prisoners to use their names. I waved my hand at her impatiently and said, "Yes, yes, I know. Tell me your name."

"Magdalena."

I nodded slowly, "That's a lovely name. Where are you from?"

"Budapest," she said, swallowing a mouthful of roll.

#

And so my atonement project proceeded in spite of my realization that it wasn't to be my salvation, and I treated it like an engineering task. Each day I came and got her from the living quarters at Crema IV and took her over to Crema V. I gave her some extra food and we talked, though she was reluctant

Melting Point

to say much. I learned that she had come in on one of the Hungarian transports and been one of the very few selected to live. Almost ninety percent of the people in those transports had been killed upon arrival. The rest had been selected for the various jobs in the camp. Magdalena had been assigned to the Sonderkommandos, a wretched job but one that provided a little more food and future than the average prisoner got. Until now.

In the meantime I talked with my Aunt to see if they would be willing to take on another servant or field hand. Mary seemed willing, but Uncle Carl would have none of it. Servants cost money; money for food, clothing, whatever. I told him I would use some of my pay to help feed her, but he just snorted at that idea. This did not bode well for my plan. If I couldn't get Magdalena a job on my Uncle's farm, I didn't have any way to save her from the purges.

After only ten days she seemed to be a little plumper, which I took to be a good sign. Mostly her body was hidden behind the baggy dress, so it was hard to tell. She was looking a little less pale, too. We had also made great progress removing the wiring, fans, fuses, ducting and other salvageable parts. There were still the oven muffles to be dismantled, but not much else. I had even taken the doors off and wrapped them for shipment somewhere. Anywhere away from the Russians would be fine with me.

On Thursday, October 5, though, she was looking pale again. After working only a short time, she came over to where I was working.

"I need some help," she said between heavy breaths, leaning against the oven wall.

I looked at her and she was looking pale again, and sweating. "Sure, what's wrong?"

"I'm . . . I'm having a baby," she said, wincing hard.

Having a baby.

Birth and Rebirth

Anywhere else on earth, that would be a wonderful event. In Auschwitz, it was a death sentence. The rule in camp was that either the baby died in birth, or both the mother and baby would be killed. Women prisoner doctors assisted most of the births, and because of the 'baby or both' rule, most babies born in Auschwitz did not survive more than a few moments after birth. Better to save the mother alone, than to save neither mother nor baby, went the common thinking.

My atonement project is having a baby. How could this have happened? I had been working with her for a couple of weeks now, and it was all in danger of coming unraveled over a baby. I hadn't noticed because of the baggy clothes and her otherwise emaciated state.

"I'll get you a doctor," I said.

"No!" Magdalena was in pain, but she was also worried.

"You need help, and I can't provide it," I said in exasperation.

She looked at me with pleading eyes, "My husband and children are dead. My parents are dead. This baby is all that I have left. If a doctor comes, it won't survive."

"But, I don't know anything about delivering a baby."

"I do. All you have to do is help. Please," she implored.

This was crazy. "Let's say the baby is fine – what are you going to do with it? You can't take it back to the barracks."

She started crying, and looked desperate. "I don't know. I just know that this baby *has* to survive. It's all I have left."

I took a deep breath. *Now what?* Help her have the baby, fine. But let the baby live? If we're caught, I'll be put to death for helping! *This was crazy.* She was desperate and not thinking clearly. But, on the other hand, if we could give the baby to someone outside the camp; maybe someone in the

Melting Point

underground. There was the prisoner underground, everyone knew that. Maybe they have contacts on the outside.

"Do you have contacts outside the wire? Maybe someone in the underground that can help? You can't take care of the baby. We have to give the baby to someone else, at least until the camp is liberated by the Russians." *Well, everyone knows the Russians are coming, why not give her some hope?*

She thought a moment, wincing in pain, and then shook her head and said, "Well, there's 'Asylum Strike,' and they have been attributed with many acts of resistance. But I don't know how to contact them."

"Yes, I have heard of 'Asylum Strike' but how would we make contact?" I said doubtfully.

Magdalena briefly looked at me suspiciously, as if wondering if I would betray the resistance group, but then she winced in pain and started to cry. "I don't know. I only know that there's a story about the group. There's supposed to be an old carving in a tree over in Auschwitz One with the initials 'A. S.'. It's right in the shadow of the commandant's house. People say 'Asylym Strike' started there in Auschwitz One, maybe from the start of the camp. It gives people courage. But I don't know how to contact them."

A. S.? Carved in a tree in the original camp, by the commandant's house? A. S.; Albert Stohl.

I carved those initials in the tree years ago before the war. It seemed like an eternity ago, when my brother was alive, the world was at peace, and we had our whole lives before us. Now, a resistance movement has sprung up, rallying around my initials. They must have thought hard to assign meaning to the initials. *A.S. – 'Asylum Strike.'* Was it just the hope of doomed prisoners to believe that there was a resistance movement? Grasping at any hope, they invent the 'Asylum Strike' resistance group as a reason to cling to life? I didn't know and, at the moment, couldn't worry about it. I said, "Well, let's deliver the baby and then see what we can do."

#

The birth remains a blur in my memory. I remember lots of blood and lots of crying. Magdalena did most of the work, but I clamped the umbilical cord with pairs of vice grips and cut in between them with wire cutters. It was like cutting a rubber hose. All the while, I was worrying about what to do with the baby if it survived.

When it was over, I went back to Crema IV and told August Brück that I needed Magdalena for the night to do some additional work. He gave me an insolent grin and winked at me. I just nodded at him and grinned. Let him think what he wants. When I went back to the otherwise deserted Crema V, Magdalena was there with her newborn infant. They were both sleeping. I took a bucket of water and washed the blood from the concrete floor down the big drain in the corner of the room.

What was I going to do? I had no clue how to contact the 'underground,' let alone any people outside the wire. I can't let the baby stay in the camp, and I can't let Magdalena stay in Crema V with her for more than another few hours. She has to get back to her usual routine. I had to think, and think hard. The more I thought about the 'Asylum Strike' movement, the more I realized it was probably just dreamed up out of hope. In any case, I couldn't walk around asking people where the resistance folks were – that was crazy too.

By dawn the next morning, Friday, I had my answer. I'll take the baby to Aunt Mary. She'll have to take care of the baby for a short time, and then I'll get Magdalena a job at their farm somehow. I proposed the idea to Magdalena.

"I don't want to leave my baby – she needs me," she said, looking worried.

Melting Point

"It will only be for a couple of days, and then you'll be working on their farm and be with your baby again," I said, reasonably.

After some discussion, she relented. "Well, that is probably the best we can do," she said, looking at her child, a girl. "Please take good care of her; she's all I have."

"I will," I said.

She furrowed her brow and spoke softly to the baby. "I will always love you. If I don't see you soon, I'll be waiting for you by the gates of heaven. Then we can be together for eternity." She kissed her and worriedly handed the naked baby to me, tears streaming down her face.

"I promise you that you will both survive, and will be reunited very soon," I said. *What have I gotten myself into?*

I bundled up the tiny girl in a blanket and managed to fit the blanket and baby into a large satchel. I made sure enough air got through the satchel's lining so the baby wouldn't suffocate. I borrowed a bike from the camp, and set out in the cool of the early morning. The baby slept most of the way to the farm, but woke up and then cried for the last couple of miles.

#

Aunt Mary was not at *all* pleased.

"Albert, what are you doing? Where did you get this baby?" Aunt Mary, looking very concerned, said loudly over the wailing as she held up the baby. "Is it yours?"

"No, not exactly," I said, shaking my head. "It belongs to one of the prisoners. It would have been killed if it stayed at the camp. She asked me to take it until she can come and care for it."

Aunt Mary blustered for a moment as if to refuse to take it, and then looked into the scrunched up face of the baby, its face bright red. With a sigh and then a loud 'humph,' she took the baby into the kitchen and handed it to Etta, who had come to see what was going on. Mary got the baby some goat's milk, dipped her finger into it and then stuck her finger into the baby's mouth. The baby quieted down and drank hungrily from the fingertips as first Mary, and then Etta fed it tiny bits of milk over and over.

"Where is the mother?" asked Mary. She was quieter now that the baby had stopped crying.

"She's still at the camp. She's the one I had asked you about taking on as a farmhand, auntie."

As the recollection came over Mary's face, she slowly shook her head and said, "But Carl will never agree to have another farmhand here. He told you that, Albert."

I looked at the two women helplessly and said, "But what can I do? If she stays in Auschwitz she will be killed. I can pay for the mother's food. Just let her stay for a little while – the Russians will be here in a month or two anyway."

"I hear a baby!" Uncle Carl had returned. "What's going on? What's that about the Russians? Are you on about that again, Albert?"

"This baby is from a woman in the camp," I said reasonably. "I just need you to take care of this baby and her mother until the Russians arrive. I'll pay for her keep."

Carl looked at the baby as though it were a goat patty. "We're not running a nursery here for your convenience, Albert. I have enough trouble keeping track of the hands as it is, without more. And a baby! That is totally out of the question."

Melting Point

Mary said to Carl, with a private wink to me, "Well, let's let them stay the night, anyway, and then we can figure out what to do tomorrow. Etta, do you mind taking care of her for the afternoon?"

Etta had been feeding the baby and bouncing her up and down. The baby looked quite content. Etta looked content too. "What's her name?"

I said, "Her mother hasn't named her yet."

Carl peered more carefully at the baby and said with a trace of disdain, "Well, it looks healthy, anyway. Don't want to be spreading disease."

Mary smiled at me and raised her eyebrows. Carl might be softening.

#

After dinner it was Carl who sat with the sleeping baby in his lap as he rocked in front of the fire. He spoke softly to me, "It's not that I'm trying to be cruel, Albert, but we just don't have room for another hand, and one with a baby wouldn't get much done."

"It would only be for a short while," I said.

"Yes, I know, only until the Russians come," Carl said ruefully.

Mary suddenly thought of something. "What if one of the other farms around here needs someone? Maybe we can ask around and find work for the mother somewhere else."

"Someone who can take a mother and baby?" Carl looked skeptical. "That's asking a lot."

"All right, it's settled, we'll take the mother just as long as it takes to get her a new place to work," said Mary with a broad nod to me. "This weekend Etta and I can care for the baby. Albert will return to the camp tomorrow and bring the mother over as soon as he can."

I breathed a big sigh of relief. Now, all I had to do was to convince Karl Bischoff to let me take Magdalena away. This plan might actually work!

Birth and Rebirth

Asylum Strike

This time, Magda had a look of fascination on her face. The winds had picked up in Bodega Bay, but the rain had stopped completely.

"Am I named after this woman you were saving?" Magda asked.

"You have to wait and see," I said mischievously.

"Oh, you! Don't keep me in suspense like this!"

"Alright, alright," I said, laughing and holding up my hands in mock defeat. "We did name you after this woman. Her courage impressed us."

"Well, where is she now, did she make it?"

"That, you *do* have to wait for," I said.

I went to the kitchen to get some coffee; I needed some energy to get me through the rest of the story. The coffee was cold, but I microwaved a cup.

Tony poured himself a cup of the cold coffee too, and waited to put it in the microwave after mine. "That Bischoff fellow was really your friend, wasn't he."

"Yes, he was, Tony," I said, removing the coffee cup from the microwave.

Melting Point

"It's just so weird to think of someone who was in charge of all those ovens and gas chambers as *nice*." Tony shook his head as he placed his coffee in the microwave and shut the door. "I imagined maniacal fanatics, people you couldn't even talk to."

"Oh, we had those too," I said, laughing. "That Irma Griese woman I met at Höss' birthday party was like that. She loved to be cruel to prisoners, and she fits the image of the fanatical Nazi."

After taking his hot cup out of the microwave, Tony and I walked back into the living room.

"I'm glad to see mom in the story now," Magda said to me. "And you did save her from the camp, after all. You got her to your Aunt and Uncle's farm to work there. You saved her life."

"Yes, I did that, and I think it is one of the reasons your mother liked me," I said. Trying to lighten the mood, I added "That, and my boyish good looks." After some chuckles, I said, "Now let's finish this story, shall we?"

#

I had set the final parts of my great plan for salvation into motion. The baby was safe at my Aunt and Uncle's farm, and I would bring the mother there as well. By now I knew that this might not be *my* salvation, but maybe it would be Magdalena's and her baby's. My luck just had to hold out a little longer.

That Saturday, October 7, 1944, I rode the bike back to camp. As I got closer, I heard sirens from within the camp. At the camp itself, the gates were closed and the guards had strict instructions not to let anyone in or out.

"What's going on?" I asked the young guard at the gate.

"Some sort of an uprising. It's been busy here all morning. They don't tell me much, though. But no one goes in or out until it's over."

"Well, guess I'll just go into town and have some beer," I said, more cheerfully than I felt. The guard gave me a look as if he would like to go too, but he was stuck at his post.

I rode down to the town and over to the Hotel Herz. There was a nice bar there, where a German could get some decent beer. The talk around the bar was about the camp. No one knew what was going on, but everyone knew that something *big* was happening. I didn't like the sound of that, and hoped that Magdalena was keeping out of sight.

As night fell and no word came that the camp was opening, a number of us displaced workers asked for a room at the hotel. There weren't enough rooms to accommodate us all, so people doubled and tripled up in a room. I didn't get a room, but got to sleep on a sofa in the lobby, a wool blanket my only companion. I tossed and turned for a while.

I had gotten the crazy plan this far. I hadn't counted on a baby, but so far that part had worked itself out. I got my aunt and uncle to sort-of agree to take Magdalena; now I just needed to *get* her there. I wanted to get her out of the camp Sunday if I could. The faster I got her out of there, the better. Hopefully Karl Bischoff will help me get her assigned to the farm.

As it grew later, I found myself staring up at the ceiling. The old hotel's paint was peeling in places, and the ornate chandelier was covered with dust, its oil-burning lamps long dark for lack of fuel. With no excess fuel for heating, the October chill worked its way through my blanket. Now that I was so close to finishing my plan, was this going to atone for anything I had done, anything I had participated in?

No. It's just the right thing to do. I suppose that, in and of itself, is a start.

I tossed and turned on the lumpy sofa, worrying about Magdalena, the Russians, my brother, the war, and my future until I fell into an exhausted sleep a couple of hours later. I woke up late on Sunday morning, and then only

Melting Point

because of the people talking and smoking in chairs near me in the lobby. I went over to the restaurant at the hotel, only to find from other workers there that the camp was still closed. This wasn't looking very good.

In the meantime all I could do was wander around the town of Auschwitz. Still called 'Oswiecim' by the natives, this area was still the pretty, medieval town with a central square that I remembered. I could still recall the birds devouring the remains of Herman's and my lunch on the bench in the square all those long years ago. As I sat back down on that bench and looked around, I realized with great sadness that no one would ever again think of this as just another pretty town. Its name will be forever associated with mass death and the worst that humans have to offer each other. I walked from shop to shop, the cold fall breezes blowing through my hair, trying to recall how I felt the first time I had been here at this town. Everywhere I looked, though, there were signs of how we had changed this town. Signs all over told people what they could do, when they could do it, how to act respectfully to Germans, and so on. Germans had redesigned part of the city to house the civilian engineers and scientists who would work up at the synthetic rubber factory nearby at Monowitz, now called 'Auschwitz III.' They had *cleaned up* the town of its old, its poor, the Hassidic Jews, and other *undesirable* inhabitants. The rest were here to serve Germans in some form or another. Shopkeepers, hotel owners, street sweepers, they were all here to make German lives more livable. That's all. I shuddered at the magnitude of what we had done. I shuddered at what the Russians would think of us when they got here.

#

On Monday, we were finally allowed back into the camp. The guards were nervous and the civilian workers were ordered to see their supervisors. I headed towards Karl Bischoff's offices. On the way, I passed by many dead prisoners splayed on the ground, clouds of small black flies already buzzing around their heads. I saw one wall with 'A.S.' etched into it. I shuddered at

Asylum Strike

that. When I got to the architectural offices, there were a few of Bischoff's men there, including the architect Erik. Erik handed me a pistol and some bullets.

"Carry this at all times, loaded," said Erik. "You can't trust any of the prisoners anymore. Be careful. And be glad you weren't here," Erik said with a shudder.

Karl Bischoff came out of his office with one of the construction foremen. There were now seven men in the office, most of the remaining staff he had. They were all unshaven and looked tired. Their clothes looked rumpled, as if they had slept in them. On their desks were strewn water bottles, dishes with half eaten sandwiches, and bowls with some soup in them. Apparently these men had lived here in the office for the weekend.

"What happened?" I asked of the group.

Karl Bischoff slumped down into a chair near me. He put his feet onto the nearest desk, the dried mud from his boots dropping clumps of dirt onto the desktop.

He sighed, "Where do I start? Apparently, the Sonderkommandos in Crema IV had been smuggling in explosives from the Monowitz construction site and storing them in the broken Crema IV ovens. Saturday, one of the German Kapos found out about it. The Sonderkommandos killed him and detonated the explosives. Then they started attacking SS men with axes, hammers, bricks, anything they could get their hands on. They set fire to the building. There were all those bales of hair drying up in the attic, which burned really well."

The hair had come from the heads of prisoners, and would have eventually been woven into socks, blankets, fuses, and other products. Karl cleared his throat, took his feet off his desk, stood up and walked over to a bottle of mineral water and took a swig from it. He offered me some. I hated the taste of the mineral water, myself, but the tap water came from the river and

Melting Point

was still polluted. The prisoners drank it after it was boiled, but I wouldn't touch the stuff.

"No thanks," I said, turning down his offer.

Karl swallowed another mouthful of water and said, "The Sonderkommandos over in Crema II, where some of the ovens were operating, heard the explosion. I guess that was a signal to start a planned revolt. August Brück happened to be over in Crema II at the time, which was unfortunate for him. Apparently they opened one of the doors from a running oven and shoved him in."

I winced at that thought. It's hard enough to get near to a hot oven door when the ovens are going, I can't even imagine what it must have felt like to be pushed into the oven. I hoped he was dead or unconscious at the time.

Karl took another swig of water and swished it around in his mouth before swallowing. "They killed a couple of men that way. They beat another guard to death, and then made a mass escape."

Karl set the nearly empty bottle down and returned to his seat. "They tore down the fence between Crema II and the Women's camp and broke out and ran. They eventually barricaded themselves in a small barn a mile or two from here. The guards were shooting prisoners as fast as they could. They killed everyone in the barn. The guards have been on a rampage ever since."

Karl sighed and rubbed his eyes. "At least two thirds of the Sonderkommandos were killed. Maybe two dozen guards."

That would be over 400 men and women. Was Magdalena one of them? I felt flushed and I suddenly had a terrible headache.

"Can you imagine it?" Erik said with a shudder. "Being shoved into a hot oven, most likely while still alive? Those barbarians."

#

I never saw Magdalena again. I don't know if she was involved in the revolt or not, though she certainly had the ability and motive for it. She may have just been a victim of the reprisals afterwards. In all the confusion, it would have been impossible to tell. I wonder if she took solace in the fact that her baby was safe. Or, did she really know that the baby *was* safe? And for that matter, *was* the baby safe? I had saddled my Aunt and Uncle with an infant and no mother to take care of her.

At the first opportunity I went back to the farm to tell them the bad news. I was surprised by Uncle Carl's reaction. He said quietly, "Well, I wasn't too excited by taking the mother, but none of this is the baby's fault. She's welcome here."

Apparently he had grown to like the baby over the past several days. It helped that Etta had taken most of the burden of caring for the child.

Etta said to me, "You should name the child."

"Me?"

"Well, with her mother and father gone, now, you are the closest thing she has to family," Etta said.

"You have become her surrogate mother," I said. "Etta, perhaps *you* should name her."

Etta looked off into space for a moment and then said, "Magdalena. Let's call her by her mother's name. The name may be all she has left of her real family. Since you saved her, she should be Magdalena Stohl."

The Russians are Coming!

Magda let out a loud scream of shock and disbelief. "*I'm* the baby! I'm the daughter of Magdalena!"

Tony, Amanda, and Tom all looked stunned.

"Yes, Magda," I said with great sadness. "Your real mother was Magdalena, a Jewish woman from Budapest. That's about all I know about her."

"Then, you're not my father," Magda shook her head. "And mom wasn't... wasn't..." She stifled a sob.

"We both loved you very much. Like our own daughter. Really, Magda..." I said, reaching for her with some desperation.

"I know," Magda said, pulling away, with some sadness and disappointment. "I can't **believe** you and mom never told me this." Magda sighed, "Please, just finish the story, Albert."

I didn't know what else to say to her. Maybe she'll calm down a bit by the end. I continued the story.

#

Life and death went on at Auschwitz and throughout Europe. That Tuesday, the tenth of October, Soviet troops captured the city of Riga. There was a camp there as well. The next Saturday, the Allies liberated Athens,

The Russians Are Coming!

Greece. Around camp on that same day, a week after the revolt, we had the 200 remaining Sonderkommandos at work tearing down the walls of Crematorium IV. The walls already had holes in them from the explosion, but the brickwork was still stubborn and took a fair amount of effort to break down. I directed workers to take out some of the remaining salvageable metal parts of the ovens for shipment west. The Sonderkommandos had once been on increased rations, but now were back on the meager regular rations. Because of this, the heavy work of tearing down the walls caused dozens of workers to die of exhaustion.

#

There were more escapes from the camp, a symbol of the general breakdown of order. Part of the problem was that SS men were transferring out in large numbers to be in the SS army. Some left because we needed the men in the army, and some because they didn't want to be the ones left here when the Russians arrived. Another problem was that many of us were trying to figure out what we were going to do when the end came; guards looted what they could, and some even felt compelled to do good deeds, probably in exchange for letters of support from the prisoners. For example, late in October one of the guards tried to smuggle out a number of prisoners under the guise of taking a load of laundry out of camp. He wasn't careful, though, and another man reported him. The four Poles and an Austrian were taken out of the laundry chest, tortured and hanged. The guard was sent before a brief SS tribunal and shot.

Crema V had been stripped of its metal parts by now and I felt it was no longer safe to keep my precious stones in one of the crevices of an oven there, so I hid them just outside the camp in a secluded outcropping of rocks. It was in a clump of trees by the side of the road, so that I could pretend I was just 'taking a leak' when I went to visit the pouch of diamonds.

Melting Point

#

At the very end of October, the very last trainload of prisoners to be gassed at Auschwitz arrived from Theresienstadt. After that, Cremas II and III were used only occasionally as prisoners who had been at the camp for some time died or were killed. But, there were no more trains.

#

Late in November, Heinrich Himmler officially ordered all of the gas chambers and ovens demolished, and the ashes dug up from their pits and removed for scattering elsewhere. The Russians were close, and it was time to pretend nothing ever happened here. Cremas II and III were taken offline and we set about destroying the buildings. Given that there wasn't a lot of time before the Russians were to arrive, it was decided to blow up the buildings rather than remove the bricks and scatter them. We put 100 women to work over in Crema III making holes in the bricks for the dynamite. It was slow work, and as time went on we added more women to the task. When they finished with Crema III they went on to Crema II, and finally Crema V. I also supervised some details of women removing the last of the metal oven parts, ductwork, and wires.

There were two kinds of pits in the camp; those used to bury ashes from the ovens, and those used to burn bodies during the recent Hungarian operation. By early December, we had teams of men and women digging up the ash pits and dumping some of the ashes into the river and scattering the rest over the nearby forest floor. The pits that had bodies in them had not all been covered properly, and so other teams of prisoners were filling in and leveling off those pits, and planting trees on them to hide them. Still more prisoners were leveling off the ground on which Crema IV had stood, where we had done a more thorough job of removing the building. Soon, most other work in

The Russians Are Coming!

Auschwitz had come to a halt as more and more prisoners were assigned to the task of erasing the evidence of our guilt.

#

In Mid December, the 'Battle of the Bulge' started in the west, with a million German men and fresh equipment. This was exhilarating for us because of the renewed hope it gave, but when it collapsed around Christmas due to the sheer power of the Allied forces, we became gloomier than before. It didn't help that the Allies continued to bomb nearby industrial areas seemingly at will.

#

Christmas was bleak. I spent it with Albert, Mary, Etta, and baby Magdalena, but it was a somber occasion. The Russians were just a few weeks away now, and occasionally you could hear the very distant rumble of bombs and artillery. The front was uneven, and in places the Russians were fairly close. If Etta was happy that liberation was near, she didn't show it. I think she realized that the Russians were likely to be cruel to the Poles too, given that they had invaded half of Poland back in 1939.

#

In the first half of January, we finished removing all the parts we could from the Cremas. Most of the parts managed to get onto trains bound for Gross-Rosen, another camp to the west. Whether they would ever be able to make use of them depended on how long Germany held out. Not all the parts made it out, because rail traffic became much more sporadic as the Allied planes destroyed our tracks, junctions, bridges, engines, and everything else it takes to make a railroad work. By mid-January, rail service had been completely destroyed in our area.

#

Melting Point

By January 17th, it was just about over. As the Russians captured Warsaw, we made our last roll calls at Auschwitz. 67,012 prisoners were counted. That didn't include the few thousand who were too sick to report to roll calls. It would be a staggering number of people if it weren't for the fact that we had killed maybe 30 or 40 times that number of people over the years. Our able-bodied prisoners had spent their last few weeks destroying barracks and finishing the preparation for destruction of the Cremas. They had been filling in pits and planting trees on them; digging up ashes and removing them; leveling off ground where buildings had stood; burning papers and records from our offices; and all kinds of other cleanup efforts.

On January 18th long columns of prisoners started on a march out of camp towards Germany. Columns marched out all that day and the next day, each with a small number of camp guards to watch over them. There were very few guards for each group, but the prisoners were so emaciated, weak, and sickly that they wouldn't cause much trouble. The plan was to get to the nearest functioning rail junction and place them on trains for their journey to other camps. As it turned out, they had to march to the Polish border town of Gleiwitz, a journey of about three days. The weather was very cold and there was snow on the ground. The prisoners had thin clothes and shoes. About a quarter of the prisoners died en-route from the long march, their bodies left by the side of the road. A total of 66,000 prisoners left over those two days, leaving a large number of very sick and a few healthy prisoners behind.

I stayed behind with a small group of men and prisoners left to finish the demolition of the camp. On January 20, Corporal Perschel and other men of Karl Bischoff's command detonated the explosives that had been placed in the walls of Cremas II and III. What was left was a jumble of concrete and brick. Karl Bischoff and I turned our attention to the final work on preparing Crema V for demolition. At the same time, prisoners were destroying the various sheds and huts we had used, such as 'The Little White House.'

The Russians Are Coming!

Corporal Perschel's men next turned their attention to the burning of the storehouses. When prisoners got off the arriving trains, their luggage was collected and taken to a special area of the camp to be sorted for re-use. In addition, when prisoners disrobed in preparation for going into the showers or the gas chambers, all their belongings were gathered and also taken to this special warehouse area of the camp. The items were then sorted, categorized, and shipped out on trains back to Germany or other destinations. For example, Germans who lost their homes due to the bombings received new clothes and other personal items for their use; items that came from facilities like ours. Arriving prisoners that were to stay at the camp and not be gassed immediately still had to relinquish their personal items, only to receive others from prisoners who had arrived before them. In a great tragic-comic opera, prisoners gave up their own clothes and shoes only to get other people's clothes and shoes, often ones that were ridiculously proportioned. For example, Magdalena was wearing the baggiest of clothes when I knew her. That was not uncommon.

Over the years, then, thousands of tons of personal effects had been processed and shipped out of the camp. When the Hungarians arrived, there were an overwhelming number of personal items to be sorted, cataloged, and shipped. The SS and prisoners in charge of that effort had fallen behind, their work load being so great. Now the rail line into the camp had been destroyed, and it was very difficult to get materials out. As a result of all this, the storehouses were still fairly full.

There were thirty-five large warehouses, filled with all kinds of loot. Clothes, shoes, glasses, suitcases, pictures, silverware; anything people could bring in a suitcase.

The warehouses were located to the North East behind the location of Crema's IV and V. The SS decided that they would take the few days that were left to make one final pass through the warehouses, get the most valuable of the

Melting Point

loot, and then let Perschel and his men burn the buildings. So, starting on the day that the majority of prisoners had left the camp, they took a few hundred prisoners and went through the items in the warehouses. What was valuable enough to save and easily load onto a truck was shipped out. The rest, the vast majority, was left in the warehouses. When they had finished with one warehouse, Perschel set it ablaze and went onto the next warehouse. Plumes of white and black smoke went up from the wooden buildings as their contents burned.

Because of the limited number of trucks that could be spared, the SS men had to be very selective, and therefore spent too much time on each warehouse. They managed to sift through only about five or six warehouses per day, coming up with a truckload or two in each warehouse they picked over. Some warehouses burned fairly quickly, but others burned slowly because of the lack of fuel and the snow that dampened the wooden buildings.

The last day for the camp in German hands was January 26, 1945. On that day, we finally blew up Crema V. I was there to witness that, but I was very nervous because you could clearly hear from the not-too-distant explosions that the Russians were very close. On this day, too, the SS men set fire to the last of the warehouses. Bad weather caused the warehouses to be stubborn and not burn as fast as desired, and so when the Russians arrived the next day, they found six of the thirty-five warehouses still fairly intact.

Years later I would find out that in those six warehouses, or about 16 percent of the total, were such items as 836,000 women's coats; 348,000 men's suits; 43,000 pairs of shoes; 14,000 carpets; 14,000 pounds of human hair; and tens of thousands of glasses, toothbrushes, shaving kits and so much more.

At the time, though, I didn't worry about warehouses; I was more worried about getting out of camp. We had finished destroying Crema V and I had the pistol given to me after the revolt. I decided against taking much else,

The Russians Are Coming!

as we had a long walk to the trains as well. Karl Bischoff and his few remaining men and I joined the group of men gathering near the front of the camp in preparation to leave. A few hundred prisoners, the last to march out of the camp, had just started to leave with a small team of guards. I was feeling nervous and stressed from the closeness of the Russians, and I was anxious to get going.

#

From the other side of the camp we suddenly heard a lot of gunfire.

"The Russians!" I said with great alarm.

"No, no Albert, that's too close, it's the guards," Karl said reassuringly. After a moment, he stopped, looked down at the ground, and said quietly, "It must be the Sonderkommandos."

The guards were apparently killing the last of the Sonderkommandos, some 200 women who had been left behind to help out to the end. Their bodies joined the hundreds of others lying on the ground.

It was finally over for Auschwitz. A long column of prisoners, guards, and contractors like me walked west away from camp. We left some 7,000 people behind, mostly women, too sick to move. Whereas the Sonderkommandos were witnesses to the *machinery* of death, these prisoners, if they survived, were just witnesses to the death. That seemed to make a difference to the SS, somehow.

The rail lines were down and we weren't sure how far we would have to walk. The earlier groups had walked for days; I hoped our group wouldn't have to walk as far. Though, I had a different destination in mind for myself; I needed to take the baby to safety. I also needed to make my aunt and uncle take refuge from the Russians, even if they didn't flee back to Germany with me. The air was cold, and the road was slushy. I carried my pistol for safety, and I stopped by the clump of trees to gather my small pouch of diamonds to

Melting Point

take with me. It occurred to me for the first time that the diamonds might help me survive; they were 'portable wealth.'

"No, I must return them, or donate them, or something," I said angrily to myself. It was frustrating, because it was clear that there was almost no one to return the diamonds *to*.

When I got to the junction in the road that would take me to my aunt and uncle's farm, I stopped Karl Bischoff and shook his hand.

"I'm going to my aunt and uncle's farm, see if I can talk some sense into them about leaving," I said.

Karl took my hand in his, looked me in the eye and said, "Goodbye, Albert. Take good care of yourself. I'm proud to have worked with you."

"I was honored to serve with you, sir," I said in reply. Then I lowered my head and looked at the ground, at a loss for words. I looked up again and our eyes met. Karl nodded at me and walked away.

I left the column of people, including those I had worked with for years now, and headed towards my aunt and uncle's farm. With a last wave goodbye and a promise to myself to try to catch up with the column sometime later, I walked quickly down the center of the road, my boots squishing in mud and dirty snow. My shorter leg was a little stiff today from the cold and I limped rather more than usual. The cold air made my breath freeze up on my face, and my nose felt as if it was frozen. There were some clouds out and the sun was beginning to set.

Now away from the crowd, the distant sound of cannons was more pronounced. Somehow when I was with people, the distant thunder of the cannons hadn't bothered me as much. Now, they were a reminder that the Russians, and the end, were drawing near.

I mumbled under my breath, "Damn Russians."

The Russians Are Coming!

When I finally reached the gate to my aunt and uncle's farm, I paused to gather my breath and collect my thoughts. What could I say to my aunt and uncle to make them leave their home, their farm, their life? They must leave, or the Russians will surely kill them. And they must leave *soon*. It was getting dark, and we should all leave tonight. By morning there would be soldiers here.

I felt through my coat pocket for the thousandth time since leaving the main road and the stream of people. Pistol. Pouch. It was a nervous habit.

I walked through the gate and crunched through the deeper snow on the walkway to the old farmhouse. The farmhouse, barn, and shed stood like silent sentinels in the vast white fields of snow. The only light for a mile around was coming from the farmhouse. That didn't bode well for us. Reaching the steps, I trudged up the stairs and banged my boots on the iron scraper outside the entranceway to shake off snow and mud. The door opened, and my Aunt Mary came out onto the porch.

"Albert, what on earth are you doing here? We weren't expecting you!" She opened the door for me and let me move by her, into the house. She helped me take off my coat, and hung it up near the fire to dry. The room was stuffy and warm, smelling of wood smoke and greasy sausages.

"I'm sorry, Auntie, but I had to come," I said. "The Russians are close, and it's time for us to go." I looked at my Uncle Carl, sitting at the dinner table, and added, "Time for us *all* to go."

Uncle Carl shook his head and said, as much to convince himself as us, "They won't bother us. I'm just a lowly Polish farmer. They'll need farmers. They won't bother us."

I felt my frustration grow. I didn't want to confront him, and wanted to keep my tone calm, but I *had* to convince them to leave. I said, reasonably, "You're not Polish. You're German. They won't care about anything but

Melting Point

revenge now. You and Mary are in great danger. You can come back later when things have calmed down, but you *must* leave with me. Tonight!"

Uncle Carl grew red in the face and pounded his fist on the table as he said, "This is *my* home. This is *my* farm. I am Polish with German ancestors. I had nothing to do with this awful war. I had nothing to do with all that rubbish *you* were involved in. It's *you* they are hunting, not me! I'm not leaving!"

My face flushed, and I was unsure what to do. I felt stung by what my uncle had said, but there was truth in it. I opened my mouth to protest, but Aunt Mary shushed me and said, "We'll be all right here, dear. You and the baby must leave. They won't like the baby."

For the first time, I became aware of Etta holding the infant in a dark corner of the room. Etta smiled up at me, I could feel my heart melting and I smiled back at her and the baby. The baby was thin and frail, with her perfectly round face and scrunched up nose. She looked like a thin bulldog puppy, as she looked up at me with her large round eyes.

"Etta, are you and the baby prepared to leave tonight?" I asked. "It will be a long walk, so we should bring plenty of supplies."

"I am ready, Albert," Etta said in her Polish-accented German. "And Magda here was born ready to leave this place."

"Good. Let's pack some things," I said. I turned around and faced across the small room to where my aunt had sat down at the table with Uncle Carl. With a pleading look and some desperation, I said, "*Please* come with us."

Uncle Carl's face softened. He took Mary's hand, and said to me, "Take good care of the baby. This is our home, and we'll be just fine here. The three of you must leave, though. Magda must live her life elsewhere. That's all that matters now." A long tear came from Mary's eye. She nodded at me and tried to smile, as the tear slid down her cheek.

278

The Russians Are Coming!

They knew they were in serious peril, but chose to stay here and brave it out rather than fleeing and trying to come back home later. It was bravery I had seen before among victims at the camp. Bravery I had never felt.

Etta packed some things in a knapsack and I got together some food for the journey, with Mary's help. I wasn't sure how I felt about a long journey with Etta, whom I barely knew, and an orphaned baby. I needed Etta to care for the baby, as I knew nothing about babies. Surely, though, I can find somewhere for the two of them to stay once I get over into Germany. Then I can go back to work in Erfurt. If we can't win the war, then I'm sure we'll negotiate a peace and I can get on with my life.

Mary called from the other room, "Albert, I hear something!"

I rushed into the front room and then stopped and listened. I heard a distant snapping, almost like twigs breaking. I knew at once what it was, and could feel the blood draining from my face and my stomach tightening.

"That's gunfire. The Russians are near. It's too late to leave now, they'll see us against the snowy fields," I said, running my hand through my hair.

"Out in the barn the door to the root cellar is hidden under hay," Carl said quickly. "Get in there and wait for them to leave. Mary, go with them and cover the door back over. I'll douse the lights."

Everyone jumped into action. I pulled my boots and coat back on, grabbed the knapsack, checked again for the pistol and the pouch. I followed Mary and Etta, now with Magda wrapped in a shawl, outside. I saw that there were already lots of footprints in the snow from earlier in the day, so our new footprints wouldn't be suspicious. The last of the day's light was quickly fading.

Reaching the barn, the four of us went inside. A lone goat looked up at us and bleated with a baleful cry. Mary shushed the goat as she brushed aside some hay and pulled up a trapdoor that was imbedded into the floor. I helped

Melting Point

Etta, still carrying Magda, down the steps into the cellar. I started down the stairs, then looked at my aunt and pleaded, "Please come down here with us."

"Nonsense, my place is at Carl's side. Besides, who would put the straw back over the door? We'll be alright," Mary said, smiling at me. She handed me an unlit candle she had brought from the house, and I reluctantly continued down the stairs. Mary closed the door over us. Then she brushed some hay back over the door and headed back to the farmhouse.

The cellar was cool and dry, but was warmer than being outside where the snow was, and that was a relief to Etta and me. I struck a match and lit the candle. The cellar was small, designed to keep food cool in the summer. There wasn't much food in here now, but there were a couple of crates that I arranged as a makeshift bench. There was just enough room for the three of us and our pack, so Etta and I sat very close together, Etta cuddling Magda.

In the dim yellow light of the candle, I studied Etta's clear and smooth skin from just a few inches away, and thought again how beautiful she really was. She may have looked plain from a distance, but I liked the curve of her ski-jump nose, and the way her thin lips curved around, like the lines on a fine violin. She was strong in body and in spirit, while I was weak in both.

"Beautiful," I mumbled.

"Yes, she is," Etta said, looking at Magda. She sighed deeply and added, "My parents, my sister, and my brothers are all dead now. The only family I have is sitting here in a root cellar waiting for the Russians to come and kill us. If it weren't for Magda that might even be a relief. But Magda deserves better."

"You're Polish, the Russians aren't mad at you," I said, hoping that she wouldn't agree and leave me here alone.

The Russians Are Coming!

"At the start of the war, Germany invaded Poland, but so did Russia. They split us down the middle. Do you really think the Russians will treat us any better than you did?"

I wasn't sure whether I should feel insulted or relieved. I didn't have long to ponder, though, because Magda scrunched up her face and strained, turning pink as she filled her diaper.

I sniffed the air and groaned. "Trapped in this tiny cellar with that smell. It might be better to face the Ru ..."

As if on cue, there was a loud bang from above. The Russians had arrived. I felt sick with the realization that the bang was probably a grenade. Next, we heard muffled shouting and the pops of rifles. I sucked in some of the foul air and a tear started to well up in my eye, as I thought of Mary and Carl in the farmhouse. Etta placed her hand on mine.

The shouting came nearer, and then boots could be heard on the floor of the barn above us. The Russians were searching for more people to shoot. Magda was done filling her diaper and decided to let 'mom' know it was time to change her, in the time-honored method. She bawled and kicked and fussed, as Etta tried to calm and shush her. Above, the boots stopped moving.

Etta stuck her finger in Magda's mouth to shush her, but that didn't help. The boots resumed moving, but without the shouting. Etta tore off the dirty diaper while at the same time shoving Magda's head up under her sweater and letting Magda at her breast. She tried to wipe Magda as best she could. Magda wanted nothing to do with Etta's breast, being that it was dry, and continued to fuss, the sound now muffled a bit by the sweater. The boots above came closer.

I was breathing hard and looking desperate. I had the gun tucked in my belt, why hadn't I thought of that? I reached into my over coat and under

Melting Point

my sweater and pulled the pistol out. Etta looked terrified at me and hissed, "No! There's too many of them. You'll just get us killed!"

I looked at her with wild eyes, undecided as to what to do. I remembered the candle, and rested the gun on my knees, leaned over, and blew out the flame. I could feel my heart pounding in my chest. Etta was next to me, rocking Magda and breathing heavily, though I couldn't see her at all. I was fingering the gun, wondering if I would have the courage to use it. Magda was starting to calm down, and her cries were still muffled from being up under Etta's sweater.

Above, the boots were almost on top of the trap door. Just then, the goat bleated at the Russians. After a brief pause, the Russians laughed and started to move out of the barn, dragging the goat with them, bleating its mournful cry. After waiting a long minute to make sure they were gone, I lit the candle again. Etta finished cleaning up Magda and put her in a clean diaper. Magda settled down, much more content.

"Magda sounds like a goat," I whispered with a small smile of relief.

Etta smiled weakly back, narrowed her eyes at me, jabbed my side with her elbow, and said, "The goat sounds like Magda." She gave Magda a bottle of milk to drink.

Magda settled in for a nap, and Etta and I sat in silence with just our thoughts. Gradually the smell of the candle helped to damper Magda's smells. Occasionally we would look at each other and smile a weak smile, each trying to reassure the other. I hadn't eaten in some time, and so despite the unpleasant odors, I rummaged around the knapsack and found the cheese, wrapped in a thin cloth. As I unwrapped it, a small locket fell out. Puzzled, I opened it. Inside were pictures of Mary and Carl from many years ago. In the dim light of the candle, I could just make out a tiny inscription on the back that read, "To my lovely Mary, from your adoring Carl – love forever".

The Russians Are Coming!

Mary knew she was likely to die. I lost my appetite then, and showed the locket to Etta. She put her hand to her face. I put the cheese and locket back into the knapsack. Mary knew.

After two hours or so, we could hear more sounds from the Russians. This time, the Russians appeared to be leaving. They sang some sort of patriotic song, and it faded into the distance as they left. We waited a few more minutes, and then, at Etta's prodding, my stomach churning from hunger, the smells and my fear, I blew out the candle and cracked open the trap door.

A waft of icy cold fresh air came in through the crack. I didn't like the cold, but the smell was a whole lot better than what Magda had left us with. I couldn't see any activity, so I opened the door farther and crawled out, lowering the door behind me. I looked around, but it was deathly quiet, and I concluded that the Russians had indeed left. I went back to the cellar door and opened it. I helped Etta and Magda, now safely back in her shawl, up through the door. I then returned to the cellar to fetch the knapsack. I came back up the short cellar stairs and closed the trap door for the last time. Slinging the knapsack over my shoulder, I led the three of us, crunching through the snow, to the farmhouse.

We could see the destruction even from the outside. All of the windows had been blown out. The goat was outside the door, lying in a pool of its own blood, its throat cut, with chunks of meat carved out of its lifeless body. I eased the door open and stood in the doorway, a pained look on my face as I surveyed the room. Etta, behind me, couldn't see inside, but she could guess what I saw.

The Russians had thrown a grenade into the room before they entered it. The grenade had shattered the windows, killed Carl and Mary, and left metal fragments embedded into the walls. The Russians had also feasted on the food in the house and fried up some of the goat. Everything was shot up, kicked

Melting Point

around, and smashed. Pictures had been torn from the walls, drawers pulled out and strewn around, jars smashed, curtains torn.

After shock, I felt anger. How could these barbarians do this? How could they be so uncaring as to sit in the farmhouse and eat the food of a dead farmer and his wife? They must be caught and punished. Then I breathed a large sigh and realized that they wouldn't be punished, they were the new masters and **we** Germans were the barbarians.

Outside, Etta, getting colder from standing behind me, said quietly, "We must go now."

"Let me at least bury them," I said, wiping my eyes.

"No. I'm sorry, but there is no time. We have to leave *now*."

"But, I . . ."

Etta cut me off. "Now!"

I nodded and turned, the knapsack on my back, and followed Etta as she led the way across the field; Magda snug in the shawl and her cocoon of clothing. To the east was the bulk of the Russian army. We couldn't go east. We could clearly see the Russian's footprints heading north-west, so we headed south-west. I had replaced the pistol in my belt, and nervously touched it every few minutes to reassure myself that it was there. I also checked frequently for the small velvet pouch with diamonds tucked deep into my pocket. Pistol. Pouch. Pistol. Pouch.

After several hours of walking we reached a road, and headed west. We trudged on a few more hours and we came to a small village. From there we managed to hitch a ride on the back of a farmer's cart heading west. We were exhausted.

I never did find a place to leave Etta and the baby. I didn't really *want* to leave them; I loved the infant and felt a responsibility for her and Etta. They

The Russians Are Coming!

stuck with me all the way back to Erfurt. It was easy to find temporary housing there, as many thousands of families were homeless and in temporary shelters. We decided to 'play house' in order to raise the baby without any suspicions. Since I still had my special clearances from the SS (from Karl Bischoff), anytime people questioned us I simply showed them my SS credentials and we got pretty much anything we needed.

I wrote a letter to my mother telling her about my situation, and asking her if Etta and the baby could stay with her at our home in Dresden for a while until we can relocate them somewhere appropriate. I never got a reply. On February 13 and 14, my home city of Dresden was bombed. Our house, along with thousands of others, was destroyed. I never heard from my mother again. For awhile I held out hope that she would be found alive somewhere. The more stories that came out of Dresden, though, the more it became clear that I would never hear from her again. I drifted from rage to fear to guilt to numbness. Etta and the baby became a great comfort to me, and a reason to continue living. I hadn't been able to help my brother or my mother, and my father was still missing; but I *could* help one small baby and her adopted mother.

#

There wasn't much to do back in Erfurt. The war was rapidly coming to a close, with daily news of more and more defeat. Gitta the secretary was still there, though she volunteered a lot of her time at the hospital. She was cool towards me, which was fine because I didn't want to have to explain to her why I had a woman and child living with me. In fact, I didn't tell anyone at work about them.

News of German-held positions being retaken by the Allies became routine. Routine, that is, until General Patton's US Third Army took Buchenwald in mid-April. This was the first major concentration camp taken back by the western Allies. When the Russians had captured Auschwitz they

Melting Point

tried to tell the world about the horrors that had been found there. The rest of the world tended to discount what the Russians said, in part because the Russians wouldn't invite foreigners to the camp to see for themselves. I had the sneaking suspicion that, had we not destroyed the crematoria, the Russians might have pressed it into service for themselves. As it was, the Russians set about finishing the synthetic rubber plant at Monowitz, a plant that is used even to this day to make rubber.

The allied newspapers carried pictures of Buchenwald, including pictures of the ovens. In one, a half-cremated skeleton lay in the upper oven cavity, ready to be moved to the lower oven. The pictures were fuzzy enough that you couldn't clearly make out the inscription on the oven door, 'Topf.' The army knew, of course. And those of us at the company knew. And we were scared.

#

On May 8, 1945, Germany surrendered. Germany was divided up between the Russians and Allies (America, France, and England). Erfurt ended up in the 'American Zone', for which we were all thankful. On May 30, the U.S. Military Police finally showed up at our offices. We frankly were surprised at how long it took them to find us, given that Buchenwald was liberated a month earlier. They asked Gitta for the people in charge of the cremation ovens, and Gitta stalled them for a while pretending not to understand their translator's German. When the Police got agitated, Kurt Prüfer came out of his office to her rescue. I watched from a cracked open door in an office at the end of the hall.

"I'm the man you seek," Kurt said to the translator.

"You are the one in charge of the crematoria?" asked the translator.

"Well, not in charge, but I am the chief designer," replied Kurt calmly.

"Who is in charge, then?"

The Russians Are Coming!

"Ludwig Topf is the overall manager," Kurt said, but added, "but I managed the various accounts for him."

After conferring in English, the translator said, "All right, we'll get back to you, but let's first talk with Mr. Topf."

Kurt bowed slightly and led the way towards old man Topf's office. I thought he should have identified Ernst-Wolfgang Topf as the leader, since he was the conniving mean brother. Ludwig was always a gentleman, and, ever since Kurt Prüfer had saved him from military service, was very gracious towards us all. Still, Ludwig was technically in charge.

The men all passed by the office I was peering out of and walked down towards the big corner office occupied by Ludwig. It was locked. The MP's banged on the door and shouted for him to open it.

Poor old Ludwig. His family's business that had been built through generations of hard work had all come to this – he was in charge of a company that engineered mass murder. Through innovative engineering ideas his firm had outbid the competition for work being offered by his government. Against incredible shortages of equipment and manpower, his company had managed to build crematoria unsurpassed in capacity and fuel efficiency. In any other circumstance he would be a civic hero, and his accomplishments would crown his long years of work. Now his family name would be forever stained; forever linked with places like Buchenwald and Dachau and Auschwitz. Ludwig had a portrait of his grandfather on his wall, and I could imagine Ludwig feeling the old man's accusing stare.

A shot rang out from within the office. The MP's drew their weapons and kicked in the door. Slumped in his chair, blood splattering the wall from where the bullet had exited his skull, was Ludwig Topf. At the end, he took the honorable way out, something I didn't have the strength to do. His brother, Ernst-Wolfgang, while devastated in the turn of events, refused to even

Melting Point

acknowledge his involvement with the furnace part of the company.

After all that, the MP's were content to arrest Kurt Prüfer and talk to him off and on over the next many days. I went and visited him in the makeshift prison they had set up; I took him food and news. The MP's didn't search our offices or take anything from there; they seemed content just to talk with Kurt.

Fourteen days after arresting him, they let Kurt go. As soon as he got back to the office, he went into Ernst-Wolfgang's office and shut the door. The next thing we knew, they both came out and told everyone to gather up the various contracts the firm had signed with the SS and destroy them.

"They would be our undoing," Kurt said. Ernst-Wolfgang agreed.

They had finally let Kurt go because he convinced them that our operations were not the murder of the gas chambers but the hygienic job of disposing of the bodies in a sanitary and respectful way. He even convinced the Americans that they should order some crematoria from us in order to help dispose of the thousands of dead bodies from the war still awaiting burial! It was to be one contract we would never fulfill.

#

At about the same time, the Allies had reached agreement on the new German dividing line between Russia, and the Allies. Erfurt was to be turned over to the Russians! When the Americans pulled out on June 21, just a week after Kurt got out of custody, Ernst-Wolfgang and his wife went with them. So did Etta, Magda, and I. Kurt Prüfer, Karl Schultze, and others stayed. On July 3, 1945, the Soviets marched into Erfurt, and I didn't hear any more news from that town until decades later.

Etta, Magda, and I made our way to Spain, then Cuba, then New York, then eventually California.

Bodega Bay, California

The first golden rays of sunlight were rising from the east. The ocean and the surrounding hills were bathed in an orange glow. I felt old and tired. I was emotionally spent. I had told the whole awful story to my daughter and her family, and now it was over; the story, my life, my family's love for me, everything.

"So now you know the complete and disgusting truth," I said dejectedly.

Silence.

Magda finally spoke up, a little angry, "So, I'm not even. . . your daughter."

"No."

"And, mom wasn't . . . mom."

"No."

"I'm Jewish," she spelled it out after a moment. "I'm a Hungarian Jewish woman, living with Catholic adoptive parents for 55 years." She snorted a short laugh, "That's unbelievable." She frowned.

Silence.

Melting Point

"Did you and Mom love each other?"

I nodded, "Your mother was beautiful and strong willed. She always seemed to know just what to do. She didn't let me brood about the past, but always looked to the future. Yes, I loved her; I still love her. I will always love her. And, I think she loved me too."

"You never had any other children?"

"No."

"I'm getting a headache, I am exhausted and I need to go lay down." And with that, Magda got up and left the room.

There was an awkward silence as Tony, Amanda, and Tom sat there, unsure of what to do or say next.

Amanda broke the silence by asking, "You said you heard later what happened to the people you worked with; what *did* happen to them?"

I thought I had been finished with the story, but with Magda gone it felt good to talk again. "After the Berlin Wall fell in the late 80's, and with the later warming relations between East and West, I found out more about what happened after we left Germany."

"In early March of 1946, Rudolf Höss, the commandant of Auschwitz, was captured by the British and tried both in Nuremberg and in Poland. He was hanged at Auschwitz, in front of the old Crema I, a dozen yards from his former house and from the tree where I carved my initials.

"Irma Griese, the woman I danced with at Höss' birthday party, was sentenced to death for 'crimes against humanity' at the Lüneberg trials. She really deserved it for the way she treated prisoners.

"My coworkers Kurt Prüfer, Karl Schultze, Fritz Sander, and Gustav Braun had all been arrested in Erfurt in early March of 1946. Apparently it took the Russians eight months to figure out what we had been doing. Fritz Sander

Bodega Bay, California

died of a heart attack at the end of March, or so they said. Gustav Braun was sentenced to 25 years in a Gulag, but released in 1955 after 9 years. In 1952, Kurt Prüfer died of a brain hemorrhage while serving a 25-year prison term in a Gulag. I shudder to think what they did to give him the hemorrhage. I don't know what happened to Karl Schultze.

"In 1949, Ernst-Wolfgang Topf started a new Topf heating company in Wiesbaden. It lasted until 1963, but was never very successful. However, he got a patent for a method of fueling furnaces with animal fat. The idea was to capitalize on what we had learned in the camps – human fat can help fuel the fires of a crematorium if managed right. The SS at the original Auschwitz prison had discovered it. Kurt Prüfer had designed it into the ovens in Crema's II and III, where Sonderkommandos would carefully select the right mixture of fat and thin bodies to maximize the fuel. We proved the idea successful in Poland on over a million test subjects, my colleagues suffered and died in Gulags for it, and Ernst-Wolfgang got a patent on it to make money off the idea.

"Ironically in all this, Karl Bischoff, the SS major who oversaw the construction of the furnaces and gas chambers for Auschwitz, apparently led a quiet life in Germany. I heard that he died in 1950. He was an architect and designer, as responsible for the deaths at Auschwitz as any of the Topf employees, maybe more so. I wish I had been able to see him one more time. I'd like to know how **he** felt; how **he** coped with what we did.

"At the Nuremberg trials in 1946, Herman Goring and other Nazi leaders were sentenced to death by hangings. Their bodies were cremated in the Topf ovens at Dachau. Ironically, that was the very first oven that we installed, if you recall, stealing the thunder from the Allach company, and launching Kurt Prüfer and the rest of us on our destiny."

#

Melting Point

We were all tired from the overnight storytelling, and so went to our rooms for some needed rest. I was still worried about Magda and whether she would ever speak to me again. I lay down on the bed and stared at the ceiling.

"Well, Etta, I've done what you asked. Now she knows. They all know. Now what do I do?"

I slept, dreamless, for several hours. No curly-haired girl, no Etta, nothing.

I woke up in the early afternoon. I splashed some water on my face and combed what little hair I had left and went out to the kitchen. Magda was the only one up, sitting on the couch, next to a pile of Kleenex. I hesitated when I saw her. Her eyes were red from crying. I thought maybe I should go back to my room.

"Oh papa, good, you're up. Come sit with me," she said, patting the cushion next to her.

I went over to the couch and sat at the desired spot. She put her arms around me tightly and kissed me.

"Thank you for telling me the story. It really hurts, but at the same time it feels good to know the truth." She gave me a weary grin and said, "I always thought there was something odd about our family. Now I know."

I found it hard to talk all of a sudden, I wiped away a tear as I stammered out, "I… I'm so sorry, Magda. I love you so much; I have loved you ever since that first day when you were born. We should have told you years ago, but I begged your mother not to tell you, because I felt you would hate me."

She looked up at me, "Hate you? How could I ever hate my father? I'm shocked, yes. Surprised, a little hurt, but hate? No. You are and always will be my dad. I . . . I hate what you did; I hate what you were; but I have so many good memories of you and mom that I see you almost as two different people. It will take some time to reconcile them together, but I will **always** love you."

At that we both broke down and cried. We clung on to each other and sobbed for quite a while. It felt good for my heart to have let all this out finally, and she still loves me!

#

At dinner, everyone was up and packed and ready to head home. The mood was quiet and everyone was somber. We would have this one last small meal together and then head back inland. As we snacked on cheeses and bread, with butter and olive oil for dipping, I had one last thing I needed to discuss. I pulled out a small pouch from my pocket and held it over the table. I slowly turned it over and dumped out its contents.

Almost one hundred diamonds poured onto the table. Most were fairly small, a half carat or less. A few were larger. Most of the larger stones would have been shoved out of the ovens with their owner's remains, after all.

"Would you folks help me find some way to use these to help the victims of the holocaust and their descendents?" I asked of Magda.

Tom whistled and said, "That's a fortune in diamonds!"

Tony picked up one and studied it closely. He grinned and said, "Wow, you weren't fooling, you really found all these diamonds? What are they worth?"

I nodded, "Yes, I really found these in the ovens, and I figure each one is worth about 15,000."

"No, not that much," Tony looked at me with one eyebrow raised. "These are too small. Maybe more like 750 to 1,000 dollars."

"Not 15,000 dollars," I clarified. "15,000 lives."

Tony's smile fell and he very carefully put down the diamond.

Melting Point

"All those people," Amanda said, shaking her head. "What a loss. And because of who they *were*, rather than for what they *did*."

Magda looked at Amanda, and then at the stones and thought a moment. "Amanda, you know how you have been talking about adopting an orphan from Rwanda?"

Amanda, sensing the usual fight, said cautiously, "yes . . ."

Magda looked at Amanda. "I think that is a wonderful idea."

Bodega Bay, California

Notes

This book does not seek to justify or excuse the actions of the hundreds of thousands of mostly unknown men and women who helped contribute to the murder of millions of people. However, to help understand how people could come to terms with themselves and their actions in dealing with organized mass murder, I have created a realistic, somewhat sympathetic, Holocaust perpetrator. This will offend some readers, and I'm sorry for that. But, if we are to prevent another Holocaust, we must understand why it happened, and why seemingly normal people went along with it. This is one attempt at that understanding.

Albert Stohl and his family are inventions, as is Gitta, the receptionist at Topf. Albert's buddies in college are invented. The rest of the characters in the book are real. I have no knowledge of the discussions that took place or of the specific mannerisms of the people involved, so of course that is all made up.

The companies of Topf, Allach, and the others all existed and played their parts in history as described. The various events in the life of Auschwitz are real, including the construction, the problems with chimneys, wiring and electrical fires, and the like. The trial of thieving SS men, thwarted by the mysterious burning of the building behind the first crematorium, is real, though it is not known how the fire started or who did it.

The extermination of the Hungarian Jews in the summer and fall of 1944 happened as described, and many of the written stories by Auschwitz survivors came from people who arrived with the Hungarian Jews and managed

Melting Point

to survive until the end. As far as is known, this was the most concentrated of the floods of people brought to the camp; prior to that trains would arrive from elsewhere in Europe at a slower, more 'manageable,' pace.

There were several small acts of sabotage and a few escapes. I described the largest act of sabotage where the Sonderkommandos, realizing their end was near, revolted. Brave men and women smuggled dynamite from the construction site at Monowitz over to the Sonderkommandos, who stored the explosives, of all places, in the broken furnaces of Crema IV.

There is still a fair amount of debate over such issues as how many people died at Auschwitz. This has been an ongoing debate since the end of the war. Shortly after the war it was reported that the Polish government said that six million people died there, but apparently that was a misinterpretation of the assertion that six million Poles died in the Holocaust, not specifically at Auschwitz. About half of the six million Poles were Jews.

There has been further confusion by folks who looked at the camp from a 'capacity of death' viewpoint. That is, they examine the theoretical capacity of the ovens, multiply that by 24 hours and come up with the number of people killed based on the claims of the survivors that the ovens were 'working full time.' As we've seen in this story, based on evidence, the furnaces were often not working at ALL and never worked at their rated capacity. Also, the survivors were likely witnesses during the peak period at the end when the Hungarians were arriving, and at that time the ovens really were operating as much as possible.

Folks who have tried to examine train schedules and transfers in and out of the camp come up with estimates from one to two million. I have used the estimate of one and a half million. We'll never know the exact number.

Further Reading

Selected Bibliography and further reading

- Anatomy of the Auschwitz Death Camp. 1994 by Yisrael Gutman and Michael Berenbaum, editors. Pub in assoc with the US Holocaust Memorial Museum. A series of articles looking at everything from the camp history, resistance movements, oven construction, and other aspects of the camp. Many of the scenes in <u>Melting Point</u> were inspired by this book.

- Auschwitz 1270 to the Present by Debórah Dwork and Robert Jan van Pelt. W.W. Norton & Co. 1996. A tremendous record of Auschwitz, the town it bore the name of, its place in this millennium's history, what it looks like today, and of course, how it developed during the war.

- Five Chimneys – A Woman Survivor's true story of Auschwitz, by Olga Lengyel. © 1947 by Ziff-Davis, my copy is 1995 by Academy Publishers. Olga was on the trains from Hungary and was a doctor, so she was able to survive by working in the hospital. She tells the story of babies being killed at birth to save the mother, which helped me form the subplot of Magda's birth in the story.

- Hitler's Willing Executioners – Ordinary Germans and the Holocaust, by Daniel Jonah Goldhagen. Vintage Books (a division of Random House) 1996. Documents that the people involved in the holocaust were ordinary

Melting Point

people and policemen. This book started me thinking along the lines of what would it be like to be just another German drafted into this endeavor.

- The Rise and Fall of the Third Reich – A History of Nazi Germany, by William L. Shirer. 1959 (but my Touchstone Edition was first published after 1990). The definitive work about Hitler's rise to power, his successes, and his failures. Not a chronicle of battles, but of the politics. Much of the early part of <u>Melting Point</u> is based on the information from here.

- The World Must Know – The History of the Holocaust as told in the United States Holocaust Memorial Museum by Michael Berenbaum, Ph.D. Little, Brown, and Co. 1993. A good overview of the holocaust, with a big emphasis on the victims, their remembrances, and photos. The curly haired girl and her guardian walking along the path were inspired by stories from here.

- Albert Speer: His Battle with the Truth. 1995 by Gitta Sereny. Vintage Books, a Division of Random House. Albert Speer was 'Hitler's architect,' but as told in <u>Melting Point</u>, he became the overall manager of wartime construction. He maintains in his own books (both excellent: 'Spandau Diaries' and 'Inside the Third Reich') that he knew nothing of the goings-on at the various death camps, yet he was responsible for the use of slave labor in factories. Factories that he visited and so couldn't help but see what was going on. For me, this helped crystallize my view on how someone can fool themselves and others for a long time. Albert Speer was the ultimate Albert Stohl.